CAN WE KNOW?

Answering the God Question

Blessings,
Tom Shetler

Can We Know?

Published by Thomas Shetler
3226 Hill Ridge Drive
Eagan, MN 55121
Email: tomshetler@hotmail.com
Website: www.tomshetler.com

Cover design by Susan Shetler
Cover photo by Ashley Teets
Interior design by Bethany Press International
Printed by Bethany Press International

ISBN: 978-0-615-25518-7

DEDICATION

To my mother, Dorothy Shetler, whose faithfulness to the One who can be known, enabled her children to find Him. Her compassion and servant's heart revealed not only the transcendence of those values, but the One from whom they arise.

ACKNOWLEDGEMENTS

Special thanks to Chris Soderstrom for a first-class job of editing and for showing a passion for the book that rivaled my own. Thanks to Marnie Fujii for proofreading the book and giving many helpful suggestions. Also, I am deeply grateful to my amazing wife, Susan, for her efforts in designing the cover and for her constant encouragement. Thanks also to my sister and brother-in-law, Tim and Kathy Dahlstrom, for their wise counsel and review of the manuscript. Finally, I want to thank Tom Hulting and Alec Brooks for looking at the manuscript early on and providing valuable input and encouragement.

CONTENTS

CHAPTER ONE

CHANGE—FOR BETTER OR WORSE

Consider how the world has changed in the last two hundred years. We've gone from oxcarts to space shuttles, kerosene lamps to PCs, the Pony Express to the Internet. No generation in history has seen greater technological advancement.

However, the changes that have had the deepest impact on people's lives have not been those of which we're most aware. We've been most profoundly affected by developments in philosophy and theology. In a momentous shift from God to no gods, Western civilization has traded its religious and spiritual heritage for secularism and naturalism. More than ever before, we are questioning the fundamental value of religion in general and Christianity in particular.

Previous generations believed faith was a force for good in the world. Just half a century ago, parents considered religious training one of the essential elements in their children's moral development. "The family that prays together, stays together" was a frequent public service message of the time.

Beginning in the 1960s another cultural attitude began broadly to emerge. People offended by the mere mention of religion began to take legal action. In response to one lawsuit, the Supreme Court outlawed formal prayer in American public schools. After another, the Court banned public-school Bible reading.

The courts were responding to the petitions of a secular minority. In seeking to protect an alleged right to not be exposed to religious messages, the justices permitted the Constitution to be invoked. This approach to human rights—somehow traversing from freedom *of* religion to freedom *from* religion—placed the United States of America, through reference to its founding legal document, far along the road toward becoming a secular society.

Whether or not we meant to, we've made secularism our prevailing cultural philosophy. In the name of "protecting minority rights," we've prohibited public religious expression. But the courts that handed down these rulings never would have agreed to such restrictions if they did not agree, in principle, with the basic Enlightenment view of religion.

The "Enlightenment" leaders questioned religion's *value* because they first questioned its *validity*. They maintained that religion is a holdover from ancient delusions and pre-scientific superstitions that long have ruled humankind. Accordingly, for the sake of progress and for our ultimate welfare, it was said, religious belief must be reduced or eliminated.

THE DIRECTION AND THE DESTINATION

At the *personal and private* levels, America is a Christian nation. At the *public and political* levels, though, we are secular. In the realms of legislation and education we have moved away from the faith of our fathers. Publicly, the apathy toward or rejection of anything religious has dramatically reduced the level of moral and spiritual knowledge among the general population.

Before the twentieth century, most people in the West believed that the universe has a Creator and that we ourselves are both spiritual and physical beings. They embraced the reality of life after death, with heaven as the reward of the righteous and hell the punishment of the wicked. The church, the university, and the state all spoke the same message, and Christianity was the Western worldview.

There were a number of accompanying benefits. Included was the promise of a better life after the sufferings of this present, less-than-perfect world. Such hope sustained people in their daily lives and enabled them to endure their trials, knowing that whatever they faced in the here and now, their faith would uphold them and carry them to the day when all struggles will cease.

Faith also provided a foundation for justice. If God ultimately is opposed to evil, then we are joining Him in the fight against suffering. We are, in fact, doing His work. Hospitals, schools, orphanages, and other philanthropic vehicles throughout the world were born and built out of Christian belief.

The pursuit of equality and justice in Western societies is a direct consequence of Judeo-Christian values: namely, the sanctity of human life and the existence of an absolute moral standard. This worldview called individuals to personal integrity and created cultures that emphasized honesty, fairness, and faithfulness in its citizens. While not everyone lived up to these virtues, their establishment in the larger society elevated the level of integrity.

On a personal level, the Christian worldview provided a high view of humanity. Man was created in the image of God. In theory, this meant that human life is sacred and that each individual life is significant. As a result, education was extended to the masses and freedom became a right, not a privilege:

> We hold these Truths to be self-evident, that all Men are created equal, that they are endowed by their Creator with unalienable Rights, that among these are Life, Liberty, & the Pursuit of Happiness.[1]

Western civilization has taken the lead in universal education and suffrage and in racial and gender equality. The West has never been perfect in any of these regards, but its values raised the issues, encouraged the progress, and facilitated the benefits we enjoy today.

From the beginning of the twentieth century, we have been on a philosophical and political journey in a different direction. We are becoming a secular society; we are pluralistic; we define ourselves by not having or even allowing a dominant religious persuasion. Our universe is vastly larger, more complex, and more mysterious than our ancestors ever conceived it to be. In regard to the nature of reality, certainty and authority are relics of the past, and we are adrift in a sea of agnosticism.

As a result, we must make personal choices in regard to morals and values without the aid of sacred text or even cultural consensus. The world religions are still options, but that's all they are: buffet dishes among a multitude of alternatives. This "certainty of uncertainty" has produced an ideological and social revolution of unimaginable proportions. The forces of theological skepticism came to fruition in the twentieth century, which wrought the furthest-reaching upheaval, most devastating warfare, and greatest loss of life of any historical era.

The devastation is not just cultural or social; it is also deeply personal. In the early 1980s, talk-show host David Susskind (1920–1987) interviewed a British novelist whose 23-year-old son had committed suicide. When Susskind asked what could explain this tragedy, the man gave two reasons. First, this generation, unlike its predecessors, is convinced that death is the end of personal existence; therefore, death is the ultimate escape from the pain of reality. Second, in his suicide note, the young man had written, "I have done everything there is to do in life and find that nothing is worth doing twice."[2]

With the loss of belief in the transcendent and supernatural has come the loss of belief in the transcendence and significance of life itself. While we live in the age of the most remarkable technological advances in the history of the human race, we also live in an age characterized by the loss of life's meaning, of moral boundaries, and of overarching hope.

Many have asked how this generation, which has so much abundance, which knows so much freedom, which has access to entertainment and information at unprecedented levels, likewise could be so filled with disillusion. The answer is that it's a generation without a sense of larger purpose for their lives. This despair is the Enlightenment's true legacy: We are a culture without faith and, thus, without hope. The two are vitally connected, and we cannot have one without the other.

Be appalled, O heavens, at this;
be shocked, be utterly desolate,
declares the Lord,
for My people have committed two evils:
they have forsaken me,
the fountain of living waters,
and hewed out cisterns for themselves,
broken cisterns that can hold no water.[3]

The question of our time will be whether Western civilization can survive such a serious challenge. In the mid-twentieth century we feared a nuclear holocaust, but in many ways the loss of meaning that accompanies theological skepticism is a greater more substantial threat to our existence, because its destructive force is at work on the very foundations of our culture. Already we are far along the road that leads toward our doomsday. If we continue with secularism, we will find, to our horror, that we have no defense against our moral and social dissolution. We will have gravely misplaced and misdirected our energy, and we will have discovered that "The Hollow Men" by poet T. S. Eliot (1888–1965) was an oracle:

> This is the way the world ends
>
> Not with a bang but a whimper.[4]

THE RELIGIOUS QUESTION

Despite our pursuit of secularism, the central question facing the West is still "the religious question." How we answer it will determine our place and very likely our duration in the drama of human history. For now we have decided, collectively, that religion is unnecessary and irrelevant. This book seeks to determine whether or not our assessment is correct. Our examination will address both the historical process that brought our culture to its current perspectives and the ideological process that has resulted in today's Western worldview.

The question can be divided into two essential queries: (1) Does God exist, and (2) if He does, can we know that He exists? We have come to our present societal status based upon the answers the intellectuals of recent centuries have given. One reason for the Western opposition to religion is the widely held belief that science already has answered the first part—"Does God exist?"—with a resounding *no.* When the most learned among us say God is a myth, it's hard for the rest of us to disagree.

In addition, many philosophers for the past two-plus centuries have posited that certainty about knowledge is beyond the grasp of finite human beings. Religious claims to be able to define or explain God are seen, commonly, as the height of presumption. Even if there is a God, He is beyond our capacity for empirical knowledge;[5] anyone who claims to know Him is a fool or a scoundrel.

Our culture's movement from belief to secularism, from faith to agnosticism, reversed the order of the questions about knowing God. Enlightenment scholars *began* with the epistemological question of knowledge about God[6] and, from the answer they formulated, came to their ontological conclusion about His existence.[7] We will attempt to follow that process in the order it occurred.

All ideas have consequences; the bigger the idea, the more significant the results that flow from it. One of the reasons we can be confident that the question of God's existence is among the most primary of all human inquiries is the dramatic effect it's had upon our society. And, no era in history has proven this question's importance more clearly than our own.

THE CONTEMPORARY ERA

The contemporary world can be described broadly by three concepts: secularism, relativism, and pluralism. A *secular* culture is one in which reality is defined and explained in purely nonreligious terms. Religion is allowed as an individual option, but for issues of import to the culture as a whole (such as education and public policy), religion is denied any place. In practice, secularism sets itself in opposition to spirituality, outlawing its expression in public life.

A *relativistic* culture is one in which moral values are believed to be relative to society, to personal beliefs, or even to one's present circumstances. Relativism denies (or significantly reduces the number of) unquestioned moral values, either within a culture or cross-culturally; relativism assumes that these can and should change. The problem for most relativistic societies is that the change is not toward what earlier generations called moral progress but toward a regression in values, which creates a people who are becoming increasingly permissive and, concurrently, are receiving negative results from the behavior that comes out of their beliefs.

A *pluralistic* culture is one in which any number of beliefs, philosophies, and lifestyles are acceptable to the larger society. We do not mean by this that all religions or moral systems are somehow true. Rather, relativism and pluralism say that it's impossible to know which, if any, is ultimately true, so it's up to each person to decide what's true for himself.

In the end, this is not a declaration that everything is true but that nothing is true. The intellectuals who ushered in the modern age described themselves as "agnostics," meaning those who possess "no knowledge" of things eternal.[8] We, their philosophical grandchildren, have inherited the whirlwind of their unbelief.

WHERE DO WE GO FROM HERE?

This is not the end of the story, however. Such a reduced view of ourselves and of our world has left many people profoundly dissatisfied. The discontentment that began with the existentialist philosophers[9] spread to the artists and musicians; today, it affects a considerable portion of Western culture. Despite repeated attempts to create a completely secular society, we presently are undergoing a spiritual revolution. The nineteenth- and twentieth-century intellectuals expected universal scientific education to end religious belief in the West. In this new millennium, though, people are as intrinsically spiritual as they've ever been.

For example, university-trained nurses are seeking to use New Age practices in hospitals, sensing the patient's "aura" and seeking to aid the healing process by meditation.[10] Our bookstores are filled with volumes on spirituality and the spiritual pursuit. Postmodernism is a pervasive reaction against the modern monolith; many have sought to find meaning through neo-paganism. To the chagrin of those who want a purely secular culture, people are rejecting the West's formerly dominant objective-naturalistic worldview[11] and are embracing mystical and spiritual explanations for the universe.

Nevertheless, we have not yet come full circle. We began as a religious culture built around the teachings of the church.

We became a secular culture built upon the assumptions of the scientific age. We are becoming a spiritual culture again, but this time in a search for personal meaning in what more and more people believe is a purposeless universe and thus a senseless reality. In most cases this religious search is individualistic, seldom connected to a traditional religious community. Thus, we still are not establishing a devout consensus that can function as a societal foundation. We are still a nation that has changed gods, and the results, both corporately and individually, continue to be disastrous.

❖ ❖ ❖ ❖

We have asked, "*Does* God exist?" and "Can we *know* if He exists?" We must look now at the historical process that brought us to the agnostic answer, which is "I don't know and neither do you." We must also ask if the agnostic answer is correct. Examining the ideas that led us to our present status will enable us to decide if this really is the best or only option.

---

[1] From The Declaration of Independence. (On the document titled, "A Declaration by the Representatives of the United States of America, in Congress Assembled.")

[2] The David Suskind Show. PBS: February 1982.

[3] Jeremiah 2:12–13 ESV

[4] Thomas Stearns Eliot, "The Hollow Men" in Poems 1909–1925 (London: Faber & Gwyer, 1925).

[5] "Empirical" refers to knowledge gained by direct personal experience, using the physical senses.

[6] Epistemology is the study of how we achieve knowledge and of our certainty in regard to that knowledge.

[7] Ontology is the study of the nature of being and existence.

[8] See Ronald W. Clark, The Huxleys (New York: McGraw-Hill Book Company, 1968). Thomas Huxley first defined agnosticism this way: "Positively the principle may be expressed, in matters of the intellect, to follow your reason as far as it may take you, without regard to any other consideration. And negatively: in matters of the intellect, do not pretend that conclusions are certain which are not demonstrated or demonstrable. That I take to be the agnostic faith, which if a man

will keep whole and undefiled he shall not be ashamed to look the universe in the face, whatever the future may have in store for him" (emphasis mine).

[9] Existentialism, a philosophical system initially developed by the Danish thinker Søren Kirkegaard, postulates that personal existence is the chief and ultimate reality for all human beings. Kirkegaard was a Christian who believed that even though God cannot be explained or defined, and even though His existence cannot be rationally proven, He can be experienced, and this experience comes through Jesus Christ. The later French existentialists Jean-Paul Sartre and Albert Camus implied that what we make of our lives, personally, is entirely up to us; we are all alone in a godless reality. Generally, beginning with Kirkegaard, these philosophers sought to retain the realities of hope, goodness, and meaning in a universe that arose purely by chance and as a result of natural forces. In order to do so, they (the existentialists) had to move into the realm of the irrational. Their desire for goodness and meaning were based not on historical or scientific knowledge but on an intuitive hope that somehow truth and justice exist.

[10] Dennis McCallum, The Death of Truth: Responding to Multiculturalism, the Rejection of Reason and the New Postmodern Diversity (Minneapolis: Bethany House Publishers, 1996), 60–61.

[11] The modern West's "objective-naturalistic worldview" has been built upon empiricism. The view maintains that knowledge comes entirely through scientific experimentation and direct personal experience; it heavily emphasizes the use of outside observation (objectivity). It's also naturalistic in that it supposes everything in our universe to have arisen entirely by the interaction of natural forces. Only nature and nature's forces exist; the supernatural is either completely out of the picture or a figment of humankind's imagination.

CHAPTER TWO

HISTORICAL DEVELOPMENT (PART I)

How have we become a secular culture? Why are we pluralistic and relativistic? And now, why are we embracing New Age spirituality? Let's begin by noting that there are four eras related to the religious beliefs of our civilization.

Prior to roughly CE 1700, Westerners primarily held to the teachings of orthodox Christianity and believed they had unassailable reasons for doing so. History, philosophy, and experience all joined together to support faith in the God of the Bible. From Augustine to Zwingli, the great thinkers were theologians. Christian themes permeated the arts and letters—think of Dante's *Inferno*, Michelangelo's works in the Sistine Chapel, Leonardo's *The Last Supper*.

Little wonder Europe defined itself as "Christendom." We might call this "the age of *rational belief*."

❖ ❖ ❖ ❖

The period from broadly 1700 to 1900, the Enlightenment age, brought the initiation of a pervasive "liberation" process from beliefs and traditions that some had come to maintain were inhibiting human progress. Included among these was the Christian religion. Intellectuals began to argue that by casting off the yoke of the past, a new day would dawn for the freedom and fulfillment of humankind.

However, there were insufficient reasons for hoping this would lead either to liberty or to progress. In fact, Enlightenment thinkers were borrowing the hope of Christianity while rejecting the foundation upon which that hope rested.

People continued to operate under the premise that history is linear and teleological (moving toward an ultimate goal); again, though, this is the distinctly Christian view of history. The ancients had seen history as cyclical; the honest secularist must see it as a series of random events. Enlightenment intellectuals believed progress was built into the structure of nature itself and was inevitable. They would come to discover this to be neither reasonable nor true. We must call this "the age of *irrational unbelief*."

❖ ❖ ❖ ❖

In the first half of the twentieth century, Western culture came to grips with the Enlightenment's conclusions. As Friedrich Nietzsche wrote, "God is dead … and we have killed him."[12] A universe without God is a dark and empty place; there is no room for the significance of man, of history, or of anything transcendent. Philosophy, art, literature, and music began to reflect the stark realizations of a solely material world. Two catastrophic wars that wrought unprecedented carnage would prove our confidence in progress and technology to be unfounded. Reason would take us to the brink of the abyss, forcing us to face the implications of a godless reality. We will call this age "the age of *rational unbelief*."

❖ ❖ ❖ ❖

Beginning in the 1950s and 60s, people began to reject Western naturalism in hopes of finding a metaphysical reality.

Timothy Leary, Alan Ginsberg, and others sought to lead a generation out of the technocratic wilderness into the promised land of transcendental experience. The path to nirvana moved from hallucinogenic drugs to Eastern mysticism; the influence of New Age philosophy continues, as many today are on a spiritual pursuit. Now, however, it has become a search not based on history, evidence, or even logic, instead taking place in the world of crystals, channeling, and Zen riddles. This is the world of experience, and thus we currently live in "the age of *irrational belief*."

THE AGE OF RATIONAL BELIEF : PRIOR TO CE 1700

During the Middle Ages (c. CE 400s to 1400s), philosophy and theology were one. Theology was considered "queen of the sciences," and philosophy was her handmaiden. The conclusion of philosophy was that the universe could not have existed forever, nor could it have created itself.

Theology—the knowledge and understanding that arose from what was believed to be God's revelation of himself—gave further substance to philosophy's conclusions. Philosophy said that God must be eternal and transcendent, and, in so doing, it confirmed the testimony of the Scriptures: "In the beginning, *God*...."[13] Philosophy and theology, reason and faith, worked together to give a logical explanation for reality.

As a result, for the first sixteen hundred years of Western civilization, the vast majority of people believed in God and accepted the church's teachings. The mysterious circumstances of life were more likely to be defined in supernatural than in purely natural terms. In the pre-scientific age, God was the reasonable and sensible explanation for the universe's beauty and complexity. How could such a marvelous world exist without Him?

In the medieval period, people were taught that the church is God's voice on earth. What the church taught through the Bible, along with its sacred traditions based on Scripture and history, was considered a divine revelation upon which were built the guidelines and expectations for society and for life. Accordingly, people looked to the church for the answers to life's significant questions.

In many ways this was a codependent relationship. The church considered itself to be the repository of divine truth and the only legitimate teacher of humankind, and for nearly a thousand years in Europe it was. Yet the church likewise depended upon the people and the people groups it cared for, and its massive financial appetite alone led to growing political and religious manipulation. The sale of church offices and the promise of paradise for a price were just two egregiously visible symptoms of an unhealthy relationship between the church and the people.

RENAISSANCE AND REFORMATION

With the coming of the Renaissance (c. 1400s–1600s) and the Reformation (c. 1517–1648), all this began to change.

The Renaissance—the rebirth of art, literature, science, and philosophy in Europe—emerged from the rediscovery of Greek and Roman (classical) art, literature, science, and philosophy.[14] One central theme of the Renaissance was *ad fontes*, which is Latin for "to the sources." Scholars began to seek the writings of the ancient world and to study them in their original languages. This approach, likewise adopted by Christian theologians—when combined with a strictly literal interpretation of the Bible (*ad fontes*)—would lead directly to the Reformation.

One noteworthy Renaissance byproduct was the development of classical humanism and, thus, the study of the humanities. Many leading thinkers of the period, including Desiderius Erasmus (1466–1536), Philipp Melancthon

(1497–1560), and John Calvin (1509–1564) are often described as humanists; "humanism" in this regard indicates their concentration on human art, human culture, and human life.[15] The Renaissance was part of the Age of Faith, and its standard-bearers saw no dichotomy between the aims of humanism and the creeds of religion. They were merely shifting the *focus* of intensive study from God to man; they accepted the existence of God as self-evident, and they held man to be His highest creation, worthy of examination.

Nevertheless, gradually, among intellectuals, the Renaissance would expand an increasingly perceived separation between faith and reason that—after gradually developing for hundreds of years—finally would eventuate in the secularism of our own day. The initial rift of this separation had begun to form earlier, in the debate between the realists[16] and the nominalists,[17] during the Scholastic period, which we will examine shortly.

❖ ❖ ❖ ❖

The Renaissance humanists and reformers exposed hypocrisy and corruption in the church; they also began to show that the church had been lying to maintain its political power. For instance, Lorenzo Valla (c. 1406–1457) revealed that the document known as the *Donation of Constantine*, upon which the papacy based its claim to all of Europe, was a forgery, written not by Constantine but by zealous monks centuries after his death.[18]

Martin Luther (1483–1546), John Calvin, Ulrich Zwingli (1484–1531), and others called into question the institution's authority to speak for God, demonstrating contradictions between the teachings of the church and the teachings of the Bible. The reformers were able to make a distinction between the church and Christianity, and where the church departed from biblical Christianity, they departed from the church.

In addition to all its positive effects, though, the Reformation produced a series of devastating religious wars in Europe that further weakened the authority of the church, Catholic *and* Protestant. By the time of the Enlightenment, people weren't looking for a reformation; they were pursuing revolution. There would be two revolutionary goals: the overthrow of oppression by the monarchy (the end of feudalism) and the end to oppression by the church (the end of the primary bastion for the "opiate of the masses"[19]).

THE SCHOLASTIC MOVEMENT

The first great revolution that produced our current civilization was not a political or military uprising; it was an intellectual revolution. The paradigm shift that would be elemental in producing the modern world actually had its roots in the earlier Scholastic movement. During this time, scholars like Peter Abelard (c. 1079–1142), William of Ockham (c. 1288–c. 1348), and Roger Bacon (c. 1214–1294) had begun to discuss the *limits of reason*. The notion that reason has a ceiling would play a crucial role in establishing a new pathway to knowledge—knowledge not through deduction from a known truth to a particular question, but through induction from a particular fact or discovery to a general conclusion about the nature of reality. As much as anything else, it is this transition *from deduction to induction* that defines the development of the world we live in today.

Deductive reasoning, an important element of logic, reasons forward from a known truth. For instance, to explain a specific event, deduction starts with an accepted fact and then builds upon that fact in the process of discovering the answer. The answer to "Why is a blade of grass green?" comes from what we know about chloroplasts, the green organelles (cell-subunits) that conduct photosynthesis and partially comprise the blade.

Deduction, then, assumes a fully accepted body of truth from which further conclusions can be reached. We use deduction to find conclusions about specific questions using the catalog of knowledge we've developed over the millennia of human history.

Regarding deduction, the ancients believed truth to be a concrete reality that exists beyond our world; the Stoics called it the *Logos*, while the Egyptians called it *Ma'at*. This truth was seen to be the product of the eternal Mind who established the world, and since we humans are gifted with minds, it was maintained that we have a connection to the eternal realm.

According to the Greek philosophers, we must, therefore, educate our minds in the guidelines of reason in order to discover those truths that exist behind or beyond our world. These rules of logical deduction were considered the only necessary tools for the discovery of truth. In pursuit of truth, the carefully trained mind was perceived to be superior to experience or to observation, which were labeled as too imprecise and subjective to be trusted as sources of truth. The eyes could be tricked; experience was fickle and could be misinterpreted. The trained mind, following the surety of logic, enabled people to deduce the secrets of life from the body of eternal truth that lay at the universe's foundation.

❖ ❖ ❖ ❖

Returning to the Scholastic movement, we note once more that its rise brought significant challenges to long-held beliefs about the capabilities and limits of human reason. The original debate within Scholasticism revolved around the question of whether or not Plato was correct in his description of reality. Plato (c. 427–347 BCE) had theorized the existence of an ultimate "pattern" for everything that exists in our world. For each of us, as individual men or women, there was a perfect man or woman in the mind of God. Our job, as individuals, is to understand as much as we can about this perfect human and seek to pattern our lives after it.

The same was held to be true in the realms of law, politics, society, and so on. These eternal patterns, or principles, were called "universals."[20] The universals were held to be the all-encompassing truths that governed all existence, the unseen realities of which our physical world is a mere shadowy reflection.

In essence, the Scholastics were asking, "Is the individual man a reflection of the universal man?" (as said Plato); "Does the universal man exist *in* each individual man?" (as said Aristotle); or "Is the universal man a figment of the imagination—does only individual man actually exist?" (as said Democritus). They were engaging in a debate, then, about the nature of reality and how we come to know that reality. The battle lines would be drawn between those who believed that truth is learned through deductive reasoning from known facts to conclusions about specific realities, and those who believed that truth is discovered inductively, through questioning and experience.

Inductive reasoning, which involves the asking of questions, the gathering of facts, and the application of criticism to reach a general conclusion about an aspect of reality, lies at the heart of the scientific method. This was the era in which the emphasis on induction as the pathway to discovery and to knowledge was born. The method of scientific reasoning we take for granted today was once considered revolutionary, but induction would come to dominate the search for knowledge because it would prove to be so effective in revealing the secrets of the natural world.

FAITH *VERSUS* REASON?

Eventually, the Scholastic discussion concerning metaphysics[21] would expand to address the roles of faith and reason in the acquisition of knowledge. As we said in chapter one, the question of God's existence was not their first question; for them, the question of knowledge preceded it. These men accepted the existence of God as self-evident; however, they began to debate how much of reality humans could know with the use of unaided reason.

The dispute began with the question, "Do we know by reason, or do we know by faith?" While in a rationalistic and secular age this question makes no sense, in the age of faith it made all the sense in the world.

On one side were men such as Anselm of Canterbury (c. 1033–1109), who declared, "I *believe* in order to *understand*."[22] This stance was an affirmation of an eternal body of truth from which all of life's questions can be answered. Submitting one's reason to the Scriptures was part of one's Christian responsibility, on a par with following the church's moral teachings. Reason still was given a place in confirming and reinforcing the wisdom of revealed truth, but where reason and faith seemed to conflict, reason always yielded.

This view didn't eliminate investigation or even speculation; the mind, however, was to search for what had always "been there" but as yet remained hidden by ignorance and sin. Reason was encouraged in the pursuit of truth; it was to be utilized for discovering that which has existed in the mind of God for all eternity. Thus people were to use reason to discern the natural law and to mine the depths of Scripture.

Later Scholastic thinkers, led by William of Ockham, would sharply disagree, arguing that the divine is unknowable by our finite minds. Their insistence, in effect, was that God is as distanced from us as quantum mechanics would be from an ant—that we have no capacity for comprehending the eternal and infinite. They came to the conclusion, as churchmen, that the only alternative for humankind is to accept, on faith alone, the teachings of the church. This was *the radical separation of faith and reason*; one of its large-scale consequences was *the elevation of the church as the only pathway to God and truth*. Hereby was laid the groundwork, not only for the Reformation, but also for fideism[23] and for the neo-orthodox theology[24] of the twentieth century.

❖ ❖ ❖ ❖

As the Middle Ages progressed, the debate intensified. Thomas Aquinas (c. 1225–1274), seeking to come to terms with the philosophy of Aristotle (384–322 BC), believed that reason can be enlisted in the cause of faith and that Christian faith is reasonable. He systemized Aristotle's thought into five significant philosophical proofs for God's existence,[25] but he understood that even with such strong arguments reason would not *replace* faith. In Aquinas, faith becomes a volitional decision (a choice of the will) that is *supported by* evidence and reason.

The most pervasive consequence of this conflict was that reason and its offspring, science, were cut apart from theology and faith and, increasingly through the subsequent centuries, perceived as the pursuit of a qualitatively different category or kind of knowledge. Roger Bacon, at the end of the Scholastic era, advocated what would become known as the inductive method; later, Sir Francis Bacon (1561–1626) would expand this into the scientific method, and the rest *is* history. The scientific age was built upon the presuppositions of autonomous reason, empiricism, and naturalism.[26]

REALISM AND NOMINALISM

At its foundation, the Scholastic debate was between the concepts of realism and nominalism. The Scholastic era began with the predominance of *metaphysical realism*, the belief in a transcendental reality that exists beyond this world regardless of whether we affirm it. It progressed toward a predominating nominalism, the belief that only the here and now is real *in our experience*, and that the transcendent is far beyond human discovery.

In the end, Ockham and nominalism won the day, and the emphasis upon immediate personal experience opened the door for naturalism. The old way of realism was called the *via Antigua;* the newer way of nominalism was called the *via moderna*, and the titles are telling, for the latter truly would come to usher in the modern era.

Nominalism's complete separation between faith and reason elevated individual perception and discernment over institutional doctrine and made reason the sole source of truth in the natural realm. Accordingly, the Renaissance and a portion of the Reformation were built upon nominalism; Martin Luther's famous declaration of conscience, based upon his personal discovery of the truths of God's Word, is a powerful example of nominalism's influence on the reformers.[27] Realize, too, that the Reformation would then be taken to its logical conclusion in and through the Enlightenment.

THE AGE OF RATIONAL BELIEF : SUMMARY

We called this "the age of rational belief" because reason was used to defend faith. But reason, a double-edged sword, can be used to defend faith *or* to destroy it, and the debates of this era would cast doubt upon reason's capacity to produce faith. Even so, the churchmen who argued for the radical separation of faith from reason truly felt they were defending faith from the fickleness of human thoughts.

William of Ockham accepted God's existence and the church's teachings *without question,* maintaining that they must be believed on the basis of authority alone. He never saw the down-the-road implications of his approach. He didn't foresee an age when nothing would be accepted on authority except that which could be empirically verified. If God's existence cannot be established by reason, what happens to belief in God when reason itself is enthroned as king?

Once more, the great paradigm shift that produced the modern era was from (A) deductive reasoning as the primary pathway to truth to (B) growing and then utmost confidence in the inductive reasoning of the scientific method. *In the ancient and medieval world, logic and reason had been used to discover the right Answers.* People came to the church or the university to receive wisdom from on high; truth was accepted on the authority of the one giving it.

Education was through the catechism as students memorized the correct answers to life's essential questions. For example, the most influential Age of Faith textbook was *The Four Books of Sentences*, a gigantic systematic compilation in which a set of church-approved solutions are given to the most significant inquiries. Written by the scholar Peter Lombard (1100–1160), *The Sentences* for three centuries was the primary textbook of the great European universities.

By opening wide the door for inductive reasoning, the Scholastics of the late Middle Ages enabled the scientific age and laid the intellectual foundations for the modern world. *In the modern era, logic and reason are used to ask the right Questions.* Truth is discovered *from* nature and *from* reality as we probe, experiment, and question. As a result, nothing is accepted on authority (in theory, at least); everything must pass the verification tests either of science or of logic. Today the goal of education is to create critical thought, which is seen as the ability to question and think independently of accepted views.

For this reason, the church of today can no longer just tell people to believe. They won't believe without evidence. The church cannot appeal to biblical authority; people today will ask how we know the Bible is true. The church can no longer operate on the old paradigm of the *Answer* as it interacts with the rest of the world. It must learn how to operate in the realm of the *Question*: Can such a complex and beautiful world have arisen purely by chance? Why do we have a conscience when we are supposed to have arisen from a process that only values survival? Why are the teachings of Christ at the pinnacle of human ethics?

❖ ❖ ❖ ❖

We began by saying that the question of God's existence is related to our ability to know. The age of rational belief—the age of the church, so to speak—ended with serious questions about our ability to *know* the answers to life's most significant metaphysical questions. As we enter the Enlightenment—the age of the philosophers, and of irrational unbelief—we will only see increasing epistemological skepticism, or mistrust of knowledge gained by reason.

---

[12] Friedrich Nietzsche, section 125 ("Parable of the Madman") in The Gay Science (orig. published 1882; 2nd ed. 1887).

[13] Genesis 1:1 ESV, emphasis mine.

[14] As knowledge of the world outside Europe expanded through the growth of trade and, ironically, the Crusades, classical art and thought (particularly that of Aristotle) became the subject of study for European artists and scholars. This also created opportunity for the study of characters and subjects outside the biblical realm, and for the beginning of secular art and literature.

[15] As opposed to materialist humanism, which rejects the supernatural; we'll specifically revisit this in chapter 13.

[16] This form of realism held that the metaphysical realm described by the Greek philosopher Plato is the ultimate reality. Truth, beauty, goodness, justice … all exist in their pure form in the realm of "God," who is Pure Mind. Humans are connected to this realm through our mind; by the development of reason we discover our access to this reality.

[17] Nominalism arose from the supposition that the realm of God is beyond human knowledge and, therefore, must be approached strictly by faith. Nominalists rejected the notion that our minds are connected to the mind of God; hence, our minds do not have access to the realm of ultimate truth, beauty, and goodness.

[18] See Kenneth Scott Latourette, A History of Christianity, Volume I (New York: Harper & Row, 1953), 633–34.

[19] Karl Marx (1818–1883), from the foreword to Critique of Hegel's "Philosophy of Right," ed. Joseph O'Malley, trans. Annette Jolin and Joseph O'Malley (Cambridge: Cambridge University Press, 1970; manuscript written 1843.

[20] One of the most important "universals" was the natural law, the set of absolute moral principles believed to govern human life and society. It is right at this point that the debate between absolute moral values and relativistic morality began.

[21] Metaphysics (from Greek terms meaning "above/beyond the physical") is the philosophical discipline of studying aspects or principles of reality that are above (beyond, transcendent to) any particular scientific discipline. The aim of metaphysics is to examine and explain the nature of the universe and of existence.

[22] Anselm, in de Veritate (Stuttgart: Fromann, 1966), emphasis mine.

[23] Fideism is the emphasis on "faith as belief," without supporting reasons. Fideism, the "leap of faith" that arose from the theological existentialism of Søren Kirekegaard, is central to the teachings of neo-orthodox Christianity today. Fideism assumes that faith must be primarily irrational, a purely subjective hope.

[24] Neo-orthodoxy was born from the writings of the German theologian Karl Barth (1886–1968). In the face of rampant early-twentieth-century anti-theology, Barth began to use all the Reformation terminology and teachings in his preaching; simultaneously, he continued to hold to Enlightenment beliefs about the Bible and Christ. Barth thus used the rhetoric of historic Christianity but without the conviction that it has any basis in history or reality. In neo-orthodoxy, the gospel becomes a series of inspiring ideas and concepts that have no connection to an actual transcendent reality in which we can reasonably believe.

[25] In his Summa Theologiae (1265–1274), Thomas Aquinas presented these arguments: (1) All things are in motion, thus there is required an unmoved mover who is God [the first cosmological argument]; (2) All things require a cause and cannot have caused themselves, thus there is required an uncaused cause who is God [the second cosmological argument]; (3) All things that now have being do not exist necessarily, but there is required a necessary being for all else to exist, thus the need for God [the third cosmological argument]; (4) All mankind has an innate moral sense because they were created by a moral God [the moral argument]; (5) The universe shows evidence of design and purpose, thus the need for an intelligent designer [the teleological argument].

[26] We'll be looking extensively at empiricism and naturalism in upcoming chapters.

[27] For instance, at his heresy trial (see brief explanation at en.wikipedia.org/wiki/Diet_of_Worms), Luther declared, "Unless I shall be convinced by the testimonies of the Scriptures or by clear reason ... I neither can nor will make any retraction since it is neither safe nor wise to act against conscience. Here, I stand. I can do nothing else. God help me. Amen."

CHAPTER THREE

HISTORICAL DEVELOPMENT (PART II)

THE AGE OF IRRATIONAL UNBELIEF 1700–1900

The rise of secularism did not begin with the rise of science; the scientists of the seventeenth through early nineteenth centuries were nearly all Christians. (For example, Robert Boyle [1627–1691], Isaac Newton [1643–1727], Michael Faraday [1791–1867], and Louis Pasteur [1822–1895] were outspoken in defending the faith). Secularism arose from philosophy and from rejection of the church's authority. Through the church's self-inflicted loss of moral and political status in the post-Reformation religious wars, people began to feel free to reach their own conclusions about reality.

Thomas Hobbes (1588–1679), Baruch de Spinoza (1632–1677), Jean-Jacques Rousseau (1712–1778), and François-Marie Arouet de Voltaire (1694–1778), among others, had written scathing criticism against the church and lived to tell about it. Voltaire, deeply angered by the atrocities of the

Thirty Years War, expressed his animosity by ending every letter he wrote, for the rest of his life, with the phrase "Crush the Infamy" (of the organized church). The politically minded Hobbes was called an "atheist" (he was more likely a deist) because of his views on the church as expressed in *Leviathan.*[28]

These men were primarily philosophers; remember that since the latter years of the Scholastic movement, philosophy had been further and further separated away from theology. By now, philosophers assumed either a world governed only by natural forces (naturalism) or a world created by a God who had left it entirely to its own devices (deism).

DAVID HUME

The most radical of these philosophers, and eventually one of the most influential, was David Hume (1711–1776), the first significant empiricist.[29] Empiricism lies at the very foundation of modern naturalism; far in advance, Hume anticipated the widespread skepticism of the twentieth century, and, like so many Enlightenment intellectuals, he considered religion to be a monumental evil. Religion had been the source of terrible violence over the previous two centuries, as Protestants and Catholics battled relentlessly. Hume believed that, for the good of humankind, religion—at least the Christian version of it—must be abolished.

> If the religious spirit be ever mentioned in any historical narration, we are sure to meet afterwards with a detail of the miseries which attend it. And no period of time can be happier or more prosperous, than those in which it is never regarded or heard of.[30]

We'll return to Hume shortly. For the moment, note that Enlightenment philosophers arose at the beginning of the scientific era, and that the very use of the word "enlighten-ment" implied an emerging (real and/or perceived) from dark ages of superstition and ignorance. In this view, religion was a thing of the past, a product of human inability to understand the mysteries of the universe. If society truly were to progress, then the old explanations for reality must be replaced by a new scientific framework.

It's ironic that the scientists of this era did not share the philosophers' desire for a purely secular worldview. The conclusion of their study was that the intricacy of the universe demanded a Creator to explain it. They believed they were discovering, with their science, God's very handiwork; they described their efforts as "thinking God's thoughts after him."[31]

The philosophers, on the other hand, had already come to their antireligious conclusion. Looking at science from the outside, they saw it as the "replacement" for Christianity in the West. Beginning with Hume, they equated science with naturalism, assuming that science would, by definition, oppose and eventually destroy spirituality.

The Enlightenment had more than just this secular blueprint; as Denis Diderot (1713–1784) would say, "Men will never be free till the last king is strangled with the entrails of the last priest."[32] Again, they wanted an end to their era's *two* overarching forces of oppression: feudalism and the church. In seeking to eliminate religion's influence, the chief figures of the Enlightenment stand in contrast to the earlier Reformation leaders, who understood that while the church had harbored corruption and abuse (few people experienced the church's fury to the level many of them did), it was also inconsistent with Christ's teachings and had lost sight of some key gospel truths. For the reformers, *the church—not Christianity—was the problem.*

In addition, the Reformation, with its emphasis upon human equality (both as beings made in God's image and as sinners in need of His saving grace) and the priesthood of all believers, opened the door for the theological and philosophical justification of democracy and laid the ground for its emergence in the West. The preamble to the American Declaration of Independence, which affirms human rights and divine creation, is a reformational statement gleaned from biblical Christianity. No other concept had as substantial an influence on the overthrow of European feudalism and the Western monarchies.

❖ ❖ ❖ ❖

How can we say that the Enlightenment agenda *by itself* did not produce the modern world?

First, that agenda would have forced the removal of "Creator" from the Declaration of Independence and, with Him, the basis for "inalienable" rights. For instance, the societies produced by Marxist thought have denied and repressed individual freedom in order to further the ends of the state; atheism dramatically shaped that ideology's view of humankind. Under Marxism, collective goals take precedence over the desires of the individual, and, historically, the rights of humans inevitably end up crushed under the ideals of humankind. If man is just a product of nature, no more than an intelligent animal, then why shouldn't he be regarded only in terms of his usefulness to the state?

Second, that agenda would have diminished and reduced the Declaration's high view of humankind itself. One need only look at our Supreme Court's 1973 *Roe v. Wade* decision to see the difference between the convictions of America's founders and the tenets of Enlightenment secularism.

We also can compare the French and American Revolutions to comprehend this discrepancy. The French Revolution was a clear expression of Enlightenment values, beginning with the desire for "liberty, fraternity, and equality"[33] but ending in the Reign of Terror and Napoleon's oppression. That uprising failed because it had no sufficient foundation to build a just society and because it possessed an erroneous view of human nature.

In contrast, the American Revolution succeeded because it was correct in its beliefs about humankind—it was consistent with the way people actually are. We are "glorious ruins," as the theologian Francis Schaeffer (1912–1984) would say;[34] we're made in God's image, but we also are contaminated by sin. As a result, individuals can be given freedom, but governing power must be held in check as each branch of government watches and balances the others. The belief in man as a creature of great worth who is flawed by sin is the biblical view of human nature, and its revolutionary historical success stands as significant evidence for the validity of biblical Christianity.

❖ ❖ ❖ ❖

David Hume, a Scot, lived on the idealistic side of the French Revolution. He died more than a decade before its principles were put into practice; thus he compared the bright hope of the Enlightenment to the ugly reality of Europe in his day. He lived on the idealistic side of the scientific revolution as well. People had not yet used science to obliterate whole cities, nor was there any anticipation of the environmental and sociological problems associated with the technological revolution. Hume could write, "Generally speaking, the errors in religion are dangerous; those in philosophy are only ridiculous,"[35] because he never saw the horrors of social Darwinism and of nihilism as, for instance, revealed in the Nazi death camps. Like so many Enlightenment stalwarts, Hume was an ideologue, and at the center of his credo was the elimination of the Christian "superstition."

HUME'S NATURALISM

Hume first attacked natural theology, the belief that God's existence could be established from examining nature. At that time, most scientists considered themselves natural theologians—Sir Isaac Newton, for example, wrote as much on theology as he did on science—and again, for them, the role of science was to unfold the genius of God from the created order. Hume's initial assault was against the concept of *causation*.

At the center of that era's natural theology was the cosmological argument, which states that God is the first and ultimate cause of all things. Hume tried to argue that it's impossible to determine a cause by a subsequent effect. In other words, we can only say that something was caused; without the ability to carefully examine the process while it's occurring, we can't necessarily say what caused it. The argument originally fell on deaf ears; the complexity of the universe demanded a reasonable explanation, and an eternal Creator made more sense than any other possible answer. We may not have been able to "see" God create the world, but its majesty demanded an intelligent, personal, and all-powerful Creator nonetheless.

It's important to note, however, that Hume's perspectives were already cemented. He thought and wrote, not to discover truth, but to present his own settled view of what people needed to believe in order to achieve progress and freedom. He set out with a goal—the elimination of religious belief in society—and he was remarkably deliberate in his strategies.

Hume's approach of seeking weak points in prevailing arguments used to defend faith would become a characteristic of the Enlightenment philosophers. They *began* by rejecting Christianity and, like student debaters, crafted their arguments, not in pursuit of answers but in the specific aim of defeating their foe. They already had made up their minds: religion was the product of ignorance and superstition that must be eliminated for the good of humankind.

Accordingly, these challenges were not developed by sincere pursuers of truth but by people intent upon the intellectual destruction of a worldview. They were like reactive schoolchildren, making up a game's rules in order to guarantee their own victory. The point, in this regard, is that we must realize we are not in a philosophical discussion but rather an ideological debate.

David Hume was not engaging in an essentially philosophical dialogue on the validity of cause and effect. He was attacking the belief that God is the first cause of everything that exists. He was willing to reject the authenticity of cause and effect if it would lead to his desired conclusion, the denial of God's existence.

HUME'S VIEW OF MIRACLES

Hume's most lasting impact has come from his argument against miracles, which were understood at the time to be the strongest evidence for the Christian faith. The nineteenth-century German deconstructionist, theologian David Strauss, in speaking of Charles Darwin, stated clearly the Enlightenment view of the miraculous: "He [Darwin] has opened the door by which a happier coming race will cast out miracles, never to return."[36] Before Darwin, Hume attempted to argue against belief in miracles using philosophy, and while the idea that miracles are impossible was fostered by his arguments, he never said this; true to his strict empiricism, he only said that miracles are highly improbable.

Nevertheless, by invoking the laws of nature, *against* which he had previously argued in denying cause and effect, Hume then paved the path for one of the next era's main arguments against the miraculous. That later thesis states that a miracle is impossible because it is a violation of one of nature's laws. For now, though, even Hume had not been so bold as to assume to know the ultimate condition of the universe; he maintained that nature has no "laws," that what we call "law" is simply that which we've become accustomed to expect from the regular operation of natural forces. In fact, he said there's no guarantee that just because something has happened one way a thousand times before, it must happen that way again in the future.[37]

All the same, science eventually would refine his view to say that whenever a certain mechanism or force is present, we can expect that certain results will follow. Thus a stone dropped from a two-story building will always fall to the ground because of the force of the planet's gravitational field. An astronaut, far above the earth's surface, could release that same stone and watch it float in front of him.

❖ ❖ ❖ ❖

Hume was correct in maintaining that nature does not have inviolable "laws." Rather, nature contains mechanisms that produce the usual effects we see and hear around us. However, naturalism, the philosophy that emerged and developed from his thinking, would come to declare that nature does have laws and that those laws are ultimate and immutable. Naturalists alleged that even God, if there is one, couldn't perform a miracle because it would break *nature's laws.* In other words, every event that has ever occurred must have had a *natural* cause. Since by definition a miracle must have a non-natural cause, it is a violation and is considered impossible.

Naturalism insists that no event in nature has ever required us to resort to a supernatural explanation, and no event ever will. Naturalism says that such an explanation is a failure to be *scientific* and is, in essence, the lazy way out, bypassing sufficient research to discover the event's actual cause. Naturalism's foundational assumption is that *all* existing things had a natural cause. The only possible way for naturalism to give any place to a Creator is in the case of God "working through" nature. This has led to attempts to make evolution compatible with Christian faith by stating that God is "behind" it.

❖ ❖ ❖ ❖

Nevertheless, *the so-named laws of nature are only inviolable if nature is the ultimate reality.* That is to say, if only natural forces and objects exist, then every event in the history of the universe can only be the result of the interactions within nature. If, on the other hand, God is the ultimate reality and, as the Bible says, He created nature and rules nature, then miracles are not only possible, they are to be expected.

Those who use this argument to deny miracles have already decided there is no God; one substantial obstacle they face is the vast number of miracles people have experienced. Antagonists must seek to explain miracles away as superstition, delusion, or trickery. The problem is that so many apparently supernatural acts defy these explanations. The presence of miracles in human experience is a significant reason why religious faith never has been and never will be eradicated from society.

David Hume's weightiest argument against miracles was that a true miracle has never been witnessed by impartial and reliable witnesses and that, presumably, one never will. (Again, he also assumed that there is no God to produce them.) All miracle stories have been either from ignorant people giving supernatural explanations to natural events or from imposters seeking to deceive and control others.

Hume's contention, which he put forward in the eighteenth century, had a major problem: the universe. When the scientists of that time were using science to validate God's existence, it was hard for him to maintain that religion is unscientific. Hume did realize that many things known in the world of his day defied a natural explanation; his hope was that someday science would be able to explain everything in natural terms, and that belief in miracles then would cease. For those who anchored the Enlightenment, this would become a self-fulfilling prophecy.

Hume is one of the pillars of the empiricism that came to dominate the West. Scientists literally now are indoctrinated in the belief that only natural forces are at work in the natural world. Naturalism says that if something cannot be discovered with the physical senses or with physical instruments, then it's an unreality. Because no physical instrument—including human eyes and ears—can detect God, He does not exist, despite the display of beauty and order in nature.

HUME'S OVERALL CONTRIBUTION

Once again, David Hume's views were not widely accepted in his own day. Most scientists of that time were men of faith, and natural theology, the view that nature's wonder and beauty reveal the God who created them, was widely embraced. It was during this era that Robert Boyle established the Boyle Lectures, a series of public speeches in Christian apologetics. The most influential writer in natural theology was William

Paley, a contemporary of Hume who for that period had the more prominent influence. For instance, Paley's books (he also wrote on ethics) became required texts at British universities for a hundred years. Hume's work would not become dominant in Western philosophy until almost the twentieth century.

Today, however, the impact of David Hume (and Immanuel Kant—see below) has led many to believe that the matter is closed—that miracles and the supernatural realm *certainly* do not exist. The writings of Hume and Kant are often considered to have ended the debate; now, in many circles, rather than having to examine the evidence and discuss the issues, one need only defer to one or the other and the discussion is over. In the first years of my teaching, one of my apologetics students told of a paper he wrote for a composition class at the University of Pittsburg, seeking to defend Christ's resurrection. In response, his professor wrote, "You obviously have never read Hume," and gave him an F. The instructor made no attempt to interact with the arguments or examine the data; he simply deferred to Hume as if that were the final word.

IMMANUEL KANT

Immanuel Kant (1724–1804) is the most influential philosopher of the last three hundred years. His explanations on the limits of human reason have deeply influenced Western values, beliefs, and behavior, and his greatest impact was his contribution to the Enlightenment. Describing this, theologian R. C. Sproul (b. 1939) writes, "In comparison [to Kant] the American revolution was a trifle. The United States declared political independence of Great Britain; Kant declared intellectual independence of God."[38]

Whereas David Hume laid the philosophical foundation for naturalism, Immanuel Kant opened the West to relativism. His philosophy was built upon the question of knowledge: how much of reality can we actually know? He replied that *we only truly know our perceptions of reality—and not reality itself.*

Kant made the distinction between *phenomena* (our experiences) and *noumena* (the thing in itself). In other words, when we "touch" an object, such as a chair, we are experiencing the sensations produced by the nerve endings in our fingers, which are translated by our brain into the experience of "touching" the chair. But we do not by that experience know what the chair is really like; our sensations of things—seeing, hearing, and touching—are disconnected from the reality of the things in themselves.

Kant took this even further in saying that our mind *gives* structure to the universe itself. The apparent order in the universe, according to him, actually is a product of our mind's ability to organize and categorize thoughts and perceptions and of our desire to come up with a reasonable explanation for things.

❖ ❖ ❖ ❖

In reply, one is led to ask how our minds, allegedly products of this irrational and unstructured universe, came to be rational and structured.[39] To say that the order in the universe is a figment of our mental processes is to cast doubt on the reliability of our faculties. If we can no longer trust our eyes, our ears, or our minds, why do these faculties "see" and "hear" and "contemplate" order and beauty? Why are they able to make distinctions and discern patterns in nature? Most of us, and the natural sciences as well, would say that we perceive order because order truly is there for us to perceive.

KANT'S ANTINOMIES

For the reasons just given, this part of Kant's epistemology was not to be his most enduring legacy; it was his antinomies that would change the world. The antinomies were efforts at showing contradictions in the classical arguments for God's existence. From before the time of Thomas Aquinas, philosophy had presented what many felt were such "proofs," put forward in the same fashion by which one would prove a geometric axiom. Kant would seek to show that these arguments were not based on unquestionable certainties.

He began by demonstrating that the universe had to have had a beginning in time and *cannot be eternal* (because an infinite regress of cause and effect is impossible). Yet there also must have been a moment before the beginning occurred, and a moment before that, and so on; hence, in contrast, the universe *must be eternal.* As well, based on Euler's Principle (the least-action theory),[40] the universe *must be finite in size*; yet if we were to reach the universe's "outer wall," we would ask, what's on the other side of the wall? And what's beyond that? Therefore, conversely, the universe *must be infinite in size.*

Kant likewise extended the antinomies to issues such as free will and the existence of God. The effect was to put all foundational inquiries into the realm of mystery, that which is beyond our ability to know. One writer has described Kant's conclusion as,

> We cannot know whether or not there is a God, whether or not there is a soul, whether or not there is real freedom, whether or not there is immortality, whether or not there is a purpose in the world, whether or not suffering has meaning, whether or not life has meaning.[41]

He is thus the father of modern agnosticism, which holds that we cannot know—in fact, will never know—the answers to life's most important questions.

Kant's lifework, then, was the setting of parameters around the extent and degree of human knowledge. To summarize: Humankind, even collectively, is limited in its ability to know. There are dimensions beyond our reach and questions for which we have no answers. Every person, therefore, is required to make assumptions about the nature of reality without the luxury of certainty. He can hope his beliefs are true, but he cannot know whether they are true.

G. W. F. HEGEL

Every significant philosopher after Kant accepted his conclusions and used them as the starting point for his own work. The next thinker to shape the Western worldview was Georg Wilhelm Friedrich Hegel (1770–1831). If there is no dichotomy between truth and untruth (so suggested Kant's antinomies), then "truth" is temporal and relative. As would be said by many today, "truth" is an artificial construct created by the culture in which we find ourselves; it is not eternal and absolute but something that can change with the passing of time and circumstances. As a result, morals and values are relative to our time and place.

Hegel's theory of development would be an attempt to explain historical progress and to justify the *zeitgeist* optimism about the power of reason. He declared that when two contradictory ideas meet in the arena of history, they battle, literally and figuratively, and in the end they emerge as a single new, better, and stronger principle that elevates humankind. Hegel maintained that man's struggles throughout history were the source of progress from barbarity to civilization, and that this upward process would continue. His description of the "dialectic," truth changing and improving over time through the clashing of ideas, was a description of the Enlightenment belief in the *inevitability* of progress. The principle of the dialectic would be at the heart of Marxist thought and of Darwin's evolutionary theory.

❖ ❖ ❖ ❖

In response, Hegel's model has no support in either reason or history. There is no rationale for believing that the conflict of two ideologies necessarily will bring about the emergence of something better—it's just as likely that something worse will result. If the universe is governed by purely natural forces (i.e., if there is no God), then it has no bias toward good or bad, progress or regress, construction or destruction; it will take whatever path that cause and effect make for it.

The Enlightenment faith in the inevitability of upward human progress was an irrational hope based on overconfidence in science and the power of reason. The collective horrors of the twentieth century made a quick end of this unfortunate expectation.

The relativism that continued to emerge from Hegel was an attempt to set aside the inexorable law of non-contradiction. Kant's principle of the uncertainty of human knowledge could never eliminate this fundamental tenet of reality. His or her belief system notwithstanding, *every* human being in *every* culture operates—pragmatically—from this basic assumption: if something is true, its opposite must be false. As Francis Schaeffer showed,[42] the relativism that persisted through Hegel's philosophy only works in theory; in practice, people follow the law of non-contradiction.

For now, relativism has won the day in the West not because of logical superiority but because it allows people to set aside immutable moral standards and live what they consider to be a liberated lifestyle. Nonetheless, in truth, evil *is* evil and good *is* good; God will not be mocked, and we are continuing to reap the whirlwind of our persistent defiance.

CHARLES DARWIN

Before we move on to the next era, we must examine one more person, Charles Darwin (1809–1882), for in many ways his work would be the linchpin that connected together all these other ideas and gave them credence. Darwin's writing is the fulfillment of Hume's hope that a natural explanation could replace what previously could only be explained supernaturally. It is not an exaggeration to say that naturalism could not exist in the West without the underpinning of evolutionary theory.[43]

> Vainly did we philosophers and critical theologians over and over again decree the extermination of miracles. Our ineffectual sentence died away, because we could neither dispense with miraculous agency, nor point to any natural force able to supply it, where it had hitherto seemed almost indispensable. Darwin has demonstrated this force, this process of nature; he has opened the door by which a happier coming race will cast out miracles, never to return. Everyone who knows what miracles imply will praise him, in consequence, as one of the greatest benefactors of the human race.[44]

For his generation, Darwin provided the weapons needed to overcome the influence of the aforementioned William Paley, who had argued that the intricacy of the universe was clear evidence of it having been produced by an intelligent creator. Paley used the analogy of a watch, which, by its contours, by the complexity of its inner workings, and by its function of communicating data, is plainly of human (and intelligent) design. It would be unthinkable to attribute such complexity to chance or to natural processes. In the same way, when we see far greater levels of complexity in the universe than that which human intelligence can produce, it should be unthinkable to attribute them to chance. The far more satisfactory conclusion is to attribute the world to an intelligent creator, the "Divine Watchmaker."[45]

We noted earlier that Paley's writings were part of the British university curriculum for over a century; Darwin himself had been required to read Paley and was profoundly influenced by his views. By adulthood, though, he had rejected Paley's conclusion not because his studies in naturalism led him to do so but because of the problem of evil.[46] He wrote in a letter to a friend, "My theology is a complete muddle; I cannot look at the universe as a result of blind chance, yet I see no evidence of beneficent design of any kind in the details."[47] Darwin would come to call himself an agnostic, but the reality of suffering and his belief that the Bible was contradicted by geological findings led him toward what amounted to practical atheism.

NATURAL THEOLOGY'S MISSING INGREDIENT

The philosophy that was starting to take hold, and would eventually take over, was *methodological naturalism.* The problem with the *natural theology* of that era was that it failed to present a fully biblical picture of the world. In saying that the universe was designed, Paley and the others pointed to all the beneficent adaptations of creatures to their environments and all the wonderful features of the natural world. But they said nothing about the ever-present malaises of suffering, disease, or death. Scripture not only tells us that God created the world and that it was "very good,"[48] but also that the present world is fallen. Sin entered and was followed by disease and death. The universe has been subjected to "futility" and "corruption" as a consequence of human rebellion.[49]

The Christian worldview is fully cognizant of the existence of suffering and evil, and to the extent that natural theology failed to convey this, it failed to present biblical Christianity. As such, the unmistakable reality of suffering and death were considered natural theology's Achilles' heel.[50] One of Darwin's strengths was that he not only gave a natural explanation of "design" but also of the necessity of suffering in nature.

It would be Darwin's books that finally made the difference in the battle of ideologies. His theory on the origin of species seemed to provide a natural explanation for the biological world's complexity and order. He gave a purely cause-and-effect explanation for the appearance of design, and he implied that design does *not* necessitate a designer.

I believe this is the main reason for the theory's almost immediate acceptance in the intellectual community. Men such as the biologist Thomas Huxley (1825–1895), who became known as "Darwin's Bulldog," and the sociological philosopher Herbert Spencer (1820–1903), who himself introduced the phrase "survival of the fittest," found in Darwin's writings the ammunition they believed would enable them to defeat the church.

EVOLUTION'S MISSING INGREDIENT

The central advantage of *On the Origin of Species*[51] for Darwin's generation was that it gave a natural explanation to William Paley's strongest evidence for creation. Paley had maintained that every creature is perfectly adapted to its environment within the creation: a bee was designed for the production and storage of honey, a beaver was designed to cut down trees and build dams … each one had some adaptation related to its niche, and, unwittingly, each contributed to the well-being of the entire natural order. In a sense, this was to say, all things worked together for good as *God* superintended His marvelous creation.

Darwin's alternate explanation for this observed adaptation was natural selection. *Nature* provides these marvelous abilities in its creatures through a process of the accumulation of small genetic changes that enhance their ability to take advantage of their environment's special qualities. Nature "selects out" beneficial genetic change the way an agriculturist would select out the qualities he seeks to create in (for instance) a breed of poultry.

This argument is plausible, and Charles Darwin provided what he believed were numerous examples of this process from his observations in the isolated environment of the Galapagos Islands (in the Pacific, approximately six hundred miles west of Ecuador). The problem is—and this will continue to be evolution's critical weakness—plausibility is *not* proof. Darwin was not a biologist or a geneticist; he was a naturalist. His conclusions were not born out from detailed experimentation but from general observations of nature. He developed *hypotheses*, that is, possible explanations for the development of the features he was observing.

The work of science only *begins* at the development of a hypothesis; then, the hypothesis must be confirmed and refined into a theory, and then it must be tested by experiment and shown to be a repeated principle in nature. Darwin's theory of macroevolutionary change has never progressed beyond the stage of observation and speculation, and it has never been verified by experiment. In spite of this, the hypothesis has been broadly accepted within the scientific community as a law of nature.

The geneticist Richard Goldschmidt (1878–1958) spent twenty-five years trying to verify the hypothesis by mutation tests on insects.[52] His experiments completely failed to establish evolution by small incremental changes, so he abandoned gradual evolution for a theory of massive genetic change he called the "hopeful monster" (saltation).[53] Goldschmidt was considered a traitor and was widely scorned within the biological community, yet his initial concern has never been addressed. Mutation experiments have been conducted for over seventy years without showing any evidence of evolution. We will say much more about that later;[54] for now, note that the reaction of evolutionists to Goldschmidt tells us that something other than science is motivating their response.

WHY EVOLUTION?

Charles Darwin's theory of macroevolution is the cornerstone for the establishment of a secular society and a naturalistic worldview. As chemist Murray Eden (b. 1920), himself a critic of the theory, writes, "Darwin provided a program for a theory which made plausible an explanation of species without reference to a *deus ex machina*."[55] The naturalist commitment within Western culture is not made for scientific reasons but for philosophical and theological reasons. Darwinism allows people to explain life's origin and development without having to say God did it.

Darwinism would become a watershed for Western thought; the scientific community that broadly accepted the theory without question also made it dogma. Prior to Darwin, a significant number of scientists were outspoken Christians, but thereafter the percentage would steadily drop until, by the dawn of the next age, there were very few opposing scientific voices. Only in the latter half of the twentieth century did the lack of supporting evidence, in addition to other difficulties, lead to open criticism from respected scientists.

There is a growing discontent with the hypothesis as it is stated today, and, without reformulation, such as occurred in the 1920s with the development of neo-Darwinism,[56] the number of critics will continue to increase. There is no current danger that evolution will be abandoned, however, because it is the buttress of Western secularism. Too much is at stake—socially, politically, and religiously—to allow the theory to be forsaken.

THE AGE OF IRRATIONAL UNBELIEF: SUMMARY

By 1870 all pieces of the Enlightenment puzzle were in place, and naturalistic science had replaced the church as humankind's source of learning and salvation. Man was the captain of his own ship, and through enhanced education and inspired government, society could become heaven on earth. Reason and a careful study of human nature would even produce a set of moral values to replace those lost in the rejection of the supernatural (for many, these had been the only valid reason for religion in the first place).

By the end of the century the church had lost its moral authority through its persecutions, its intramural conflicts, and its religious wars; now it also lost the intellectual authority that natural theology had once given it. Now its last pillar of strength, the Scriptures, would come under attack, and the elimination of Christianity as the Western worldview's central assumption would be complete.

The *Humanist Manifesto*, published in 1933, would become the consummate expression of this faith in human reason. The manifesto aimed to provide an alternate source of purpose and morality to those who had become lost through the culture's abandonment of Christianity. For the Enlightenment, this was the "emancipation proclamation" for *all* humankind. While the enthusiasm seemed boundless, however, it was wildly unfounded, and the next generation would expose the fallacies on which it rested as optimism eventually yielded to despair.

---

[28] Leviathan was first published in 1670.

[29] Empiricism argues that only what can be physically seen, heard, touched, or otherwise sensed is real. David Hume said that any book not containing mathematical or empirical certainty is mere "sophistry and illusion" and should be committed "to the flames" (Enquiry Concerning Human Understanding, "Of the Academical or Sceptical Philosophy," Part III [Oxford: Clarendon, 1975, orig. published 1777]). He was, of course, not advocating book burning; rather, he was showing his disdain for metaphysics.

[30] David Hume, Dialogues Concerning Natural Religion, ed. Dorothy Coleman (Cambridge University Press, 2007; orig. published 1779 [posthumously]), 220.

[31] This quote from the astronomer/mathematician Johannes Kepler (1571–1630) became a motto of many eighteenth-century scientists.

[32] What Diderot actually wrote, in Les Éleuthéromanes, was "Et ses mains ourdiraient les entrailles du prêtre, / Au défaut d'un cordon pour étrangler les rois." ("And his hands would plait the priest's entrails, / For want of a rope, to strangle kings.") It seems that either he also said the phrase in its popular form, or that someone else later interpolated it.

[33] Originating in this form during the Revolution, "Liberté, égalité, fraternité" would later be made the motto of France.

[34] See Francis A. Schaeffer, The Mark of the Christian (Downers Grove, IL: InterVarsity, 1970) and The God Who Is There (Downers Grove, IL: InterVarsity, 1968).

[35] David Hume, A Treatise of Human Nature: A Critical Edition, eds. David Fate Norton and Mary J. Norton (Oxford: Clarendon Press, 2007; orig. published 1740), 272.

[36] Cited in Daniel Taylor, The Myth of Certainty: The Reflective Christian and the Risk of Commitment (Downers Grove, IL: InterVarsity, 1999).

[37] Hume, op. cit.

[38] R. C. Sproul, Classical Apologetics: A Rational Defense of the Christian Faith and a Critique of Presuppositional Apologetics (Downer's Grove, IL: InterVarsity, 1984), 30.

[39] We'll get to this, straightaway, in chapters four and five.

[40] This is "the principle that, for a system whose total mechanical energy is conserved, the trajectory of the system in configuration space is that path which makes the value of the action stationary relative to nearby paths between the same configurations and for which the energy has the same constant value. Also known as least-action principle." (Cited from answers.com)

[41] At www.friesian.com, see "Religious Value and the Antinomies of Transcendence after Kant." At www.friesian.com/antinom.htm, see also a presentation of the antinomies.

[42] See Schaeffer, The God Who Is There, especially pages 13–14 (in chapter two), 46 (regarding the law of non-contradiction), and 134–35 (in "Finding the Point of Tension").

[43] Evolutionary theory should properly be differentiated between microevolution and macroevolution. Microevolution, the capacity for genetic changes within species, has been demonstrated in agriculture, animal husbandry, and gardening. Mendel's Laws, which are the basic principles behind genetics, have been proven experimentally and are properly called genetic laws. Macroevolution, which is genetic change between species, is exactly what Darwin meant by "evolution." Macroevolution has never been proven by experiment or demonstrated in practice.

[44] In Taylor, The Myth of Certainty, again quoting the skeptical theologian David Strauss.

[45] In William Paley, Natural Theology, or Evidences of the Existence and Attributes of the Deity Collected from the Appearances of Nature (orig. published 1802). Paley wrote: "In crossing a heath, suppose I pitched my foot against a stone, and were asked how the stone came to be there; I might possibly answer, that, for anything I knew to the contrary, it had lain there forever: nor would it perhaps be very easy to show the absurdity of this answer. But suppose I had found a watch upon the ground, and it should be inquired how the watch happened to be in that place; I should hardly think of the answer I had before given, that for anything I knew, the watch might have always been there.... There must have existed, at some time, and at some place or other, an artificer or artificers, who formed it for the purpose which we find it actually to answer; who comprehended its construction, and designed its use.... Every indication of contrivance, every manifestation of design, which existed in the watch, exists in the works of nature; with the difference, on the side of nature, of being greater or more, and that in a degree which exceeds all computation" (emphasis mine).

[46] We will address and examine evil at length in chapter twelve.

[47] Cited in A. E. Wilder Smith, Man's Origin, Man's Destiny (Minneapolis: Bethany Fellowship, Inc., 1975), 200.

[48] Genesis 1:31.

[49] See Romans 8:19–22.

[50] More on natural theology in chapter five.

[51] Fully titled On the Origin of Species by Means of Natural Selection, or The Preservation of Favoured Races in the Struggle for Life (London: J. Murray, 1859).

[52] See Richard Benedict Goldschmidt, Theoretical Genetics (Berkeley: University of California Press, 1955). Goldschmidt said, "Nobody has ever succeeded in producing a new species, not to mention the higher categories, by selection of micro-mutations."

[53] Saltation, or massive genetic change in a relatively short period of time, is the assumption behind the later theory concerning macroevolutionary change called "punctuated equilibrium."

[54] See chapter six.

[55] Murray Eden, ed., The Mathematical Challenges to the Neo-Darwinian Interpretation of the Theory of Evolution (Cambridge: Harvard University Press, 1966), 5.

[56] Neo-Darwinian theory originated from the need to explain how genetic change might be able to leap across the species barrier demonstrated by Gregor Mendel's genetics laws. The apparent candidate for this supposed process was mutation, first proffered during the 1920s. Neo-Darwinian theory, then, suggests that the dramatic macroevolutionary change alleged to have produced the various species of plants and animals is the result of genetic mutation (see also http://en.wikipedia.org/wiki/Modern_evolutionary_synthesis).

CHAPTER FOUR

HISTORICAL DEVELOPMENT (PART III)

THE AGE OF RATIONAL UNBELIEF: 1900–1950

Not so far into the twentieth century, the untenably weak foundation of Enlightenment optimism was already being exposed philosophically, and by the 1940s the political movements founded upon its assumptions were unmasked, shown to be fraudulent. George Orwell (1903–1950), himself a socialist, was profoundly disillusioned by the outworking of socialism in the communist world. Rather than newfound freedom and enlightened government, he saw inhumanity and oppression everywhere. His books *Animal Farm* and *Nineteen Eighty-Four* were exposés of the failed Marxist experiment.[57]

Even worse, with Nazi fascism, science and technology came to the service of tyranny and genocide. The two world wars crushed the former era's enthusiasm. Society was *not* getting better and better. Educated, naturalistic man could be just as cruel and barbaric as anyone who had come before him; plus, science had now given him weapons of mass destruction.

As the philosopher Albert Camus (1913–1960) wrote in *The Rebel*, "One might think that a period which, in a space of fifty years, uproots, enslaves, or kills seventy million people should be condemned out of hand."[58]

FRIEDRICH NIETZSCHE

The man who more than any other shattered the Enlightenment's illusions was Friedrich Wilhelm Nietzsche (1844–1900), who saw clearly the logical conclusion of the naturalistic worldview. Nietzsche began his career as a philologist.[59] His study of words and literature developed his remarkable skill as a writer, and he would go on to use poetry, story, and symbolism to express his philosophy.

Furthermore, his career ultimately would mirror his philosophical significance; his brilliance set him apart, even from his contemporaries, and his unique understanding of "irrational unbelief" would place him far ahead of his time. Because his vision would enable him to grasp what others had yet failed to recognize—the stark implications of a purely natural universe—he would be a lonely, isolated figure.

While a professor at the University of Basel, Nietzsche encountered two writers, the philosopher Arthur Schopenhauer (1788–1860), and the theologian David Strauss (1808–1874), who exposed him to the Enlightenment's central tenet: the end of religious belief. Schopenhauer was a Jewish philosopher who created a storm of controversy when he sought a "natural" explanation for the events of the Old Testament Exodus, in particular the parting of the Red Sea. Strauss became famous through his naturalistic explanations for the life of Christ; he would be one of the first to attempt discovering the "historical Jesus," which in turn would become the holy grail of liberal theology.

Crucially, in addition, Schopenhauer influenced Nietzsche (1) as to the power of the human will in the face of a tragic reality, and (2) in rejecting, as an irrational fantasy, belief in the inevitability of human progress.

❖ ❖ ❖ ❖

In *The Parable of the Madman*, Nietzsche wrote,

> "Where is God?" I'll tell you, we have killed him, you and I. We are all his murderers.... What did we do when we unchained the earth from its sun? Whither is it moving now? Whither are we moving now? Away from all suns maybe? Are we not continually and perpetually falling backwards, forwards, sideways, and in all directions? Is there any up or down left? Are we not straying through an infinite nothing? Do you not feel the breath of empty space? Has it not become colder? Is not more and more night coming on us all the time?[60]

Needless to say, a world without God is cold and dark. Naturalism, which is foundationally atheistic, provides no basis for the significance of life. It leaves man as a meaningless accident within a meaningless universe.

Nietzsche, believing that man *is* alone in a purposeless reality, instructed us to take complete responsibility for the direction and outcome of our human existence. He felt that our collective undertaking of this endeavor ultimately would lead to the *Übermensch* (the Superman), who finally would usher in and enthrone true human greatness.[61] In practical terms, however, *his philosophy mandated that the strong rule the weak in a ruthless pursuit of power.* Horrifically, two of the major twentieth-century political movements seized that advice and terrorized the world for a significant portion of the era. This philosophy would be called *nihilism* (from Latin *nihil*, "nothing") because it negates life's meaning.

Nietzsche's point was exactly this: a universe produced by the chance interactions of impersonal matter can have neither purpose nor import. In light of our reality—this pointless coincidence produced by senseless elements—the human personality becomes a cruel joke. We know, we care, we feel, but we are the only ones truly awake. Even the animals, with whom we share life, are at least spared conscious thought and self-awareness; they can accept their lot and their fate without any sense of injustice or betrayal. *We,* of all creatures, are to be most pitied.

❖ ❖ ❖ ❖

As Nietzsche was the period's most influential philosopher, it makes sense that his utterly bleak portrayal of the universe would be reflected in nearly every art form. Arthur Miller's *Death of a Salesman*[62] stands out among countless iconic expressions of modern-world pessimism; Miller's aptly named hero is Willy Lowman, who, as a symbol of all men, mirrors the futility of human goals and the pointlessness of human aspirations. Summarily, Schaeffer's apt description of the impact of Nietzsche's conclusions upon Western civilization was that we, as a race, have fallen below the "line of despair."[63]

If we do live in a closed universe, originated and governed by chance and natural forces, we must come to grips with this reality and respond accordingly. Again, for Nietzsche, the appropriate response was philosophically equivalent to the survival of the fittest: We must become strong and ruthless, and, through the will to power, the strongest among us must rule the weak. Nietzsche was an outspoken critic of Christianity, not because he believed the Bible was outdated or that naturalistic science made it obsolete, but because, in his view, faith not only made people "weak," it also encouraged the protection of the weak among us. *How can we face a pitiless universe and survive therein if we are not likewise without compassion?*

Subsequent years have proven that Nietzsche's *Übermensch* is an illusion and that his philosophy lived out will look like Hitler's Third Reich or Stalin's Soviet empire. Nietzsche never lived to see his thought put into practice by maniacal despots, and from his writings one must ascertain that he would not have approved. One of history's most astounding ironies is that Nietzsche intended his philosophy to stand in *opposition* to what would become known as nihilism; he posited his beliefs in the context of the escapist, idealistic politico-religious ideologies of his day. Nevertheless, he begat a world-changing movement that others took to its logical conclusion, which wrought catastrophe that was responsible for more suffering than any other single ideology, *ever*.

Camus, speaking about the Nuremburg Trials of the Nazi war criminals, said they were really about "the historic responsibilities of Western nihilism." He also wrote that "a trial cannot be conducted by announcing the general culpability of a civilization."[64] In other words, the Nazis were not an isolated expression of one man's insane ambition and demented view of reality; they were a product of the abandonment of God and of truth that was at the core of the Enlightenment agenda. The "Enlighteners" didn't originally intend to produce nihilistic nothingness, but, unbeknownst to them, the path that begins with the rejection of religion ends nonetheless with the rejection of meaning and hope.

The Third Reich and the Soviet machine were not aberrations—they were products of the nihilism that increasingly was seizing and blanketing the Western world. When man denies God, he likewise denies all that is good and just; thus did we open the floodgates for the onslaught of evil. To a devastating degree, the history of the twentieth century better demonstrates and exemplifies this principle than that of any other.

RELIGION AS A CRUTCH

Nietzsche's view of Christianity in particular—essentially, as a weakness, rather than as a strength—also would be popularized in the twentieth century. Sigmund Freud (1856–1939), the father of psychoanalysis, would speak of religion as "wish fulfillment," that is, as a product of the fear of death and a desire for an always-reliable father figure to care for us in the midst of life's difficulties. By implication, Freud, following Nietzsche, was saying that a truly courageous person is willing to face the reality of a purely natural universe, while a religious person has given in to cowardice and has bought into an invention he imagines to be a source of safety and comfort. In common terms, the opinions of Nietzsche and Freud are summarized in the statement, "Religion is a crutch for the weak."[65]

But is this really the case? *Are* the religious among us recognizable by their cowardice and insecurity? *Has* the culture's public and political rejection of religion made us stronger, more self-reliant, and more courageous?

In contrast, an examination of our youngest generations can't help but highlight the level of expressed dysfunction in their lives. In many ways they measure themselves by their anxiety disorders, their attention deficits, and their use of medications available for coping with stress. Postings on Internet "friend" sites largely read like the ramblings of amateur psychologists diagnosing the myriad maladies of empty-souled, brokenhearted people.

The belief that we are random accidents in a meaningless universe will lead us not toward the will to power but to fatalism, to despairing self-pity. Atheism will not make humankind stronger. We only become weaker as we lose the will to live in what we believe is a pointless, unanimated reality.

❖ ❖ ❖ ❖

Much of the contemporary era's artistic expression is a manifestation of this corporate loss. For my generation, that of the 1960s, two movies succinctly expressed the angst of a purposeless existence. In *The Graduate*,[66] the question is, why should I enter the status-quo, generally accepted adult world, the world of my parents, with its patent hypocrisy and worthless values? The answer of the 60s was, I won't waste my life in the world of Mrs. Robinson; I must find a new way—in fact, I must *make* a new way. The counterculture[67] was really an exodus from the conclusions of the previous two hundred years of Western society.

Even more powerful was *They Shoot Horses, Don't They?*[68] The images of this film, indelibly etched on my mind, depict a young man and woman, each on their own journey, meeting at a dance marathon during the Great Depression. The man, a sailor, soon discovers that the woman desperately needs the prize money being offered; he agrees to be her dance partner.

Together they fight through the fatigue of dancing day after day, until they find themselves one of the last couples still standing. As they near what appears to be success, the manager of the contest lets them in on a little secret: it's rigged, and there is no prize money. The young woman, filled with disillusionment and despair, puts a gun to her head but is unable to pull the trigger. The man, in what he perceives to be an act of mercy, takes the weapon and puts her out of her misery. In the last scene, as he stands before the judge to defend his action, he declares, "They shoot horses, don't they?"

I know of no movie from that century that more concisely allegorized the dilemma of Western culture. If there is no God, then life is a cruel farce, a sham throughout which we labor and sweat for a non-existent reward. Most people accept the illusion, play the game, and are none the wiser.

Some, however, discover the truth of their condition, and for them the game is over; they must now decide if suicide is an option. If man is only a product of capricious nature—if he is merely a self-conscious animal—then why *shouldn't* the wounded be put out of their misery? Think of Jack Kevorkian, for example; as disturbing as we may find the agenda of assisted suicide, it *is* consistent with the naturalism that has permeated our society.

THE ENLIGHTENMENT'S ONGOING IMPACT

We must be clear about where the Enlightenment has taken us: it has led us to the brink. Its ultimate conclusion, nihilism, is a spiritual wasteland. Humankind cannot live there any more than we could survive unprotected and without provisions in the Sahara. It is, as Albert Camus described it, the region of the *absurd:*

> If we believe in nothing, if nothing has any meaning and if we can affirm no values whatsoever, then everything is possible and nothing has any importance. There is no pro or con: the murderer is neither right nor wrong. We are free to stoke the crematory fires or to devote ourselves to the care of lepers. Evil and virtue are mere chance or caprice.[69]

The philosophers, *and* we their pupils, "professing to be wise," have become fools.[70] The Enlightenment brought us not to a promised land but into a barren wilderness, and now many of us feel we must find our own road back. We can no longer trust science or even reason; we must find other avenues. Part of the movement we call postmodernism is exactly this search for another way.

Our reaction against nihilism is intuitive; it goes fully against the intrinsic grain of our humanness. That's why Camus could not accept this moral ambivalence—because he was a person, innately human and hence imbued with the divine. Good still is and always will be preferred over evil; the core of our being gravitates toward the good and even fights for it.

> The final conclusion of absurdist reasoning is, in fact, the repudiation of suicide and the acceptance of the desperate encounter between human inquiry and the silence of the universe....
>
> I proclaim that I believe in nothing and that everything is absurd, but I cannot doubt the validity

> of my proclamation and I must believe at least in my protest.[71]

Albert Camus was willing to cling to life to continue his protest against what he described as the "silence of the universe." But if the universe truly were silent, if reality were only a *thing*, then protest would be pointless—equivalent to a man sternly lecturing the rock upon which he has just stubbed his toe. To protest is to assume there is *someone* to protest to; it is a tacit admission that deep down we don't believe the universe is impersonal or meaningless.

There's more involved here than just "reasoning." Once again, Camus was expressing his *humanity*. Something deep inside him could not accept a senseless reality. Why? If reality actually were meaningless, why, and how, should there have arisen any part of us that values meaning? C. S. Lewis (1898–1963) said, of his former unbelief,

> My argument against God was that the universe seemed so cruel or unjust. But how had I got this idea of *just* and *unjust*? A man does not call a line crooked unless he has some idea of a straight line.[72]

THE AGE OF RATIONAL UNBELIEF: SUMMARY

Possibly the most well known of the twentieth-century existentialist thinkers was Jean-Paul Sartre (1905–1980). Sartre is said to have described his philosophy as "total responsibility for a life lived in total isolation."[73] In this vein, we *are* truly alone in the universe, and what we make of our lives is entirely up to us; this is the essence of modern existentialism.

Such a plainly pessimistic view of life, which appears to be the culmination of rationalistic thought and scientific research, has led many to look for alternative approaches to "truth." Sartre himself chose actions that contradicted his amoral ideology. For example, in 1954 he signed the "Algerian Declaration"[74] in opposition to the French government's pursuit of nuclear weapons. He was sharply criticized for betraying his beliefs, but in signing the protest, he was acting as a person, not as a philosopher.

Existential nihilism still stands as a contributing factor to and presence within Western culture, but the vast majority of people in the West cannot and do not reside there. They're now like the hero of *The Graduate*; they're desperately looking for a way of escape from the lifeless, desolate terrain of a closed universe that randomly derived from and is inexorably ruled by faceless natural forces. Like Albert Camus and Jean-Paul Sartre, they have often followed their hearts more than their heads.

THE AGE OF IRRATIONAL BELIEF : 1950–PRESENT

In popular culture, the big shift took place from approximately 1954 to 1968 with the hippie movement and the formation of the counterculture. If science and technology have given us Aldous Huxley's *Brave New World*,[75] and if reason leads only to despair, then why have anything to do with them? Why not "Turn On, Tune In, [and] Drop Out," as Timothy Leary encouraged?[76] An entire generation set out on a spiritual quest, based not necessarily on reason or history but on the intuitive sense that as human beings they were more than biological machines or the accidental products of random forces.

The search took them to LSD and magic mushrooms, to Leary and Maharashi Mahesh Yogi, to Haight-Ashbury and Katmandu. Many drug users of this period were not looking for a high; they were seeking to part the veil between this world and the world of the spirit. As almost everything does in American culture, hippiedom would eventually become a form of hedonistic escapism, but it didn't start out that way. Its instigators saw themselves as spiritual pilgrims who were hoping to find the road to nirvana.

SØREN KIERKEGAARD

Francis Schaeffer called Søren Kierkegaard (1813–1855) "the father of modern thought"[77] because, more than a century before, Kierkegaard had clearly articulated the dilemma of modern man. If people follow naturalistic science, they are led to conclude that man is a meaningless accident, a freak of nature with no ultimate purpose beyond individual survival and personal comfort. Reason, meanwhile, takes one only to a dead end of hopelessness.

Kierkegaard's existentialism, therefore, turned its back on objective reasoning with the design of finding a transcendent reality in subjective experience. Kierkegaard, like Nietzsche, opposed the Enlightenment's baseless optimism; progress is not inevitable, nor, as Hegel claimed, is it built into the structure of the universe. Kierkegaard was particularly offended by Hegel's attempt to deny the law of non-contradiction.[78] That which is actually true cannot become false, and that which is truly wrong won't ever become right.

❖ ❖ ❖ ❖

Kierkegaard would profoundly influence the next generation of philosophers through three important concepts.

First, he would speak of our need to accept the reality of the "*absurd*," connecting the idea of the absurd with the necessity of faith. His famous expression "the Leap of Faith" perhaps is best conveyed by the phrase "I believe it [e.g., heaven, miracles, God] because it is absurd."[79] For him, the acceptance of a belief's absurdity was essential to accepting it by faith.

Second, he spoke of *angst* as central to the human experience. "Angst," which would commonly be translated as "fear," more properly means "discomfort" or "alienation" in

Kierkegaard's philosophy.[80] Later existentialists—in particular, Martin Heidegger (1889–1976)—would make "angst" central to their view of the human experience. Heidegger said that we find ourselves alienated from nature because while we're creatures of nature, a part of us doesn't feel at home in nature. We are alienated from God, from the truly transcendent; it's unknowable and unattainable for us. Finally, we're alienated from ourselves, finding even many of our own actions unfathomable.[81]

Third, Kierkegaard's most significant contribution probably was his description of God as "*wholly other.*"[82] In other words, for us, as finite human beings, God is a completely incomprehensible reality; the separation between God and man (one of the gospel's central teachings) is due to our inability to gain rational knowledge of Him. Kierkegaard taught that this distant, utterly transcendent God can only be approached by that needful faith-leap. The leap is based not on objective evidence but on the subjective hope that God truly exists.

On the whole, Kierkegaard's search for meaning in the realm of the irrational would (1) pave the way for the subjective to enter into Western thought, and (2) legitimize a pursuit of "truth" not founded on reason and evidence but *in contradiction to* reason and evidence.

It's important to separate Kierkegaard the philosopher from Kierkegaard the believer. He wrote extensively on the Christian life, and he was extremely critical of the empty formality he saw in so many churches. His deep desire was for a vital, life-changing relationship with Christ.

The problem was, just as his own life was compartmentalized between the philosopher living in the realm of the material (e.g., science) and the Christian living in the realm of the spiritual (e.g., faith), so his writings would only exacerbate that same compartmentalization in the Western world. Eventually an entire branch of theology—neo-orthodoxy[83]—would mirror his attempt to create a safe haven for faith, separate from the demands and attacks of reason.

THE COUNTERCULTURE

As Theodore Roszak's[84] book *The Making of a Counter-Culture*[85] vividly described, no generation took the leap of faith more seriously than that of the 1960s. The culture of their parents told them they were biological machines devoid of purpose beyond sustaining the all-encompassing military-industrial complex. They saw that world as empty and lifeless; they called it the "plastic society" and rejected it out of hand. The hippies, in seriously undertaking the leap, dropped out of default culture, doggedly pursuing a meaningful reality and seeking to create an alternative milieu based on three irrational hopes.

First, they hoped that the ancients were right and that deep within the core of nature was magic and mystery. Second, they hoped that within nature there were substances (LSD, peyote, and marijuana, for instance) that would lead them into this hidden dimension. And third, they rejected the philosophies and religions of the rationalistic West for those of the East, hoping that these were more likely to take them to the desired realm of the transcendent.

Thousands of young people joined the counterculture's "Magical Mystery Tour." They formed communes, lived in vans traveling cross-country, and sought to rediscover nature. For the majority, the tour ended in disillusionment. They found that "free love" wasn't free at all but carried the price of emotional and sometimes physical devastation. They learned that most of nature is cold, hard, and cruel; the mystery, if it exists in nature, extracts an extremely high cost. They also discovered that drugs, even those derived from "nature," are harmful and even can be deadly. In the end, most were compelled by necessity to reenter regular society.

❖ ❖ ❖ ❖

There's an amusing TV advertisement in which two early-teen boys holding cans of Pepsi watch people their parents' age, all dressed up (suits and ties, dresses and dress shoes), revisiting the scene of Woodstock. The boys stare incredulously at the antics of these obviously middle-aged people—they clearly have no idea what their parents once were into. They only know the conservative values their parents adopted *after* the 60s; they have no concept of the search for freedom and love and significance that took place before they were born.

What remains of the hippie pursuit is the quest for spiritual fulfillment. In the beginning there were two approaches: drugs and mysticism. When the former were found to be counterproductive, the pursuit shifted to the latter, which was sought through both Eastern religions and the occult.[86] The remnant of the movement today is the widespread popularity of New Age spirituality, and in many ways this is an American assimilation of the original intent. It's otherworldliness in Dockers and a Polo shirt. It's listening to Deepak Chopra on satellite radio in a BMW.

Primarily, the hippie experiment failed because American youth, accustomed to the comfort and convenience of Western technology, found they could not live the primitive, natural lifestyle for any extended period of time. The romance of nature soon wore off, and most of that generation took their places beside their parents in sustaining and enjoying the benefits of corporate America. Nevertheless, there persists a deep and abiding spiritual hunger in the West.

THE CONSEQUENCES

One critical result of the experiment's failure was that the generations following the counterculture were left without the hippie era's hopefulness and idealism. Accordingly, the options of these later generations were greatly reduced. The hippies' inability to achieve authentic community, global peace, and a viable alternative to materialistic consumption left their children and grandchildren without the better-world optimism that had been a primary reason for the countercultural pursuit.

Drugs now had nothing to do with spirituality; they became about escapism and altered perception. Society's youth also moved away from Eastern mysticism to delve deeper into the occult, and as their choices diminished they became more and more nihilistic. The music got harder, the images turned violent, clothing and cosmetics became darker, and some even moved toward self-mutilation. Colorful idealism had been replaced by icy realism: enter Punk and Goth. If the slogan of the 60s was "This is the first day of the rest of your life," in the 90s it was "Life sucks."

The 1999 Columbine tragedy, for instance, was not fundamentally about access to powerful guns or the dangers of graphic media—it was a nightmarish expression of the next generation's overwhelming hopelessness. Intuiting that they're left without alternatives in an absurd and meaningless reality, they're giving themselves over to rage and despair. This is the true horror of nihilism; most of us don't take it to its ultimate ends, most of us don't articulate its final implications … most of us don't even *realize* where it's leading us.

But kids do. And even though we don't spell it out for them, their still-creative and yet-imaginative souls are showing them where we're going. They think, *Why crawl to the finish line? If this is all there is, and if that's how it will end, then why not just be authentic about it and live out what we really believe?*

If you do not sense the desperation, the ennui, the almost suicidal abandonment of virtue, you are not sensing the heartbeat of this age. Why do rock stars dress like medieval executioners or paint their faces in demon masks? Why do they blur the lines between male and female and glorify illicit sex and brutal violence? And why does this attract young people? Ultimately because they have embraced nihilism; in light of our collective core beliefs, we've given them no other credible options.

Fyodor Dostoyevsky (1821–1881) may have defined it best:

If God does not exist,

then everything is permitted.[87]

The appeal of nihilism (and its political counterpart, anarchy) is *unlimited* "freedom." That is to say, because nothing matters, anything goes. Like a drug, it promises pleasure and excitement; also, like a drug, it destroys the life of its user.

Throughout history—and our day is no different—nihilism invariably degenerates into perversion, cruelty, and death. Those aspects of Western civilization that have incorporated nihilism are presently spiraling downward, and anyone who can stand to watch literally will see the descent toward destruction. Not long ago the *London Times* reported that an occult movement in Eastern Germany had led to the deaths of fifteen young people in two years; another fifteen to twenty in the immediate region were seen to be at risk for suicide.[88] As the culture grows increasingly decadent, its despair is rising proportionately, and this is most visible in the youth.

If we continue on our way, our growing acceptance of and even passion for "Everything is permitted" will be our undoing.

❖ ❖ ❖ ❖

Our society seems virtually oblivious to the consequences of its choices. We have swept away the church, we have sought to rid ourselves of the "middle-class morality" of social convention, and now we are pressing our central institutions—the courts, the legislatures, and the schools—to legitimize what we think we want. And, in embracing everything, we must *fool* the populace (ourselves!) into accepting the unacceptable.

We accomplish this largely through careful terminology. We are protecting "rights," promoting "diversity," and preventing "intolerance." But this is political rhetoric—we're really saying we have the right to engage in or ignore whatever we please, because essentially it makes no difference. It's both agonizing and fascinating that we must resort to deceit to achieve the goal of nihilism. That we must cheat ourselves and blind our own eyes to believe that everything is truly a right and that the "values" we're promoting will bring peace or harmony.

One classic example is the story of a mother who would not allow her son to continue in the Boy Scouts because of their decision to restrict openly gay scoutmasters.[89] Homosexual behavior is a contradiction of everything the Scouts represent; they are about instilling in young men the virtues (such as integrity and morality) at the erstwhile core of our civilization. That a mother, in the name of tolerance, would *not* want those values instilled in her son, or that she wouldn't fear the damage were he to become a predator's target, indicates how powerful and pervasive our culture's forces of indoctrination have become.

THE OBSTACLE OF OUR HUMANITY

One of the most stalwart barriers facing promoters of unlimited license is that of our humanity. Because our conscience will not allow us to knowingly promote evil, we must deceive it and even enlist it in our cause. *We must somehow make evil seem good.* But this raises a question: In an allegedly meaningless universe—in a pointless, impersonal reality—why does human nature value the good and show aversion to evil? Why have all of history's tyrants and madmen had to use "double-speak,"[90] convoluting and confusing evil with goodness, in order to unleash destruction upon the earth?

This has been confirmed repeatedly throughout the annals of time. For instance, in order to consent to mass murder, a people must have their victims defined in terms that make the victims appear to be subhuman. The extermination of millions of Jews and Gypsies during the Second World War was achieved by propaganda. The Jews, for example, were accused of elaborate conspiracies to rule the world and of acts of unspeakable cruelty—like sacrificing Gentile children for their Passover bread.[91] None of the allegations was true, but they reinforced anti-Semitic hatred that had existed in Europe for centuries.

Likewise, the genocide of North and South American indigenous peoples was justified by establishing them as "savages." In our own day, we've gone through a polarized and protracted debate about the nature of a human fetus. Our conclusion—that it isn't a human being and therefore isn't subject to legal protection—is simply another attempt to deceive our conscience and allow, or perpetrate, a murderous massacre in the name of "rights."

❖ ❖ ❖ ❖

What's the overarching point in all this? *The curiosity of conscience.* Humans are not animals; we cannot kill without justification, and we cannot selfishly satiate our own appetites without some process of legitimization. This is not to say animals are evil—they do what instinct demands, and because they do not have reason or conscience, they are innocent. Humans are different; we innately have another level of existence, of *being*. The calling to do good and to shun evil comes from within, from the voice of conscience, of reason. And again we must ask: *why?* Why, as Lewis put it, if the universe is all "crooked," do I find "straight" inside of me?[92]

This is why, at their absolute core, people *cannot* embrace nihilism. Though they may believe they have no choice but to accept its conclusions, they do not willingly do so. While a large part of our culture has abandoned itself to pointlessness, many people are frantically looking for a way out, prisoners searching for a hidden passage out of their dungeon. Their hope is to find a way of life that releases them from the condemnation of meaninglessness; we noted earlier, too, that most are following their hearts and not their heads in this process.

People of the East *and* West embrace New Age spirituality for subjective, experiential reasons, not objective, scientific reasons. The number of those who embrace this option will continue to grow in the coming years, and it will continue to receive widespread cultural and popular support. *People cannot live without hope.*

THE AGE OF IRRATIONAL BELIEF : SUMMARY

Western civilization has reached a juncture of desperation and despair. In describing its present state, we began by using three terms: secularism, relativism, and pluralism. All three ultimately are *negations*: no God, no absolutes, and no final conclusion about reality. We cannot build our lives upon these; they offer us no direction, and they leave us without hope.

We embraced them out of an adolescent desire for freedom from rules, fueled by idealism and an unwarranted optimism regarding human nature. We found ourselves badly mistaken. We had placed our faith in science and technology only to discover that they provided no foundation for morality or justice. Instead they left us alone in an impersonal universe. Scientific reasoning concluded that we're just a cosmic accident, the chance combination of molecules forming a self-conscious animal.

Reason and science, therefore, became roads to nowhere, and countless people in the West began to turn around and look elsewhere for *something* that would give them hope. They delved into existential philosophy and Eastern mysticism; they experimented with drugs; they explored the occult. They still haven't found what they need—what they were made for, what corresponds with who they are and why they're here.

The West today is searching for spiritual reality. The key question is, will the Christian church be ready to assist in the pursuit?

---

[57] George Orwell, Animal Farm: A Fairy Story (London: Secker & Warburg, 1945); and Nineteen Eighty-Four: A Novel (London: Secker & Warburg, 1949).

[58] Albert Camus, The Rebel (New York: Vintage Books, 1956), 3.

[59] Philology, which literally means the "love of words," technically is the study of human verbal communication using language. Philology focuses on the impact historical and cultural forces had and have on the development of literature and language (see also http://en.wikipedia.org/wiki/Philology).

[60] In Friedrich Nietzsche, The Gay Science (orig. published 1882; second ed. 1887).

[61] See Friedrich Nietzsche, Thus Spoke Zarahthustra: A Book for All and for None (orig. released 1883–1885).

[62] Arthur Miller, Death of a Salesman: Certain Private Conversations in Two Acts and a Requiem (New York: Viking, 1949).

[63] See Francis A. Schaeffer, The Complete Works of Francis Schaeffer, Volume 1 (Wheaton, IL: Crossway Books, 1982), 8.

[64] Camus, The Rebel, 181.

[65] Nietzsche once said that "In Christianity neither morality nor religion come into contact with reality at any point." Freud, who considered religion roughly equivalent to early-life neuroses, also said that it's an illusion, once which "derives its strength from its readiness to fit in with our instinctual wishful impulses."

[66] The Graduate. Dir. Mike Nichols. Embassy Pictures Corporation, 1967.

[67] More on the counterculture below, under "The Age of Irrational Belief: 1950–Present."

[68] They Shoot Horses, Don't They? Dir. Sydney Pollack. Palomar Pictures/ABC, 1969.

[69] Camus, The Rebel, 5.

[70] See Romans 1:22; cf. 1 Corinthians 1:18–27; 2:14.

[71] Camus, The Rebel, 6, 10.

[72] C. S. Lewis, Mere Christianity (New York: Macmillan, 1952), 45.

[73] In Jean-Paul Sartre, Being and Nothingness (New York: Citadel, 2001; orig. published 1956).

[74] This document actually was titled Declaration on the Right to Insubordination in the War in Algeria: The Manifesto of the 121.

[75] Aldous Huxley, Brave New World (Garden City, NY: Doubleday, Doran & Co., 1932).

[76] Timothy Leary, "Turn On, Tune In, Drop Out" (sound recording). Chicago: Mercury, 1967.

[77] Francis A. Schaeffer, The God Who Is There (Downers Grove, IL: InterVarsity, 1968), 15.

[78] Aristotle described this principle thusly: "One cannot say of something that it is and that it is not, in the same respect and at the same time" (emphasis mine).

[79] In Søren Kierkegaard, Either/Or (orig. published 1843).

[80] In Søren Kierkegaard, Fear and Trembling (orig. published 1843).

[81] See Martin Heidegger, Being and Time, trans. John MacQuarrie and Edward Robinson (Oxford: Blackwell, 1967; orig. published 1927).

[82] See Kierkegaard, Either/Or.

[83] See footnote on neo-orthodoxy from chapter two, under "Faith verses Reason?"

[84] Professor of History at the University of California-Hayward, Theodore Roszak has written extensively on the New Age, the counterculture, feminism, and the ecological movement. He is considered a leading spokesman for a transcendent view of nature.

[85] Theodore Roszak, The Making of a Counter-Culture: Reflections on the Technocratic Society and Its Youthful Opposition (Garden City, NY: Doubleday, 1969).

[86] The occult (the word means "hidden") is the pursuit of magical power and knowledge; it's integral to the New Age movement. The occult is mostly connected to pagan beliefs and practices that arose from ancient animism.

[87] In Fyodor Dostoyevsky, The Brothers Karamazov (orig. published 1880).

[88] Allen Hall, "Teenagers Jump to their Deaths" in the London Times (Tuesday, August 28, 2001).

[89] Information from article in the Oak Park Journal (May 9, 2001).

[90] See Orwell, Nineteen Eighty-Four.

[91] The primary source behind this legend was The Protocols of the Elders of Zion, which originated in Paris in the 1890s. This document was written by Pyotr Rachovsky, an agent of the Russian secret police, who borrowed extensively from previous anti-Semitic writings. Protocols later would be used extensively by the Nazis and is still in circulation today, adding fuel to the fire of anti-Israeli sentiments in the Muslim world.

[92] Lewis, Mere Christianity, 45.

CHAPTER FIVE

THE CHALLENGE OF NATURALISM

We have now examined many elements of and contributors to the process that led us into the Enlightenment and out into postmodernism. It's time to note one of the unquestioned assumptions behind everything that's happened to shape the contemporary world: that ours is the "scientific" age. Science, which we have come to equate with naturalism, has been granted a level of respect and authority given to almost nothing else in our culture.

But *does* science lead inevitably to the conclusion of naturalism? Is it possible to be both scientific and religious? Our society says the answer is no, and that's not solely the verdict of the secularists; at this point, those who embrace some form of postmodernism agree that science and faith are incompatible. The widely held belief is that in the pursuit of spiritual reality, we must abandon the West's scientific-objective worldview.[93]

In truth, few are willing to *reject* reason in the pursuit of personal fulfillment. It's probably more accurate to say that many who are searching for some form of spiritual reality are willing to *compartmentalize* "reason" and "faith." As such they have, so to speak, one mental compartment for the presuppositions of naturalistic science, and another compartment for the practice of meditation, prayer, yoga, and other forms or disciplines of spirituality.

It appears that the naturalism upon which science monolithically has been based is the eight-hundred-pound gorilla in the "room" of our worldview. We confront it at our peril. Yet if we want to deal with the two aspects of the religious question—"Does God exist?" and "Can we know it?"—we must.

EMPIRICISM

The foundation of naturalism is empiricism, as introduced above under David Hume. Empiricism maintains that only what can be discovered or demonstrated with a physical test can be considered real. Empiricism tells us that only those things we can see, hear, touch, or feel truly exist; this is to say, all legitimate knowledge originates from sensory experience. Empiricism denies the possibility of any nonmaterial or metaphysical existence (unless those existences can be proven by some type of inductive test or observational experiment). One poignant expression of this conviction is given in the parable of the invisible gardener, long ago put forward by the philosopher Antony Flew (b. 1923).

> Once upon a time two explorers came upon a clearing in the jungle. In the clearing were growing many flowers and many weeds. One explorer says, "Some gardener must tend this plot."
>
> So they pitch their tents and set a watch. No gardener is ever seen. "But perhaps he is an invisible gardener."
>
> So they set up a barbed-wire fence. They electrify it. They patrol with bloodhounds. (For they remember how H. G. Wells's *The Invisible Man* could be both smelt and touched though he could not be seen.) But no shrieks

> ever suggest that some intruder has received a shock. No movements of the wire ever betray an invisible climber. The bloodhounds never give cry.
>
> Yet still the Believer is not convinced. "But there is a gardener, invisible, intangible, insensible to electric shocks, a gardener who has no scent and makes no sound, a gardener who comes secretly to look after the garden which he loves."
>
> At last the Sceptic despairs, "But what remains of your original assertion? Just how does what you call an invisible, intangible, eternally elusive gardener differ from an imaginary gardener or even from no gardener at all?"[94]

Here are the presumptions of modern naturalism: that the presence of order and beauty are insufficient to prove a supernatural origin for the universe; that there must be *empirical* evidence for God's existence—we must be able to see Him, hear Him, or reveal Him through tangible experiment. In naturalism's view, an invisible God means *no* God. This, of course, is a complete surrender to materialism, the belief that only energy and matter exist, that all phenomena can be explained as resulting from their interactions, and that there is no other reality.

If God is immaterial (not composed of matter or energy), then He cannot exist. Because we cannot discover Him with any of our tests for discovering material existence, we have strong evidence that He indeed does not exist—at best He is an illusion. The ancient pre-Socratics Democritus and Leucippus were correct all along: All that exists are atoms and the void.

A RESPONSE TO EMPIRICISM

Let's begin with invisibility, which often comes up when we speak with children about God. They might ask, "If God is here, why can't I see Him?" We might respond with the analogy of a television signal, pointing out that the air around us is "filled with programs," and though we can't see them they really are there. We can hold up our hands—we can't feel the transmissions, but they actually are there. The way for us to discover them is to get a TV, which is designed to receive and use the invisible signals. Turning it on, we see what's being sent out from the station; however, even when the TV is turned on, it doesn't reveal the actual signal that produces the program in the set. The radiation remains invisible; we only see its effects.

Analogously, the Bible tells us that God is spirit, not visible to our physical senses. But just as a TV responds to and reveals the signals designed for it, so the human spirit responds to and reveals God's Spirit. We are, as it were, God's "technology." We discover Him in our spirit, because it's of the same stuff as He is: "God is spirit, and those who worship Him must worship in spirit and truth."[95]

I remember a conversation with a businessman who attended church on a regular basis even though he himself was not particularly religious. "I go because I like the feeling of peace I get when I'm there," he said. Little did he realize his TV set was on, and His spirit was in communion with God's Spirit. I trust he will eventually make the connection between the peace he was feeling and the God who is its source.

Religious experience throughout history stands as testimony to the existence of a spiritual realm beyond the reach of our physical senses and instruments. It's only in the reductionistic[96] West, and only in the last two hundred years, that we have denied the spiritual dimension of the human personality. The materialistic experiment is losing ground among the many who are searching for spirituality again.

Historically, the two primary means of verifying God's existence are (1) the evidence for His creative power as the author of the universe and (2) the moral component within human nature. The study of these observed realities is *natural theology*. We may not be able to physically see God, but His existence is essentially self-evident by what He has done and is doing in the world. In other words, we see the effects of His existence all around us.

THE COSMOLOGICAL ARGUMENT

The ancients believed that the universe itself requires the existence of the supernatural for explanation. The Judeo-Christian worldview provided the transcendent Creator as the explanation for the universe's complexity. Even in our skeptical age, most men and women find it difficult to believe the universe arose by accident; the instinctive sense that the world was created and the self-evident realization that it was intricately designed are among the reasons that more than 80 percent of Americans still believe in a Supreme Being.[97]

Beginning with Thomas Aquinas and his summarization of Aristotle's arguments, European philosophers put this intrinsic sense into a series of logical formulations. The summation of many, if not most, was *the argument from contingency*: that everything we know of in the universe, including the universe itself, depends (is contingent) upon something else for its origin and/or continued existence. For example, we humans had parents; we all must eat, drink water, and breathe air; we are dependent upon a hospitable environment, and so on.

A contingent thing cannot have created itself, nor can it sustain its own existence—it is dependent upon something outside of itself. Everything we can point to exists in this dependent state. We ask, of each thing, what is its origin and what sustains it? The intensive efforts we're expending to discover the origin of the stars, the galaxies, and matter itself all reflect the assumption of contingency.

This being the case, how do we explain the universe? If everything within it is contingent, then how does the sum of all the parts escape the need for contingency? Naturalism requires a universe that is self-sufficient and self-explanatory, but the more we discover about the nature of matter and the qualities of the universe, the more difficult to fathom that requirement becomes. It's increasingly untenable to maintain that the universe is merely a material mystery.

Children and agnostics ask, "If God created the world, then who created God?" This question assumes the correctness of contingency, that everything must have an origin and an explanation. But if *everything* were truly contingent, nothing could have come into existence in the first place. For anything to exist now, something (or someone) must exist that did not have to be caused or that depends upon nothing outside itself for its continued existence. To ask who created God, or from where did God come, is to include Him in the category of contingency; at that point, He is not God.

We have only two choices: either (1) the universe is, in some form, eternal and thus non-contingent, or (2) there is an eternal, omnipotent Creator who is self-existent. Either the universe emerged from some eternal preexistent state and achieved its incredible levels of order and complexity by natural and accidental circumstances, or it was designed by an infinitely intelligent and all-powerful God.

❖ ❖ ❖ ❖

The astrophysicist Carl Sagan (1934–1996) said:

> If the general picture of an expanding universe and a Big Bang is correct, we must then confront still more difficult questions. What were conditions like at the time of the Big Bang? What happened before that? Was there a tiny universe, devoid of all matter, and then matter suddenly created from nothing? How does *that* happen? In many cultures it is customary to answer that God created the universe out of nothing. But this is mere temporizing. If we wish courageously to pursue the question, we must, of course, ask where God comes from. And if we decide this to be unanswerable, why not save a step and decide

> that the origin of the universe is an unanswerable question? Or, if we say that God has always existed, why not save a step and conclude that the universe has always existed?[98]

In saying, "Why not save a step?" Dr. Sagan was asking us to leave out the most important step in the explanation: personal intelligence. As we look upon astounding intricacy, from the structure of the atom to the wonder of the DNA molecule, we see aspects that go beyond the accidental. To leave out the step of God is to say that the stuff of the universe—matter and energy, mindless forces and elements—randomly produced all the wondrous phenomena we perceive around us.

Consider this theoretical test: on one side of a display stands a scientist in a lab coat; in the center is the Hubble Telescope; on the other side is a pile of sand, gold, iron ore, copper, and coal. A person is then brought into the room and asked to identify the creator of the telescope—is it the scientist, or is it the stuff in the pile? Now consider the choice before us concerning the origin of the universe. How could non-living, non-thinking matter produce something that so clearly bears the marks of planning and purpose?

The order and complexity of the universe are at the very essence of its contingency. In the nineteenth century a person could more credibly suggest that it had progressed by chance and natural forces from the simple to the complex because we still had no concept of the degree of intricacy it actually possesses. Such a progression (or evolution) was conceivable then because our real knowledge of genetics, astronomy, biochemistry, and physics was relatively rudimentary. Here in the twenty-first century, we can no longer say the universe progressed from the simple to the complex; we must say it moved from complexity to even greater complexity.

THE ARGUMENT FROM RATIONAL NECESSITY

The physicists John Barrow and Frank Tipler, in their book *The Anthropic Cosmological Principle*,[99] straightforwardly present this aspect of contingency. They give a detailed listing of factors that must be "just right" for our universe to exist. This truly overwhelming list leads to the conclusion that a purely accidental explanation for the universe doesn't hold up. They also quote the work of Donald Page, with Princeton's Institute of Advanced Studies, who calculated the odds against the accidental formation of our universe as 1 in $(10{,}000{,}000{,}000)^{120}$.

No matter how long the time involved, it's only reasonable to acknowledge that chance could not have produced such intricacy. It's no use to shrug our shoulders and say that even though it seems impossible, it still must have happened accidentally. Such blind faith in naturalism is really a case of "Don't confuse me with the facts because my mind is already made up." It's also a denial of the data's significance; no amount of denial or wishful thinking will make the universe simple enough to have had a random origin.

Nor is it tenable to say, as some do, that the universe must be complex in order to produce creatures as complex as we are—to say that complexity, at any rate, is to be expected, and that we needn't resort to the supernatural to explain it. The problem with this argument is that the level of complexity is just too awesome; chance cannot produce it. Charles Darwin is said to have been troubled by the intricacy of the human eye; the complexity of sight is a *trifle* in comparison to what we now know about genetics and the biochemical systems within living organisms.

To say, in essence, that complexity isn't a big deal is again to ignore the implications of the data (as we'll continue to see). It is to be prejudicial, in the most profoundly irrational sense, against any non-natural, non-accidental explanation for the universe. It is an excuse, not a reason.

The more complex an object, the more it demands explanation and the more it displays its contingency (its dependence on something else for its existence). An aircraft at forty thousand feet is more obviously contingent than a piece of paper blowing in the wind. It is only our bias against the supernatural that allows us to ignore the evidence standing before us.

❖ ❖ ❖ ❖

Philosopher and mathematician Gottfried Wilhelm Leibnitz (1646–1716), stating his argument from rational necessity, based on the principle of sufficient reason, said that everything must have a reasonable explanation, and that because of the universe's extraordinary complexity, God is logically necessary to explain its existence. Leibnitz lived about three centuries ago; we since have learned more about the universe than he would have thought possible, yet his argument still holds. No scientific discovery has contradicted his belief; in fact, the discoveries have strengthened it. An accidental origin of the universe is more inconceivable now than ever.

The assumption of an eternal and infinite universe allowed Enlightenment philosophers to set aside rational necessity and maintain that the universe needs no explanation because it exists beyond the capacity of our finite minds. The agnostic Bertrand Russell (1872–1970) once declared that the universe is "a brute fact."[100] We can't say that any longer; astronomy now tells us it's a thing—finite and bounded—and thus in need of a reasonable explanation. In the face of massive complexity, a personal, intelligent Creator is far more reasonable than the random accumulation of chance events.

❖ ❖ ❖ ❖

Remember how significant was Immanuel Kant's theory of knowledge in the progression of shaping today's Western world?

Kant's own agnosticism was founded upon the notion that the universe itself is eternal and infinite. If this were true, then the universe indeed would be unknowable and indefinable: a material mystery. It would also not be contingent.

If, on the other hand, the universe is finite and bounded, then it is a contingent thing that requires something outside itself to explain it. This is the dilemma facing modern theories about origin: The universe, as science understands it today, is defined by age and size. It's a finite thing that emerged several billion years ago. It *is*, therefore, subject to contingency.

> For the scientist who has lived by his faith in the power of reason, the story ends like a bad dream. He has scaled the mountains of ignorance; he is about to conquer the highest peak; as he pulls himself over the final rock, he is greeted by a band of theologians who have been sitting there for centuries.[101]

PROBABILITY THEORY

In order to illustrate how important the matter of complexity is, we must turn our attention now to the field of probability. Many forms of mathematics are exact sciences, but in nature we've discovered things that must be approximated rather than designated. Probability theory began to be utilized in the study of gases and thermal conductivity, and it spread also to economics and statistics. Today it's fundamental to the field of quantum mechanics.

Furthermore, having a mathematical discipline that deals with probability means we can talk about future events with more than just guesswork. Probability theory allows us to put actual numbers to an event's likelihood. We can also predict how often a repeated event will occur in a span of time. For example, the probability (P) for rain tomorrow might be forecasted to be 40 percent ($P = 4/10$).

Let's examine probability theory's fundamental principles. A coin has two sides; if you flip it, there are only two possible outcomes, so the probability of flipping heads is one in two ($P = 1/2$). A die has six sides; thus rolling a certain number is one of six options ($P = 1/6$). If we write this as a formula, it's $P = 1/\text{number of options}$. If there are 100 options related to an event, then $P = 1/100$. The number of possible outcomes determines the probability of a single outcome, and the greater the number of options, the less the chance of a single particular occurrence taking place. To say it another way: the greater the complexity of the event, the lower its chances of occurring in nature.

When events are linked together, things get even more complicated. For example, if we want to flip two heads in a row, there are now four options for which we want only one result (2×2; $P = 1/4$). For three heads in a row, we are faced with eight options ($2 \times 2 \times 2$; $P = 1/8$). Consecutive rolls of the die coming up "3"? This yields a probability of 1/36 (6×6). In other words, the options are not added together, they are *multiplied*.

Mathematicians have developed a number of formulas to predict events in nature, but these two principles enable us to understand how probability helps us answer the questions of the origin of the universe and of life:

(1) The greater the complexity of a single event, the lower its probability;

(2) When events are linked together, their probabilities must be multiplied together.

We're more familiar with probability than we realize. We use it regularly as a measure of our confidence or concern about something happening. If a doctor tells us we have a 90 percent chance of recovery, our confidence is likely to be fairly high, even though we might also have some concern. If he were to tell us our chance for healing is 50 percent, we'd probably be frightened even as we hoped for the best. The lower the probability, the less our confidence that the desired event will occur.

Many people take the time to send in an entry for a mail-in sweepstakes, even though their miniscule chances are $P = (\frac{1}{2})^8$. That's *one chance in 200 million* (and if you look at the fine print in the sweepstakes letter, you'll see these or similar odds given). Winning against those odds is at least conceivable. There comes a point, however, when the probability becomes so low as to exceed the point of conceivability. The point where this occurs is debatable, but it certainly exceeds $P = 1/10^{100}$.

Permit me to illustrate. If we decided to flip a coin until we flipped a hundred heads in a row, would we be able to do it? The catch is that every time we flip a tail, we must start over. The probability of flipping a hundred consecutive heads is $P = (1/2)^{100}$.

This number, without fraction or exponent, would be expressed as "2" with a hundred zeros behind it. Compare that to the mail-in sweepstakes number, which would be "2" with only eight zeros (and *that* meaning just one chance in 200 million). It's no stretch to affirm that this is an utterly inconceivable event. Perhaps flipping ten or even twenty in a row seems possible, but one hundred is beyond any possibility. In fact, mathematicians consider $P = 1/10^{1000}$ "nonsensical" and a guarantee that the event could never occur in nature.[102]

The findings of modern cosmology and biology combined with probability theory provide a measure of the universe's complexity and therefore the chances of it being a product of purely accidental events. As we said, the higher an event's complexity level, the more it depends upon a sufficient cause for its existence. The universe's complexity is of such a magnitude as to render a random origin entirely incredible. The probability calculations made for significant events of nature, such as the accidental development of DNA, are numbers *far* in excess of $P = 1/10^{1000}$. This helps to explain why the intelligent design (ID) movement is growing rapidly in the scientific community.

THE ARGUMENT FROM DESIGN

At the heart of natural theology in the eighteenth and nineteenth centuries was the argument from design or, as it's traditionally called, the teleological argument. William Paley's analogy of a watch and the necessity of a watchmaker became its metaphor. The remarkable evidence of design in the universe supported the belief that it originated from an intelligent Creator; as they put it, "Design implies a Designer."[103]

One way this argument is being restated in our era is called the anthropic principle, which posits that the earth and the universe seem to be constructed in such a way as to prepare for human life. We noted that one recent version is found in *The Anthropic Cosmological Principle*, in which Barrow and Tipler present the amazing cosmological conditions required to make human life possible. The classical anthropic argument has been around since the early proponents of natural theology, pointing to the earth being the right distance from the sun to provide a range of temperatures that allow humans to inhabit. The planet's size and gravitational field; the chemical composition of the atmosphere; even the thickness of earth's crust are *just right* for the existence of life. Other essential elements to life's existence on earth are the carbon cycle, the ozone layer, the structure of the water molecule, and the nitrogen cycle.

All these elements together present a picture of the intricacy of the earth's environment that goes beyond the possibility of coincidence. For example, the ozone layer blocks out two of the most deadly bands of ultraviolet light radiating from our sun. Without this screen, all life would be "sterilized" from the planet. The ozone layer exists because the chemical bonds that make oxygen into ozone, and ozone into oxygen, are the exact match to the energy levels of those two ultraviolet bands. If any one of those four factors (O_2, O_3, UV_1, UV_2) were different, life could not exist on earth.

If there were only one or even two such "coincidences," we might attribute them to chance. But this is merely one of *hundreds* of remarkable facets that make life possible. In the face of innumerable marvels, it seems far more likely that the source is supernatural—miraculous.

What Barrow and Tipler have done with the traditional argument is add the cosmos into the equation. They examined the ratio of matter to antimatter, the expansion rate of the universe, and many other cosmological factors. Much of their work included the calculations of probability for significant events in the universe's history. After all their efforts, they came to the conclusion that the entire universe must have had a miraculous origin. Another scientist, The British astronomer Sir Fred Hoyle (1915–2001), implied that life's accidental development on earth would be like a tornado sweeping through a dump and producing an airliner.

> A junkyard contains all the bits and pieces of a Boeing 747, dismembered and in disarray. A whirlwind happens to blow through the yard. What is the chance that after its passage a fully assembled 747, ready to fly, will be found standing there? So small as to be negligible, even if a tornado were to blow through enough junkyards to fill the whole Universe.[104]

Of course, not everyone agrees. Carl Sagan, in *Cosmos*, presented an alternate explanation to the anthropic principle. He believed that the earth is perfect for life's development because, through evolution, life emerged from the elements already present in the earth's environment. He felt that "life" could theoretically emerge on an entirely different world and that those life-forms would consider their environment miraculous as well. To make his point, he put forward the hypothetical case of "cloud creatures" that might come out of Jupiter's upper atmosphere. Their environment would be "just right" for their existence, providing them food and enabling their continued survival.[105]

This may sound possible or even reasonable until you begin to ask what constitutes "life." Life is an indescribably complex state that requires the ability to reproduce, grow, respond to surrounding conditions, escape danger, capture and assimilate food, and more. There are no known or even conceivable alternatives to the carbon-based life that exists on earth.

Sagan had no evidence of his cloud creatures. The idea of Jupiter's toxic gases somehow combining to produce self-replicating molecules, gaseous "cells," and some form of energy/waste transfer system to fuel the organisms is beyond a realistic possibility. We know how those gases act, we know what compounds they produce, and nothing even remotely resembling life is possible from them.

THE ORIGIN OF LIFE

The idea that life could arise anywhere is closely related to the idea that life will arise *automatically* wherever the conditions are right. This is the foundation of the search for extraterrestrial intelligence. Evolutionists speak as if life's development is an inevitable process given the presence of water, a proper atmosphere, and the requisite chemicals for organic life. Supposedly, if life developed on earth, then it must have developed on other planets as well.

This fails to take into consideration what we have stated previously: Life is too complex to be accidental. We have no plausible explanation for the development of living organisms from non-living, inorganic matter. How can we say that life would arise automatically on some other world when we can't even say how life arose "automatically" here?

Some scientists say they are close to an answer to this question. They point to the famous experiment that produced amino acids in a sealed jar by the arcing of electricity through methane/ammonia gas. The problem they face is that the production of amino acids is a far cry from producing life. This is the equivalent of saying that because we discovered the alphabet we know how those proverbial monkeys typed the works of Shakespeare. Countless hurdles must be overcome to support a naturalistic explanation for the development of life.

DNA (deoxyribonucleic acid), for instance, is one of the most complex and intriguing molecules known to man. We've already mentioned that the probability against DNA's accidental development is eons beyond astronomical. Next is its close cousin, RNA (ribonucleic acid), which is an essential part of a living cell. RNA's complexity rivals that of DNA.

There is also the factor of protein. You cannot have a cell (the basic unit of a living organism) without protein, but the inside of a living cell is the *only* known place where protein can be manufactured in nature. This is the chicken-and-the-egg conundrum: how can a cell have developed on its own, without something to make the protein of which it is constructed? Protein is extremely complex: RNA, genes, and other elements within the cell are needed for its production.

Additionally problematic for the "automatic" development of life is this: Events that are predictable in nature have a predictable source called a mechanism. When the mechanism is present, the event will take place. There is no known mechanism for the production of life from non-living matter; therefore, it cannot be a predictable event and it surely cannot be automatic.[106] The presence of water, atmosphere, and the right chemicals is certainly insufficient to make life's emergence inevitable.

In regard to the notion of "something within nature that makes life emerge whenever the right conditions are present," we nevertheless have no idea what that something might be, or even if there could be a something. If we were truly willing to face up to the facts of what we know about life, we would not say that the accidental development of life is automatic—we would say it is *impossible*.

---

[93] Theodore Roszak has written extensively on the limited view of the universe that has arisen from the emphases on objective reasoning and empiricism (what we

can see, feel, hear, or taste) that has come to be equivocated with modern science. His book Where the Wasteland Ends is focused on the desacralized view of nature that has developed from the West's emphasis on scientific "objectivity." (Where the Wasteland Ends: Politics and Transcendence in Postindustrial Society [Berkeley: Celestial Arts, with R. Briggs, 1999; orig. published 1972].)

[94] Antony Flew, in "Theology and Falsification," University, 1950–51; from Joel Feinberg, ed., Reason and Responsibility: Readings in Some Basic Problems of Philosophy (Belmont, CA: Dickenson Publishing Company, Inc., 1968), 48–49.

[95] John 4:24

[96] Reductionism speaks to the reducing of all reality and of all explanations to the material and the empirical. Reductionism found its highest expression in the philosophy of logical positivism, wherein no expression of the abstract and intangible could be considered legitimate. Of course this was self-refuting; reductionism itself is an abstract and intangible mental construct.

[97] E.g., see http://www.gallup.com/poll/27877/Americans-More-Likely-Believe-God-Than-Devil-Heaven-More-Than-Hell.aspx

[98] Carl Sagan, Cosmos (New York: Random House, 1980), 257.

[99] John D. Barrow and Frank J. Tipler, The Anthropic Cosmological Principle (New York: Oxford University Press, 1986).

[100] Bertrand Russell, and Frederick Copleston, "Debate on the Existence of God" in The Existence of God, eds. John Hick and Paul Edwards (New York: Macmillan, 1964).

[101] In the words of the late cosmologist Robert Jastrow (1925–2008). See, for instance, at godandscience.org/love/sld014.html

[102] See Murray Eden, ed., The Mathematical Challenges to the Neo-Darwinian Interpretation of the Theory of Evolution (Cambridge: Harvard University Press, 1966).

[103] In Paley, Natural Theology.

[104] Fred Hoyle, The Intelligent Universe (New York: Holt, Rinehart, and Winston, 1984), 19.

[105] Sagan, Cosmos, 40–41.

[106] We'll consider this more extensively in the next chapter.

CHAPTER SIX

THE THEORY OF EVOLUTION

Several decades ago, a group of scientists was spending the summer doing research in Europe. One beautiful day they decided to have a picnic in the mountains, and, as scientists often do, they got into a discussion. This one, however, was unusual; it centered on alleged problems with evolutionary theory. Their interaction soon became an argument, pitting the practitioners of "hard" sciences against the biologists—the former, the mathematicians and engineers, claimed that evolution had never passed the normal tests required of scientific theories.

The debate raged on and eventually led to a symposium at The Massachusetts Institute of Technology in 1966. The discussion's transcript was published that year under the title, *The Mathematical Challenges to the Neo-Darwinian Interpretation of the Theory of Evolution.* The challengers raised five significant issues in regard to evolutionary theory.

MACROEVOLUTION: FIVE CHALLENGES

THE PROBLEM OF TIME

First, they stated that *there is not enough time, even given a billion years of organic history on earth, for the development, by chance, of all the incredible organisms in the world.* The mathematician Stanislav Ulam (1909–1984), a researcher at Los Alamos National Laboratory, said,

> We wondered [at] how it appeared extremely unlikely that in a short span of one billion years, due to successive random mutations, all the wonderful things we now see could have appeared.... It seems to require many thousands, perhaps millions of successive mutations to produce even the easiest complexities we see in life now. It appears, naively at least, that no matter how large the probability of a single mutation is, should it even be as great as one-half, you would get this probability raised to a millionth power, which is so very close to zero that the chances of such a claim seem practically non-existent.[107]

According to evolutionary theory, each organism and its unique characteristics—and there are billions of organisms on the earth—is the product of mutations. These changes, it is said, have enabled creatures to adapt and survive. The sheer number of mutations necessary for life as we know it, for all the world's organs and organisms, makes it exceedingly difficult to accept the evolutionary scenario. That number is beyond calculation.

If the theory were true, we would expect that evolution by mutation would be one of nature's obvious facts. By contrast, what we know of mutations in nature is that they are for the most part *destructive*. Therefore, we could anticipate that any *beneficial* mutations responsible for evolution were only the tip of the iceberg of all the mutations that would have had to take place in nature. Hypothetically, for the billions of beneficial adaptations we might see, there would need to be trillions of mutations (or more) to produce them.

The fact is, in nature, we do *not* see these vast numbers of mutations. The classic evolutionary explanation is that mutation takes place too gradually for us to observe it. This puts evolutionists on the horns of a dilemma: they have billions of adaptations to account for, using a process that takes place so slowly we can't see it no matter how long we observe it. How then is mutation *rapid* enough and *frequent* enough to explain the billions of creatures on earth?

THE PROBLEM OF A MECHANISM

The second issue raised by the symposium is *the lack of an adequate mechanism for the evolutionary process.* As we have seen, a mechanism is a natural element that produces a predictable event; a mechanism is the how and why of occurrences in nature. The mechanism for a tornado is a mix of cold air trapped above a mass of warm air in the collision of two storm fronts. The cold air must go down and the warm air must go up; the fastest route for this transfer is a vortex, or what we call a tornado. Whenever this condition exists, the mechanism for producing a tornado is present, and a tornado will likely occur. In describing a significant natural process, the first task of science is to define its mechanism.

From the beginning, evolutionary theory has proposed natural selection as its mechanism. However, natural selection is some distance removed from evolution's key element: genetic change. Genetic change is change in the genetic code that determines each unique organism's embryonic development. Genetic changes are *internal* to the organism; they're changes in the DNA that lie deep within the core of the creature's cells. According to macroevolutionary theory, these changes are the product of genetic mutations and other variations within the

DNA code. The hypothetical *genetic changes*, coming about through whatever cause, *must already be present before natural selection can do its work.*

For example, the common explanation for ocean-dwelling mammals is that the flooding of major portions of the earth "caused" mammals to develop fins, flippers, breathing mechanisms, and, in the case of whales and porpoises, the ability to give birth to live young underwater. By itself, though, flooding could not have produced these changes; flooding could not even exert genetic "pressure"[108] on these creatures, transforming them from land creatures to sea creatures. If something else were not at work, deep within their genomes, then evolution would be a total impossibility; in the case of sea mammals, any mutations that might enable them to live underwater could not be caused by the flooding of their environment.

This is because natural selection is *external* to the creature involved; it is a product of the environment the creature finds itself in, so it cannot *cause* the creature to evolve. Some form of internal genetic change must take place before natural selection enters the picture, because natural selection is the environmental condition that the creature adapts to and takes advantage of in the competition for survival. For example, a change in the available food supply requires the organism to change in such a way that it is able to take advantage of the new food supply. The change in the food supply, however, would not be the cause of the supposed changes in the organism. The creature must adapt to its environment, not the other way around.

In fact, *natural selection reduces the number of beneficial options that must already be available, having been produced by some sort of genetic-change agent.* Natural selection is a statistical modifier—a means of picking from a large population of random events those events one wants to keep. A statistical modifier does not cause change, and it cannot work if the alternatives are not already present.

To illustrate: If we were to sort a box of apples, looking for and removing those with wormholes (and possibly worms), wormholes would be our statistical modifier. Natural selection, according to the theory of evolution, selects those genetic changes that are *beneficial* in a unique environment, enabling the creature that has them to survive and thrive. Therefore, natural selection cannot be the *cause* of the change.

Notice as well that natural selection doesn't merely select any and all beneficial changes; the change also must fit the unique characteristics of a natural environment. This theory, then, is the ultimate expression of "good luck." Take sea mammals, for instance: at *exactly* the time their part of the world is flooding, they develop fins and flippers, and their noses are transferred to the middle of their backs? It stretches credulity beyond all limits to imagine that this could randomly occur, purely by accident, precisely when such a change is needed.

To be fair, no evolutionist would say that the sea mammals developed fins, flippers, and breathing holes all at once. They would say there was a progression that took millennia to move from creatures like hippos to seals and finally to whales and porpoises. Yet at each step, even in this process, we are faced with astounding changes in these creatures' anatomy and physiology that are caused by factors that are entirely disconnected from the conditions of their surrounding environment.

We must be clear about this: Natural selection most certainly is not the cause (mechanism) of evolution. It cannot and does not produce genetic change in any creature, and without genetic change there is no evolution.

❖ ❖ ❖ ❖

In the neo-Darwinian model of evolution,[109] genetic mutations are posited as the source of the change that is selected or rejected by the surrounding environment. Other mechanisms have been theorized, such as gene recombination, gene transfer within the genome, and so on, but realistically none has any more credibility than mutation. And this raises another problem—the problem the engineers raised in noting the lack of an adequate evolutionary mechanism. *Mutation is not a predictable event; it is an accident.* Most of the time mutation produces harmful results, such as two heads on a chicken or a calf with five legs. Whether a mutation is harmful *or* beneficial, however, it is nonetheless a random event with random results. Accordingly, it cannot be classed with all the other known mechanisms of nature, which are neither random nor unpredictable.

THE PROBLEM OF EXPERIMENTATION

The mathematicians asked a third question of the biologists: Why has the theory of evolution never been *experimentally* verified? The proponents of macroevolutionary theory certainly have been trying. Actually, their work has been going on for more than seventy years.

Scientists *have* attempted experimentally to establish mutation as a viable evolutionary mechanism. Since the 1930s they've been performing mutation tests on rapidly breeding insects, hoping to establish empirical proof. In all that time, *we do not have one example of significant beneficial change within any species.* We noted before that Richard Goldschmidt spent twenty-five years trying to prove evolution through mutation experiments on fruit flies and gypsy moths. After a quarter century of work, he came to the conclusion that evolution could not have occurred by the gradual accumulation of mutated genetic change.

These experiments have been well-designed. If evolution were true, they should have been able to demonstrate it. Again, this is particularly poignant in light of the mind-blowing numbers of mutations that would be necessary to produce the incredible diversity of organic life.

Furthermore, the tests have been based upon the widely used principle of acceleration testing: the practice of rapidly producing effects in the laboratory that would take years to observe in nature. For example, if a typical doorbell in a typical home is rung once a week, the doorbell system would operate about fifty times a year. In acceleration testing, a doorbell system would be set up in the lab, and an automated mechanism that pushes the switch would activate the system fifty times an hour, compressing and duplicating, in this instance, 8,760 hours of normal operation into one.

Through acceleration testing, mutation experiments on rapidly breeding insects can yield a new generation of creatures to be examined in a few days rather than in several months; fifty to a hundred generations can be examined in a single year. Even more importantly, while mutations occur quite infrequently in nature, in the laboratory they can be induced using radiation or mutagenic[110] chemicals applied directly to each specimen.

The result is that we can produce in a few months in the lab the number of mutations in organisms that would be expected in hundreds, if not thousands, of years in nature. By accelerating the process of breeding and inducing the presence of mutation, we are examining untold thousands of years of biological history. It is the failure of all these carefully planned experiments to produce any evidence of evolutionary change that convinced Goldschmidt: evolution doesn't work.

Supporters of evolution continue to hide behind the issue of time to explain the lack of any positive results. Again, evolution, allegedly, is too gradual for us to be able to observe it in the laboratory. But then once more we must ask, how in the world is this theory adequate to explain the earth's billions upon billions of unique creatures?

THE PROBLEM OF VERIFICATION

The fourth challenge the engineers gave to macroevolutionary theory concerned the problem of *theoretical verification*:

They asked how it was possible that *evolution has not been held to the standard of proof required of every other scientific theory.*

A theory is considered false until it is proven true; philosophers of science call this the principle of falsifiability. A fairly recent example was the announcement of two scientists that they had produced cold fusion—if this were accurate, we would have had a safe and virtually inexhaustible source of nuclear energy. Sadly, the claims did not stand the tests of verification, and the theory had to be abandoned.

Cold fusion wasn't accepted merely because those scientists said it was true, and it wasn't accepted on the basis of the data from their initial experiments (which they felt proved the achievement of nuclear fusion). The theory was considered false until independent tests performed by other scientists could verify or deny its claims. In this case it was proven false.

Every accepted scientific theory has undergone this process except one: the theory of evolution. Supporters cannot point to *one* verifying experiment. They do point to a great deal of circumstantial evidence, scenarios, and assumptions about what might have happened at different points in history, but they have no actual proof to back up their claims.

The engineers who participated in the MIT symposium stated repeatedly that from their perspective evolution was simply assumed without proof. They argued that the theory was considered non-falsifiable; in other words, it was accepted as true without the need to pass the tests of verification. They went further, too, insisting that facts were never used to "test" the theory but were always interpreted in light of the assumption that the theory was true.

One of the engineers, a Dr. Fentress, played a little trick on some of his evolutionist friends: "I reversed the data.... I wish I had recorded their explanations, because they were very impressive indeed."[111] Fentress presented false data, but it didn't matter; they didn't even pick up on the joke because, as usual, they weren't comparing evolution to actual data; they were comparing the data to the theory. Fentress was making the point that any "facts" of nature are always explained from the presupposition that evolution is a law of nature. They are never used to test the theory to determine if it is, indeed, a law.

Evolutionists will often say that a "good" theory must have explanatory power—that is, it must be a vehicle for explaining how and why things happen. Their view is that evolution allows them to explain the origin of many organs and organisms in nature. So, when they are presented with a set of features or facts from the natural world, they pull out the theory to "explain" how and why those features emerged. To them, this is the beauty and power of the theory: it provides natural explanations for remarkable phenomena.

All would be well if evolution had actually been demonstrated in the laboratory and in nature. It has not. It remains as it was in Charles Darwin's day: an untested and unverified hypothesis. As such, simply assuming evolution is true and then using it to "explain" natural facts is illegitimate. In contrast, the theory must be held up to the facts of nature and examined for verifiability or falsification. Evolution has not earned the right to "explain" nature.

❖ ❖ ❖ ❖

The evolutionists' responses to many of the engineers' criticisms confirmed that they viewed the theory as law, the hypothesis as non-falsifiable. C. H. Waddington, a leading evolutionist at the symposium, said,

> You are asking, is there enough time for evolution to produce such complicated things as the eye? Let me put it the other way around. Evolution has produced such complicated things as the eye; can we deduce from this anything about the system by which it has been produced?[112]

For Waddington, the *question* was flawed because it had the potential to jeopardize the theory's validity. He implied that evolution must be accepted without question and certainly without experimental verification. Amazing, then, that he or any likeminded scientist could consider the theory in any sense "scientific."

Murray Eden went on to press the point even further:

> It is a theory of a different kind. We may contrast it with the theories of Physics. Certainly Newtonian Physics is falsifiable.... My point is that for such a theory one could propose a crucial experiment and check as to whether or not the theory was false. This certainly cannot be done in evolution, taking it in its broad sense, and this is really all I meant when I called it tautologous.... It can indeed explain anything. You may be ingenious or not in proposing a mechanism that looks plausible to human beings and mechanisms which are consistent with other mechanisms which you have discovered, but it is still an un-falsifiable theory.[113]

THE PROBLEM OF COMPUTER MODELING

The final and possibly most devastating criticism came from a mathematician, Marcel-Paul Schutzenberger of the University of Paris: *Modeling the theory of evolution in the computer leads one to conclude that evolution is impossible in the real world.* Schutzenberger developed a simulation to mimic the accidental development of the genotype (the genetic instructions within an organism's DNA). As he said,

> Nowadays computers are operating within a range which is not entirely incommensurate with that dealt with in actual evolutionary theories.... Now we have less excuse for explaining away difficulties by invoking the unobservable effect of astronomical numbers of small variations.[114]

Schutzenberger summarized his results:

> All attempts to simulate evolution in the computer give nonsensical answers. The computer won't even show modified results, it just jams; only with input can it be made to run. No selection effected on the final output would induce a drift, however slow, on the system toward the production of the mechanism if it were not already present in some form. Further, there is no chance to see this mechanism appear spontaneously and, if it did, even less for it to remain.
>
> You can quote me experiences where things work in life, but we have a conflicting experience in the computer. Although our processes are based on the same principles as the ones you state explicitly and the probability of a meaningful change is not [even] one in 10^{1000}, it is entirely negligible.[115]

After Schutzenberger finished his presentation, Dr. M. H. Levin, a biologist, actually said, "I think the missing ingredient is that you have left out evolution."[116]

In all the years since that debate took place, to this day, none of the questions raised has been answered. Nevertheless, evolution is taught as if it *were* a scientific law. It is commonly considered ludicrous to present, in American classrooms, another view of organic life's origin. That scientists—the men and women who have committed their lives to the discovery of truth, who are likewise dedicated to the use of the scientific method to verify their discoveries—would be willing to abandon those principles to defend, irrationally, what is still an unproven hypothesis is beyond startling.

We said in chapter three that something more than "science" is at work. All of this demonstrates that evolution is not just a scientific issue. There's no doubt that evolution also is a critical sociological and political factor. It is our society declaring that it will not under any circumstance give religion a significant place.

PUNCTUATED EQUILIBRIUM

Neither the fossil record nor the classification system of genus and species shows evidence of "transition forms," or creatures that would show evolutionary development *from one species to another*. The evolutionary biologist Stephen Jay Gould (1941–2002) wrote,

> The extreme rarity of transitional forms in the fossil record persists as the trade secret of paleontology. The evolutionary trees that adorn our textbooks have data only at the tips and nodes of their branches; the rest is inference, however reasonable, not the evidence of fossils.[117]

In addition, after decades of acceleration-test-based mutation experiments, there indeed is not much more than inference to support the gradual accumulation of small genetic changes needed to produce significant evolutionary change. As a result, recent years have seen an attempt to revise evolutionary theory to make it fit more of the data. Several scientists, including Gould and Goldschmidt, proposed a new mechanism for evolutionary change called *punctuated equilibrium*.

According to this hypothesis, organic life is extremely stable and resistant to genetic change most of the time; this is reflected in the consistency between the fossil record and present existing species. However, at points of extreme stress and environmental crisis, genetic change supposedly is triggered on a massive scale. The scenario most often cited is that of a giant meteorite striking the earth and creating a catastrophe so great that the planet's entire ecosystem changes. So, when the dinosaurs died, in their place the birds and mammals arose and took over as the dominant form of animal life.

This newer theoretical version has the same problem as the old: it lacks supporting evidence. It's even more improbable than the idea of gradual change over long periods of time, because it implies massive genetic change in a relatively short period of time as the result of significant "genetic stress." This reminds one of bygone science fiction stories about the world after a nuclear war, where those few remaining "normal" people must do battle against the mutants that have arisen out of the radiation. Here's the key question: Is radiation or any other vehicle of genetic change able to make such wholesale alteration in creatures?

If genetic stress were able to produce this kind of large-scale genetic change, if "mutants" really would result, then we should see them, for instance, when we subject fruit flies to intense radiation or to mutation-producing chemicals; it seems hard to conceive of anything more genetically stressful than the experiments that currently endeavor to prove evolution. The insects literally are soaked in chemicals, or have X-rays passed directly through their bodies, yet we do not see major genetic change—we have never created a mutant. How could stress have made birds and mammals out of reptiles when it can't even turn fruit flies into something other than fruit flies?

---

[107] In Murray Eden, ed., The Mathematical Challenges to the Neo-Darwinian Interpretation of the Theory of Evolution (Cambridge: Harvard University Press, 1966).

[108] Genetic pressure is a term often used by those who support macroevolution to describe some type of catastrophic situation, such as a comet striking the earth. Allegedly, an event like that would have stimulated massive genetic mutations along with the transformation of the ecosystem, leading to significant macroevolutionary change. We will consider this when we look at punctuated equilibrium (below).

[109] On neo-Darwinian theory, see footnote at the end of chapter three.

[110] Mutagenic chemicals are chemicals that cause mutations. Many of the discoveries related to cancer-producing substances have come out of the search for mutagenic chemicals that has gone on for several decades.

[111] In Eden, Mathematical Challenges.

[112] Ibid.

[113] Ibid.

[114] Ibid.

[115] Ibid.

[116] Ibid.

[117] Stephen Jay Gould, The Panda's Thumb (New York: W.W. Norton & Co., 1982), 181.

CHAPTER SEVEN

INTELLIGENT DESIGN

There is a growing movement among scientists that fully acknowledges the complexity of organic life. Its adherents conclude that there is only one reasonable explanation for life as we know it: *intelligent design.* Some of those who've written to support this view have gone to great lengths to avoid any speculation *about* the intelligence behind this design; they carefully avoid references to the Bible or anything remotely resembling theology. They're compelled to take this approach because the main criticism of intelligent design is that it's just dressed-up biblical creationism. Their aim is to keep a wide berth from accusations of "being religious" and therefore being rejected out of hand by the scientific community.

Whether one way or any other, this is an exercise in futility. The invoking of intelligence necessarily means a supernatural origin of life. It *does* imply nothing short of a personal Creator, which, at the very minimum, is a theistic proposition. Beyond that point, it seems almost silly to deny what is so clear and straightforward.

Proponents of intelligent design (ID) are facing the entrenched opposition of methodological naturalism, which, again, insists that every phenomenon in the universe must have a natural (non-supernatural) explanation. Methodological naturalism literally outlaws any religiously affiliated answers in the name of science, no matter the veracity of the answers. The irony is that *true science is the unbiased pursuit of understanding based upon the discovery of the facts of nature.* Science cannot legitimately say that certain conclusions are unacceptable if the data supports them—it must be open-minded, allowing the findings to fit the facts, even if the results are not what was expected or even desired. Honest science will not hide its head in the sand and deny a reasonable or evident or obvious conclusion that doesn't fall in line with what was anticipated or sought.

The injustices being done in the name of science are completely untrue to science. Opponents attack ID by accusing it of being nothing more than the promotion of religion and the *denial* of science; its proponents frequently are called "pseudo-scientists," even though many have earned PhDs in scientific fields and strive to present the objective data that supports their findings. The critics seldom confront the actual data and the reasoning behind contrary findings; the opposition is almost always based on ID's inexorable direction toward a religious (and thus, allegedly, unscientific) conclusion.

For instance, neuroscientist Lewis Barker (b. 1942) was the most public spokesman for the Faculty Senate of Baylor University when it voted in 2000 to abolish its Michael Polanyi Center (a think tank for ID research). Barker complained that "the center is a promotion of creationism as legitimate science" and that "it will potentially taint the integrity of student degrees at Baylor."[118] The center was effectively closed down when its director, mathematician and philosopher William Dembski (b. 1960), was removed; its mandate changed from its original intention of research.

❖ ❖ ❖ ❖

When critics of ID do tackle the scientific factors involved, they rely on a spurious process of thought. We've already alluded to this: evolutionists appear to believe that if they can conceive of a way something might have happened in nature, they have proven that it's not only possible but even probable. To illustrate: Sir David Attenborough (b. 1926), a naturalist historian, in the BBC special *Nature*, described the dilemma that faced the early insects. The plants upon which they depended for food had grown increasingly taller, and with the development of trees their foliage was positioned formidably above the ground. As a consequence, Attenborough said, the insects developed wings where their front legs used to be, and hence, gained the capacity to fly up to their food source.[119]

Attenborough was assuming that the construction of a seemingly reasonable explanation for wings on insects is all that's needed to explain their development. But there is not one shred of experimental or fossil-based evidence to support his assumption. Despite creative imagination and ingenuity, the theory has no grounding in anything that's been demonstrated.

Allow me to present another example. The biologist H. Allen Orr (b. 1960) wrote a critique of *Darwin's Black Box*, a book by Michael Behe (b. 1952), professor of molecular biology at Lehigh University and a leading ID proponent. Behe's major premise is that many organs and organisms in nature are irreducibly complex. He maintains that something irreducibly complex ceases to function if one of its parts is missing, and an irreducibly complex system cannot have developed piecemeal because it won't work (i.e., is of zero benefit to the creature) without all its parts.[120]

Consider the eye—for instance, the formation of the lens, with its need for transparency and an exact shape that provides a precise focal length. In the organ we require for sight, we find structures of tissue and fluid that are perfectly clear, the convex shape that allows the focusing of light, and the nerve tissue that converts light into the electrical impulses that enables us to see. A partial eye is no eye at all.

In other words, evolution could not have produced such systems. Orr writes, in response:

> An irreducibly complex system can be built gradually by adding parts that, while initially are just advantageous, become—because of later changes—essential. The logic is simple. Some part (A) initially does some job (and not very well perhaps). Another part (B) later *gets added because it helps* A.... (emphasis mine)[121]

The problem? Orr has no proof that an irreducibly complex system evolved or could have evolved in the way he describes. He's really saying that because he can *imagine* how it might happen, he should be indulged in saying it *did* happen. This is a gargantuan leap, like saying that because I can envision a unicorn, one must exist (or must have existed).

One goal of evolutionary science is to develop scenarios based upon an environmental condition and a creature's needs by which natural selection could have produced some unique aspect of biological life. We already looked at the example of flight in insects. Orr actually refers to this mode of "logic" when he speaks of "part (B)" getting "added because it helps A." This implies that the organism's need somehow gives rise to its own evolutionary change; of course, in talking about purely chance events at the molecular and genetic level, this is pure nonsense. Evolutionists speak as if necessity is not just the mother of invention but the inventor too.

IRREDUCIBLE COMPLEXITY

In contrast to what its critics say, the ID movement is based on solid scientific reasoning, and its first pillar is *irreducible complexity*. Once more: All the parts of an irreducibly complex system must be in place or it ceases to function. Products of human technology exhibit this characteristic, which is likewise evidence of their design; the machine truly is the sum of its parts. The remarkable functions of so many natural organs display this high degree of order, such that the removal of one part disrupts the function of the whole; this reality is excruciatingly difficult to explain by gradual development over innumerable eons.

Let's return to Attenborough's description of the development of flight in insects. As he explained this process, it sounded so simple. All that was needed was the insect's front legs to mutate into wings, and it would be able to fly to the treetops.

Leaving aside the monstrous problem of a mutation of such magnitude that it could change legs into wings (in fact, we have never seen a mutation that produces significant structural change in any creature's anatomy), flight in insects—and birds—faces the reality of irreducible complexity. Merely having wings doesn't allow a creature to fly; a multitude of other abilities must be present at the same time. For one thing, the creature must have fatigue-resistant muscles that allow rapid and continuous beating of the wings; it cannot get tired in mid-flight without disastrous results. Neither can the wings just be flapped up and down; they wouldn't produce lift and flight but uselessly move the air like a couple of fans.[122]

Remember the comical pictures of early-twentieth-century inventors attempting to make "flying machines" by flapping wings attached to their arms? Flight requires a special pattern of wing motion, and the unique shape and design of the wing itself, to provide lift. One fascinating aspect of PBS's Nature was its slow-motion video of insects in flight, which clearly showed the requisite wing motions. In this case, the wings turned vertical on the upbeat, cutting through the air, and then at the top they turned to the horizontal, to push down on the air and lift the creature upward.

Flight, therefore, cannot be explained simply by saying that insects developed wings—those needed to be joined simultaneously to other factors essential for flight. Consider, then, all the factors coming together at the same time with a mechanism that's hardly more than dumb luck. Really? All of them, arising purely by accident, at just the time they were needed most?

Evolution faces this question with millions of structures in the biological world. One need not be an expert in probability theory to realize that the chances of this randomly occurring are beyond possibility. It is this observation of irreducibly complex structures, perfectly suited to the needs of the creatures involved, that leads to the conclusion that these structures must have been designed. And there is only one possible designer: a personal, transcendent Creator.

That such a conclusion cannot be tested directly by experiment does not mean it isn't logical or true. For neither can it be contradicted by experiment, as with evolution. After seventy years of experimentation (especially in light of acceleration testing), the conclusion that would have been reached far sooner with any other scientific hypothesis is that evolution does not work and is incorrect.

While it's true that intelligent design cannot be tested via laboratory experiment, neither can the claims of evolutionary theory be established by direct experiment. Evolutionist criticism of ID, then, could be applied to evolution, in which case the argument boils down to plausibility and possibility. Which of these options, evolution or intelligent design, best fits the data and seems most plausible?

SPECIFIED COMPLEXITY

A second pillar supporting intelligent design is *specified complexity*. Dembski, the movement's leader in this area, has earned doctorates in mathematics and philosophy and has made it his life's work to present the mathematical and logical evidence for life's intelligent design. He makes the point that nature's accidental forces can produce patterns like the even ripples of sand on a dune or frozen waves formed by the wind. These patterns are *specific but not complex*. We also see great complexity produced by accidental forces—who would want to collect and reconstruct all the parts of a building destroyed by a tornado? Here we find *complexity but not specificity*.[123]

Dembski's premise is that *only in the products of intelligence do we see the specific and the complex combined.* This principle, that specified complexity is a sure sign of intelligence, is already used in cryptology, forensic science, and the search for extraterrestrial intelligence. Once a truly complex pattern is found, be it a musical scale, a mathematical progression, or a pattern of symbols conveying a message, it's assumed to have been produced by an intelligent source.

The most amazing examples of specified complexity in nature are found in DNA and the genetic coding for living creatures. Within a creature's genome are all the instructions for its development. Analogically, the genetic code is the software that runs during the creature's embryonic development to produce all of its characteristic organs and tissues.

Our bodies, which are products of this coding, are biochemical marvels, displaying a complexity that transcends anything we can produce in the laboratory. Carl Sagan, narrating the video series *Cosmos*, removed a book from a library shelf and opened it to a page of multifaceted chemical formulas. He then stated that the human body, in digesting certain foods, is capable of chemical processes so complex that they have yet to be reproduced by human technology. He went on to say, "We have only been working on the chemistry of these processes for a hundred years or so, while evolution has had millions of years to perfect them."[124]

It's always intriguing to see evolution personified and given powers of implied intelligence. There is a vast gulf between nature's accidental forces and human creative capacities, yet here Sagan is equating the two and making length of time the only real difference between their accomplishments. It's taken us something like a century to go from the simplicity of the Wright brothers' biplane to the sophistication of a stealth bomber. How many eons would it take for nature to produce something similar?

Specified complexity is the work of personal intelligence, not unguided random forces. Time really has nothing to do with it; if only chance forces were at work, we could wait a trillion years and not see the type of specified complexity Dr. Sagan referred to in the process of digestion. If humans, with all their knowledge and skill, can't do something in the idealized and controlled conditions of a laboratory, how can we believe it would happen purely by accident in nature?

Carl Sagan's major life project was the search for extraterrestrial intelligence. SETI involved using the arrays of radar telescopes on earth to "listen" for evidence of intelligent life elsewhere. But what were they listening for? A coherent signal that contained information. The assumption was, any message that contained information must have an intelligent source. Sagan would have been satisfied if a simple musical scale or a sequence of dashes and dots (some type of mathematical pattern) were detected. At this, he would have believed he was receiving an intelligent message from an intelligent source.

In the genome of a living organism we have a sequence of instructions as elaborate as any known computer program. It took us years to decode the instructions for the human genome. If a simple message conveys intelligence, how much more a complex one? The more we discover about the biochemistry of living organisms, the more untenable it becomes to attribute their development to chance.

MINIATURIZATION

I remember attending a convention that featured a well-known futurist. His topic that day was the future of computers and the process of miniaturization. He noted that the first computer, which was hardly more than a large electronic calculator, filled an entire room (because it was made of vacuum tubes). He emphasized that today's computer chip can do vastly more than that first computer—and it's been reduced to the size of a human fingernail.

While these chips are a wonderful expression of human ingenuity, we have a ways to go toward equaling what we see in the natural world. One summer evening, as I watched a line of the tiniest ants I'd ever seen march resolutely toward a pool of spilled milk, I thought back to what the convention speaker had said. These diminutive creatures, so small that many of them would fit on my fingernail, possess capabilities that make a computer look like a child's toy.

They have self-propulsion, sense organs that allow them to see, hear, smell, and feel. The use of these senses allows them to make relatively complex decisions, such as recognize food, flee from danger, identify their "home" anthill, and perform all their required functions. They even have, to some extent, the capacity for repairing injury and for self-replication. Marveling at those remarkable creatures, I realized I was seeing complexity on a level far surpassing anything human intelligence has ever produced. As with millions of other such examples, *how* can we imagine it could have occurred purely by accident?

OTHER SELECT EVIDENCE FOR DESIGN

Within nature, countless facets are virtually unexplainable if our only option is to assume they resulted from chance forces. One of these features is *symmetry*. Symmetry is not just two eyes or two (or four or six) arms and legs; it's also the setting of these organs as the mirror image of the other, so that they coexist in a kind of constructive opposition. Without symmetry, horses couldn't run, birds couldn't fly, fish couldn't swim, and, of course, life as we know it would not be possible.

Symmetry is even more complicated than the formation of a geometric shape; symmetry is a complex shape mirroring itself and forming what we take entirely for granted, a left side and a right side. A perfectly square rock formed by the wind or waves is more plausible than natural symmetry.

Symmetry leads to another element of nature that seems only to be explained by design: aerodynamic shapes. For instance, the blue-winged teal (a rapidly flying and highly maneuverable duck) in flight resembles a swept-wing aircraft, and a porpoise resembles a submarine. When we see qualities in nature that resemble products of human design, surely it's logical to assume we're seeing the product of higher intelligence.

❖ ❖ ❖ ❖

Most birds build nests, lay their eggs, and then sit on them, allowing body heat to incubate the eggs until their babies hatch. This process is remarkable in itself, since the birds must do more than just sit on the eggs to incubate them. However, there's a bird in Australia that *literally* incubates its eggs.

It builds its nest by clearing out an area of sand, then lays its eggs in the sand and proceeds to cover them with leaves. Then it begins a process of monitoring the nest's temperature and humidity with the roof of its highly sensitive mouth; when the temperature gets too high or too low, the bird removes or adds leaves. It even *turns* the eggs at the appropriate times and superintends the nest until hatching time.

This creature is most remarkable to me, because my father owned a poultry hatchery, and I know personally all that goes into the process of incubation. Seeing a bird, operating purely on instinct, performing all the complex functions of incubation, screams out to us, "Design!"

Once more, if something like this were a rare or isolated case, we might be able to attribute it to chance, but nature literally is filled with such examples. There is mimicry, where plants look like insects to enable pollination, or where insects look like plants for protection. There are the many instances of symbiotic relationship and of precise adaptation to specific needs and conditions. Our body's hormonal system and the precise chemical balances that must be maintained for its normal functioning is an awe-inspiring feat of engineering.

Design is all around us at every level. In honesty, we must affirm the words of David the psalmist: "I am fearfully and wonderfully made."[125] Even the "ordinary" things of the natural world are truly wonders of design.

❖ ❖ ❖ ❖

I remember discussing with an evolution supporter the supposed transition from reptiles to birds. All that was needed, he said, was for reptilian scales to evolve into feathers. As I pointed out to my friend, here's the rub: there's a vast difference between scales and feathers. Comparing a scale to a feather is like comparing a cell phone to cans strung-together by a string. Feathers contain millions of interconnecting barbules that trap air when moved in one direction (thus providing lift) and allow air to pass through when moved in the other direction (thus preventing a useless fanning of air). Feathers are both very light and very strong. Their intricate shape and structure enables the wings' functioning. They are *marvels* of design; the notion that they accidentally evolved from scales insults our intelligence.

THE REAL ISSUE FOR EVOLUTIONISTS

Evolutionists acknowledge that so much in nature *looks* designed. This is why they are constantly personifying evolution and attributing purpose to what they claim are just chance processes. But their mechanism, genetic mutation coupled with natural selection, is completely inadequate to explain the inherent complexity needed to produce design. There is nothing in nature—no definable mechanism in any organism—that can sense when change is needed and then produce the specific degree of change that fits a given creature's environmental conditions. Yet because this is exactly how evolution is explained, it's here that the imagination must be employed.

Evolution is deeply embedded within the academic and scientific community. The theory has generated so much propaganda, and its basic assumptions are so uncritically accepted, that few on the inside seem willing or able to step out and meaningfully address its formidable obstacles. The clearest indication of this is the way these communities deal with opposition. Sincere and straightforward consideration of a specific objection is rare; the most common approach is some form of name-calling. They slander detractors and accuse them of attempting to impose religion upon the rest of society. But this is the strategy of politicians, not scientists; *this debate isn't about science but rather social policy and political control.* Again: *Evolution is essential for the continuation of the scientific and academic communities' commitment to naturalism and to a secular society.*

❖ ❖ ❖ ❖

In the middle of the controversy at Baylor University over the Polyanyi Institute, a writer for the *Houston Press* said:

> Intelligent Design comes with a political agenda that is far from moderate. The very way in which it formulates its scientific questions seeks to tear apart the Darwinian underpinnings that influence our laws, our public policies, our economic systems, our psychological theories, our schools, our sense of who we are … in short, our entire worldview.[126]

I very much appreciate this columnist's honesty. He is correct in saying that many of our laws and policies, and many of our assumptions about education, economics, and the social order, are based upon naturalism. The fact of the matter is, *all* ideas have political implications. If evolution is true, then indeed we should build our assumptions upon it. But if it is not, then we are guilty of building our society upon what is false, and history has proven that societies built upon lies don't succeed. All of the peripheral concerns beg the actual question: Is evolution true, or is it false?

Of *course* intelligent design has political implications. Of *course* the rejection of evolution by the scientific community would be a monumental paradigm shift for Western civilization. But where is the scientific evidence to support the theory? From the debate's first days, evolutionists have evaded this and simply accused their opposition of being "religious." Again, this claim is not made because there's genuine corroborative evidence for the theory but because it's crucial to the assumptions and beliefs of scientists and the academic community.

The primary excuse for not allowing any form of intelligent design to be taught alongside evolutionary theory in public school classrooms is that this forum is for the study of science and not religion. That is merely a smokescreen to (1) prevent dialogue about legitimate scientific concerns and (2) continue indoctrinating our culture with propaganda. Remember, the perplexing irony is that all this is done in the name of *science*, which is meant to be unbiased in its pursuit of truth.

Our society must decide if it will continue to perpetuate what may be nothing more than a falsehood to defend a politically correct secularism. We must determine if we are willing to hold the theory of evolution to truly scientific standards of evaluation. And we must press for honest debate based solely upon the scientific merits of each case.

> It's perfectly legitimate to question the theory of evolution. If you have a hard time seeing how human intelligence could have "evolved," you are not a religious fanatic; you're asking proponents of the hypothesis to provide realistic answers to substantive questions, questions they have heretofore either ignored or sopped with baseless and simplistic answers. Evolution is not supported by reason or experience—that's why, for it to stick around, it must be imposed by force.

CONCLUSION

As we've repeatedly seen, Enlightenment intellectuals hoped that science would eventually lead to established naturalism and the elimination of religious belief. In many ways this was a self-fulfilling prophecy: they wanted science to eliminate God, and so it did, that is, in the explanations that mattered most in our understanding of reality: the origin and condition of nature. But their methods weren't entirely true to science.

They first resorted to empiricism: if we can't see, hear, or touch God with physical tests or instruments, then we can assume He isn't there. Yet Immanuel Kant had shown that our senses alone are inadequate to answer such an ultimate question. Further, as we progressed in science, we discovered a great many things we couldn't see, hear, or touch but which we know exist because of the effects they produce.

Approaching the twentieth century, a second strategy was employed: methodological naturalism. This perspective assumed, *from the beginning*, that every event in nature must have a non-supernatural explanation. Science was, therefore, equated with naturalism, guaranteeing that religion would be relegated to the realm of the unscientific. When evolutionists say that evolution is a fact and not a theory, they are doing so on the grounds of methodological naturalism. In other words, all natural phenomena (such as living organisms) *must* have a natural (non-supernatural) explanation, so life *must* have evolved (because the only other option is intelligent design).

Regardless, science is science. It is not naturalism—it is the pursuit of truth using logic and the scientific method. What logic and experimentation lead one to conclude is the proper scientific conclusion. Something cannot be said to be scientific when its methodology and results are predefined.

Naturalism is the instrument through which we became a secular society. There is much at stake politically and socially in its continuation at the center of our worldview. However, and it's critical we realize this, naturalism is *not* the inevitable conclusion of a scientific study of the universe. God is not dead, and we are not alone in a meaningless universe. Bertrand Russell was incorrect when he said, "Only on the firm foundation of unyielding despair can the soul's habitation henceforth be safely built."[127] Belief in God, a personal God, is not irrational;

it is not even unreasonable. That belief is the sound conclusion of a careful examination of the world in which we live.

---

[118] See at www.baylor.edu/Lariat/news.php?action=story&story=15134

[119] David Attenborough, on Nature. BBC: March 1982.

[120] Michael Behe, Darwin's Black Box: The Biochemical Challenge to Evolution (New York: Free Press, 2006).

[121] H. Allen Orr, "Darwin v. Intelligent Design (Again)," orig. published in Boston Review (Dec. 1996/Jan. 1997).

[122] Behe, op. cit.

[123] See William A. Dembski, No Free Lunch: Why Specified Complexity Cannot Be Purchased without Intelligence (Lanham, MD: Rowman & Littlefield, 2001).

[124] Cosmos, video series. Dir. Adrian Malone. Cosmos Studios: 2002 (orig. released 1980).

[125] See Psalm 139:14.

[126]"In God's Country" (printed 12/14/00); see at www.houstonpress.com.

[127] In Bertrand Russell, Mysticism and Logic (Minneola, NY: Dover, 2004; orig. published 1957).

CHAPTER EIGHT

THE CHALLENGE OF SECULARISM (PART I)

Let's step back for a minute and review what we considered at this book's beginning.

The political outworking of naturalism is secularism, the belief that religious matters should be excluded from the public functioning of society. Our nation's founding fathers attempted to guarantee freedom *of* religion, meaning that individual Americans would be free to choose their affiliation and there would be no state-supported church that all citizens must join. They didn't mean the state should be opposed to religion; they intended to encourage the practice of faith as a right of free citizens. They understood the need for a moral foundation upon which a democratic republic could be established, and they believed religion provided it.

In the last half century or so, we've gone another direction. The laws of the land have been reinterpreted to guarantee freedom *from* religion. As a result, any form of public religious expression, no matter how innocuous, is considered illegal. We thus are not allowed to post the Ten Commandments on a courthouse wall or place a manger scene on the front lawn of city hall at Christmas.

In 1950 the New York Board of Regents established a special commission to recommend a plan for improving the moral education of the state's children. The plan was published in a document titled *Statement on Moral and Spiritual Training in the Schools*, and included was a simple, nonsectarian prayer to be recited at the start of every school day: "Almighty God, we acknowledge our dependence upon Thee, and we beg Thy blessings upon us, our parents, our teachers, and our Country."

It was a different era—today, only a few decades later, this would be unthinkable.[128] That generation saw religion as a force for good in the world, and they believed it was beneficial for children to be exposed to its influence, because it was the bedrock upon which civic morality was founded. Growing up in this period, I remember teachers encouraging us to go to church as part of our duty as citizens. Organizations like the Boy Scouts and Girl Scouts encouraged faith in the interest of developing virtue and character. One of their most important awards was the "For God and Country Award," which involved significant participation in the scout's local church or synagogue.

And we grew up believing that religion was an important part of a good life. Many parents felt compelled to provide such education for their children even if they were not particularly religious. I recall watching dads and moms who seldom attended services drop their children off at Sunday school and pick them up again when classes ended.

SOCIETY REDEFINED

In the 1960s, people opposed to or offended by religion's cultural presence began to take legal action; a minority that sought to protect its right not to be exposed to religious messages invoked the Constitution. In 1962, the Supreme Court outlawed public-school-sponsored prayer.[129] In 1963, the Court ended public-school-sponsored Bible reading in classrooms.[130]

The judiciary's rulings, *by reference to its founding document*, propelled the nation toward being an entirely secular society. By the authority of the land's weightiest legal standard, the courts began the process that would result in the strict prohibition of all public-sponsored expressions of religion. Secularism would become the culture's prevailing philosophy and official policy.

❖ ❖ ❖ ❖

We noted earlier that there may not have been a widespread societal intent to enthrone secularism. At the same time, again, the courts would have never agreed to these restrictions if they did not agree, in principle, with the Enlightenment take on religion: it's part of a pre-scientific superstition that's long ruled humankind and, for the sake of progress and for everyone's ultimate welfare, must be marginalized or eliminated. Since this conviction then became deeply entrenched in Western higher education, it should not be surprising that most of our learned professionals would question or denounce the value of religion in the larger society and thus come down on the side of those who desire pure secularism.

The message we often hear today is that religion is evil, mostly just a source of intrinsic division, oppression, and violence. For example, John Lennon's song "Imagine"[131] includes the hope of a secular utopia, a world free of conflict *because* it would be a world without religion. This baseless belief, that the end of faith will significantly reduce or even eradicate conflict in the world, is widespread and, in some sectors, growing. Christopher Hitchens and Richard Dawkins are among those who've written books promoting atheism and arguing for the complete rejection of religion as the answer to the problems of our time (and, hence, those still to come).[132]

Additionally, Enlightenment leaders *did* imagine just such a "secular paradise." On a very short list, David Hume, Herbert

Spencer, and Sir Julian Huxley (1887–1975) diligently worked to end the influence of what they considered ignorance and superstition. In the US, the educator John Dewey (1859–1952), the attorney Clarence Darrow (1857–1938), and the writer H. L. Mencken (1880–1956) sought to eliminate religious teachings and messages from both education and the broader culture. Others since have aimed to continue realizing and establishing those same goals.

BEING CAREFUL WHAT WE WISH FOR

Nevertheless, is the pursuit of a secular society in our best interests? Will it truly produce a more healthy and peaceful world? Might there be another side to the story, one we're ignoring or denying? What if religion—and, in particular, Christianity—*is* a force for good? What if the very values we cherish, the freedoms we enjoy, and the moral progress we've achieved are the result of the faith we're now rejecting?

We do have some history on the subject. Several twentieth-century nations attempted to create purely secular societies, and a few even outlawed religion all together. In attempting to eliminate faith from society, these regimes were attempting to create secular utopias. That is, societies free from the animosities and divisions generated by religious teaching and, therefore, it was supposed, free from the essence of conflict itself.

Kenneth Mischel, professor of Economics at the City University of New York (CUNY), writes, "The Utopian persistently exposes himself and those around him to the force of unintended consequences in an exquisitely heightened way."[133] The utopian notion that the elimination of religion will produce world peace suffers from precisely this myopia. A society without religion lacks the transcendent values that regulate and check our behavior.

In an authentically secular society, anything goes; *that* only works if people are perfect. When the Khmer Rouge came to power in Cambodia, their idealistic intention was to create the perfect egalitarian society. Tragically, because their goals weren't constrained or inhibited by moral principles, they came to believe their utopian ends were worthy of any means… including mass murder. The subsequent carnage—as many as 20 percent of Cambodia's people died—was not the result of religious hatred. The killings were carried out by those in pursuit of the allegedly perfect culture. History has proven, again and again, that the extinguishing of faith is no secret road to peace.

We humans have the capacity to be political lemmings, carried along en masse by the winds of widespread, fluctuating opinion. We must be careful that our views are accurate and not just popular; the problem with lemmings isn't the journey but the destination. It's certainly worth asking: Is our "progressive" view of spirituality leading us toward the edge of a very steep cliff?

❖ ❖ ❖ ❖

For earlier generations, the encouragement of religion was inspired in part by the belief that, as French historian Alexis de Tocqueville (1805–1859) wrote, "The safeguard of morality is religion, and morality is the security of law as well as the surest pledge of freedom."[134] Religion was one of the means by which justice, unselfishness, temperance, and compassion were fostered in the American people. Morality was understood to be the source of our liberty and the strength of our polity.

Again, public encouragement of religious practice had its detractors well before 1960. For instance, Mencken had been writing scornful critiques of organized religion since before the infamous 1925 Scopes Trial. Dewey and other education leaders had promoted a completely amoral philosophy of teaching and learning. However, it was not until the 60s that society's broad political will would accept the removal of religious influence from public education.

Today, the courts have determined that any level of religious connection is unconstitutional. For instance, using what's called the "Lemon Test,"[135] federal courts have prohibited the display of the Ten Commandments on public property because they "are clearly a religious document and must be excluded." Such decisions by our nation's legal authorities send this message: the menace of religion must be marginalized.

The judicial standard for American courts is no longer the *establishment* of a state religion: It has now become a vague accusation of *encouragement* or *endorsement*. The state, according to this new definition, must be completely secular—that is, there cannot be a religious bone in the body politic of society. We must be clear: *this is not what our constitution says*. We have put words in its mouth, or, worse yet, changed its wording altogether. Establishment and encouragement are two very different things. Establishment is the creation of a state-supported institution; encouragement is simply approving of a practice, idea, or activity.

The argument used today is that "public displays" lend state support to Christianity and thus disenfranchise those of other faiths or those who hold to no religious beliefs.[136] In response, though, we must ask, does the raising of religious symbols lead to favoritism or injustice? Does a Christian thereby get preferential treatment over an atheist?

Where did we get our beliefs *about* equality and justice? They're in the book that gave us the Ten Commandments.[137] Equal treatment for all people regardless of ethnicity, gender, or affiliation came from the teachings of the one born in that manger no longer allowed outside the courthouse. Judeo-Christian values have produced the highest degree of freedom, equality, justice, opportunity, and prosperity in human history; should we not acknowledge the debt we owe them and declare our commitment to continue upholding them, whether or not we hold to the religious doctrines behind them?

SECULARIST ASSUMPTIONS

The leaders who shaped our nation were opposed to a state church because of the terrible damage caused by Europe's religious wars. However, they were by no means opposed to Christianity. The main premises of that faith—a Creator God, the sanctity of human life, humankind's inherent value and equality as made in God's image, the rule of law as a reflection of both natural law and the revealed morality of the Judeo-Christian faiths—were to form our society's foundation.

So what explains the shift toward opposition to all things religious? Secularism is built upon several erroneous assumptions. First and foremost is that religion is a product of superstition, fear, and prejudice. Make no mistake: the church *has* committed egregious errors and abuses. However, the misuse of religion does not negate its value. The church that produced the Crusades and the Inquisition likewise gave the world Hudson Taylor and Mother Teresa (as well as countless other men and women so loving and devoted).

It was the church that led Europe out of the Dark Ages by preserving or rediscovering the literature of the ancient world. The church founded the Western world's renowned institutions of learning and has been a vital source of cultural literacy and education. The founding charters of the most famous US universities show they were founded by Christians for the advancement of the gospel.

A second false assumption is that religion is a source of monumental evil; that it intrinsically produces a deep-seated intolerance that has justified hatred of those outside the accepted faith and led to myriad and horrible conflicts. There certainly have been examples of religious hatred and violence throughout history; yet the life of Jesus Christ, the Prince of Peace, has moved countless millions to *renounce* bigotry, hatred, oppression, and violence.

While religion has produced monstrous evil, it has also produced inestimable good. In the larger picture of history, Christianity itself has been the world's greatest wellspring of individual and societal reform; there is no worldview or philosophy that is its equal. Our culture predominantly emphasizes the wrong done in the name of religion but seldom speaks of the goodness that profoundly overshadows it.

Just as the prominent universities have Christian roots, so also have the major medical and philanthropic organizations. The disciplines of nursing, nurse-training, and sanitation were significantly advanced by Florence Nightingale in the mid-1800s as she sought to alleviate horrible suffering during the Crimean War. Her efforts in the name of Christ inspired thousands to enter the medical profession. Look too at the names of the major hospitals in our cities—most have some religious connection: Mount Sinai, St. Luke's, Baptist General… the list seemingly is endless. Religion has been a consistent and underlying factor in the establishment of health care and charitable assistance.

Third, critics assume that a truly scientific worldview eliminates all religious explanations of reality. As such, a fully "enlightened" perspective has no need of supernatural explanation; everything ultimately will be explained on naturalistic grounds. The subjection of religion to this assumption aims to make it a component of the study of anthropology rather of theology.

SECULARIZED THEOLOGY

In the nineteenth century, a small number of influential theologians accepted naturalistic conclusions and began the process of developing a "scientific" explanation for the Judeo-Christian faith. Their hope was to make it "relevant" to the modern world. The problem is that a Christianity devoid of its central truths and the hope those truths provide is an empty shell. The actual Enlightenment goal wasn't *relevant* Christianity but *no* Christianity. These skeptical theologians were like squatters attempting to construct an edifice from discarded packing boxes after the truly valuable commodities inside had been thrown away.

The result for the Protestant denominations most heavily influenced by this process was an entire century (the twentieth) of dramatic decline. It made unbelievers of entire generations. Growing up in one of those denominations, I watched my own generation systematically leave a church they found entirely *irrelevant*.

Just as the secularization of science began in academia, so the secularization of theology began in the Western seminaries. Theologians who were part of the larger intellectual community, and who desired acceptance within it, endorsed the Enlightenment's premises and directives. Many scholars of this era primarily endeavored to explain the "true origin" of Judaism and Christianity.

They called their efforts *higher criticism,* because they were attempting to explain the origin and development of the text of the Bible; *lower criticism* attempted to understand the text itself. These men, many centuries removed from the events they were studying, and without historical or archeological evidence, presumed to be able to say what *really* happened in the ancient Near Eastern world throughout the development of the Jewish nation and its worldview. Their unspoken but actual goal: to present a non-supernatural (secular, naturalist) explanation for Judaism and Christianity.

In this vein, the first popular model for religion's origin was the "evolutionary model," initially expressed by James Frazer (1854–1941) in his book *The Golden Bough.*[138] Frazer was an anthropologist, not a theologian, but his theory became the accepted framework for higher criticism at the beginning of the twentieth century. He hypothesized that religion had evolved from primitive superstition to fully developed monotheism.

At the center of this idea was a theory of the development, over time, of the first five Old Testament books, and the corresponding theory of Judaism's progression from primitive polytheism to the strict monotheism of its present form. The critical scholar Julius Wellhausen (1844–1918) was given credit for the elaboration of this idea, which came to be known as the Documentary Theory. It stated that the Torah (and therefore Judaism itself) evolved over the later centuries from David's kingdom (c. 1000 BCE) until the period of the Babylonian exile (c. sixth century BCE), rather than earlier being written and given to Israel by Moses during the events of the Exodus. The theory concludes that the Old Testament characters and events are all part of a legend created by later Hebrew generations wanting to explain their identity as a unique ethnic group among the peoples of the world.[139]

There was likewise a parallel movement to "demythologize" the New Testament. Scholars set out to produce a natural or non-supernatural explanation for its events and its claims. They began by assuming that the accounts of Christ's life were fictions used to create a new religion.

REORDERING HISTORY

The fundamental assumption that drove these processes was the presupposition that miracles are impossible. Any miracle recorded in either Testament was automatically considered to be fictitious. Obviously, prophecies—predictions of events before they actually happened—were a particular inconvenience; so, these "higher critics" said that any fulfilled Old Testament prophecy must have been recorded after the fact and composed as a religious deception to inspire faith. This led them to many of their conclusions about the dates and the authors of the Old Testament books. In that arena, the two receiving the most attention were Isaiah and Daniel.

The critics believed Isaiah to have been written in two "halves": The first by the actual prophet Isaiah, around 700 BCE, and the second by a much later author that the critics named "Deutero-Isaiah."[140] This was based not on historical evidence but on the perceived need to date the book after the historical events it foretold.

For example, Isaiah identified the Persian monarch who would allow the Jewish exiles to return to their land. He actually named Cyrus and referred to his decree to rebuild the temple, which took place in 535 BCE.[141] But Isaiah lived well over a hundred years before this happened; thus, if the original Isaiah wrote these words, we are faced with a legitimate miraculous prophecy. For skeptical theologians, the assumption of a miracle's impossibility meant there *must* be a natural explanation, even for what seems to be a supernatural event.

The problem with this assumption—the book of Isaiah having two authors—is that there's no historical evidence to support the claim. All our ancient texts of Isaiah, including the very ancient copy (possibly as old as 100 BCE) that was found with the Dead Sea Scrolls, have all the passages of our present-day book. There is no hint or even suggestion from historical records of the Jewish people that there ever existed a shorter or split version of Isaiah.

Possibly the strongest evidence for the unity and antiquity of Isaiah is found in the Septuagint (LXX). The Septuagint is an ancient translation of the Old Testament into Greek, commissioned by the Jewish community of Alexandria, Egypt, around 200 BCE. The Septuagint includes the entire book of Isaiah as we have it today.

This means that the Jews of Alexandria, in the middle of the intertestamental period,[142] possessed and revered the same text of Isaiah that we do. Regarding the Jews—renowned for their respect for the Scriptures and, generally, for their conservatism—the idea that a "new" book or a newly expanded book could be foisted upon them and accepted as sacred text is, at best, hard to fathom. We have direct statements from rabbinical writings that while books written during the intertestamental period were considered valuable, none was equated with Scripture.

❖ ❖ ❖ ❖

In addition to foreseeing many other events, the book of Daniel predicts the conquest of Persia by Alexander the Great (356–323 BCE) and speaks of the division of his empire into four parts after his death. The Daniel of the Babylonian exile lived around 600 BCE; Alexander conquered Persia almost three centuries later. If Daniel wrote the book bearing his name, then his predictions clearly are miraculous. However, the critics' presuppositions led them to assume that Daniel was written by someone else, *after* the time of Alexander. Daniel was considered a fictitious intertestamental work.

In sharp contrast, we can be confident that Daniel *was* a real person who lived during the exile; Ezekiel referred to him in his book, which was written at close to the same time.[143] We also know that the book of Daniel was included in the sacred Scriptures at the time of the Old Testament's translation from Hebrew into Greek (c. 200 BCE). Again, an intertestamental book wouldn't have been included with the Hebrew canon; the writings of that era—for instance, the books of the Apocrypha—were *not* granted that status.

The direct statements from early rabbinical writing and from the historian Flavius Josephus (c. CE 37–c. 100) explain why a book written after the last of the prophets (Malachi, c. 400 BCE) could not be in the canon. What evidence is there that an exception was made for Daniel? The explanation that fits the data is that Daniel was written by the historical Daniel during the time of the exile.

THE HISTORICAL REALITY

Every form of this skeptical "theology" has the same significant flaw: It has no real historical support. As is the case with Isaiah and Daniel, there's no evidence from either the source documents or other ancient writings to support a number of different authors for the books of Moses or their development over the centuries from Israel's kings to the postexilic period. *The proposed radical reconstruction of Hebrew history is based on anti-supernaturalist presuppositions.*

Over time, matters have only worsened for the critics. Scholars in the late nineteenth century had claimed the Old Testament to be spurious because it refers to a supposedly mythical people called the Hittites. But then they dug up the library of the Hittite civilization. They ridiculed the Jonah story, not just for the part about the fish but also because it spoke of the city of Nineveh, which they believed was legendary. Within a few short years, archeologists uncovered the ancient capital of the Assyrian empire.

Archeology continued to unearth more and more of the ancient world and its cultural forms. Concurrently, it became increasingly apparent that the stories and details of the Hebrew patriarchs presented in the Pentateuch were consistent with that more ancient era; people in the time of the kings, for example, would have had no intimate knowledge of its specific customs, names, titles, and culture. It's exceedingly difficult to support the idea that a group of priests, several millennia after the fact, invented a series of fictional hero stories about Israel's patriarchs and included startlingly accurate details involving treaty forms, inheritance laws, and customs for surrogate parenting, as well as era-specific literary forms of names and places. Furthermore, the discoveries of records like the Nuzi Tablets and the Ugaritic Texts has forced critical scholars to rethink their view of the Pentateuch.

Concerning higher criticism's theories on the Hebrew people, archeologist Kenneth Kitchen (b. 1932) says,

> Nowhere else in the whole of Ancient Near Eastern history has the literary, religious, and historical development of a nation been subjected to such a drastic and wholesale reconstruction at such variance with the existing documentary evidence.[144]

MOVING FROM JUDAISM TO JESUS

This type of dramatic reconstruction has been attempted on the New Testament as well, with even less corroborating historical evidence (and that bar was low to begin with). It started with attempts to "demythologize" the life of Jesus. The philosopher Ernest Renan (1823–1892), who wrote *The Life of Christ*, started with the central assumption that Jesus was an ordinary human being; the miracle stories—and the primary miracle, His bodily resurrection—were religious fabrications. But Renan faced an obstacle: the dedication of the disciples after the Crucifixion and Resurrection. What can explain that?

> How did the resurrection legend originate? The strong imagination of Mary Magdalen played an important part. Divine power of love! Sacred moments in which the passion of an hallucinated woman gave the world a resurrected god![145]

Renan's explanation, however, only raises more questions. The disciples were extremely skeptical of Mary's story. Reading the New Testament, we discover it was not her testimony that convinced them Christ was truly alive but rather His appearances.[146] The disciples were not gullible barbarians; they knew as well as anyone that dead men don't come back to life. They had to be convinced by literally tangible evidence that Jesus was indeed the resurrected Lord.

Over the years, any number of theories has been put forward in the attempt to "find the historical (non-supernatural) Jesus" and to "demythologize the New Testament." The invariable problem still is the disciples and the emergence of the church. A movement of such devotion and sacrifice required a core of people who truly believed. Since the disciples, who had lived with Jesus and had seen His miracles, were the central force in the gospel's proclamation, they *above all* must have been true believers. The apologist J. P. Moreland (b. 1948) writes,

> I know of no New Testament scholar who denies that several of Jesus' early followers at least had a life changing experience they believed to be an experience of the risen Jesus.[147]

One of the most remarkable aspects of the entire New Testament record is the transformation of the disciples after the resurrection of Christ and the outpouring of the Holy Spirit on the day of Pentecost. Prior to the Crucifixion, the disciples ran in fear from the Jewish authorities; Peter didn't even dare to tell a servant girl that he was a follower of the Galilean.[148] Yet at Pentecost, this same Peter stood before a crowd of thousands and boldly proclaimed Jesus as the risen Lord and Savior.[149]

It is impossible to explain the rapid spread of Christianity without the dedication of the apostles. The early church placed tremendous emphasis on their testimony. Because they lived in a world filled with religious quackery, to guarantee the validity of the message they emphasized the integrity of the messenger. The movement that would give rise to the medieval church's doctrine of apostolic succession was a means of protecting it from innumerable false teachers.

From early on, the church was to follow *only* the leadership of someone whose appointment could be traced back to an apostle. Why? Because the apostles received the highest respect: they were the eyewitnesses to the gospel events. There is no hint from history that these men *ever* contradicted their testimony about Christ's life, death, and resurrection. According to the records, nearly all of them died for the message they proclaimed.

In the second generation after the apostles, it was those who had been their associates—men like Polycarp of Smyrna (c. CE 69–c. 155) and Ignatius of Antioch (c. CE 35–c. 107)—who were granted authority and credibility within the church. Also, of the thousands of "books" circulating, many of which claimed to be "gospels" or "revelations," the church determined to accept only those that could be clearly traced to an apostle or an apostle's close associate.

All of this demonstrates the status given the disciples in the church's formation. It was their personal recollection of their experiences with Christ that formed the central message of the Gospels, and it was their personal preaching of Christ's message of repentance and faith that established the first-century church.

THE HISTORICITY OF THE NEW TESTAMENT

In diametrical opposition to the theological outworkings of secularism, Christianity claims that the New Testament is an historical document written by those who saw and heard everything for which it accounts. The question, then, is, how do we test the claim? What level of confidence can we have that the New Testament truly is a reliable record of the life, death, and resurrection of Jesus Christ?

BIBLIOGRAPHIC EVIDENCE

There are methods to determine the authenticity and historical accuracy of any document from the ancient world. First it is evaluated by (A) the number of manuscripts available for study and (B) the time separation between the age of those manuscripts and the time the actual events were recorded. This is called the *bibliographic test*. The more extant copies, the better we're able to discover, for example, errors in copying or changes to the text over time. And the closer the manuscript is to the time of the events, the greater is our confidence in its accuracy.

Much has been written about the vast number of New Testament manuscripts available for study—let's consider just the main points. Because we possess *thousands* of copies, we are able to do comparative studies on a level unheard of for any other ancient document. Also, we possess portions of the New Testament that are only thirty to fifty years removed from the originals, and complete manuscripts separated from the originals by only 250 years. In comparison, the documents we use to describe ancient Greece or Rome are nine hundred to a thousand years removed from their originals.

Regarding the New Testament, Will Durant (1885–1981), one of the twentieth century's foremost historians, wrote,

> The contradictions [in the various manuscripts] are of minutiae, not substance; in essentials the synoptic gospels [Matthew, Mark, and Luke] agree remarkably well, and form a consistent portrait of Christ. In the enthusiasm of its discoveries Higher Criticism has applied to the New Testament tests of authenticity so severe that by them a hundred ancient worthies—Hammurabi, David, Socrates—would fade into legend.[150]

By bibliographic-test standards, the New Testament is the most validated document of the ancient world. We can be highly confident that the biblical text we read today accurately reflects the writings of the original authors.

EXTERNAL EVIDENCE

A second major examination for every historical record is the test for *external evidence*. These are references to the source document's people, places, and events that are found in other sources, such as letters, inscriptions, and books. Because of the chronological span between today and the ancient world, this is often a difficult task. However, it's tremendously important, because it can verify or nullify the source document's record.

External evidence also helps confirm the dates of the events and of the documents themselves. Therefore, it's a crucial piece of the puzzle in determining a work's historical accuracy. For the New Testament, the significant external evidence can be divided into three parts: *hostile witnesses* to the events, *friendly witnesses* to the events, and *archeological discoveries*. As a great deal has been written about these also, we'll summarize here.

❖ ❖ ❖ ❖

In many ways hostile witnesses are substantial; obviously they have no bias toward the document's claims. When they tell us Christ was an historical figure who was crucified by the prelate Pontius Pilate, we can be assured they're telling us what actually happened. The Roman historian Tacitus (c. 56–c. 117) says exactly this.[151] Even earlier, Josephus, the ancient world's most famous historian, also tells of Christ's crucifixion and messianic claims, as well as the Christian proclamation of the Resurrection.[152] Additionally, a number of Jewish writings declare that Jesus was crucified; these seek, also, to give an alternate explanation for the Virgin Birth, implying that the details of the Gospels were well known even outside Christian circles.

❖ ❖ ❖ ❖

The evidence from the friendly witnesses is overwhelming. It has been said that the early church fathers (the leaders who succeeded the apostles) quoted the Scriptures so extensively in their writings that nearly the entire New Testament could be reconstructed just from their letters. What we gain from these sources are the stories of the New Testament's composition. Irenaeus of Lyons (c. second century), for example, tells us that Matthew wrote and sent out his gospel during the time of Nero's persecution in Rome (c. CE 63–64), and that Mark, a disciple of Peter, wrote his gospel at about the same time. Eusebius of Caesarea (c. 275–339) confirms this and also says that Mark wrote his gospel "not, however, in exact order" [that is, chronologically].[153] That's a fascinating phrase, particularly in light of Luke's opening statement in *his* gospel:

> Inasmuch as many have undertaken to compile an account of the things accomplished among us … it seemed fitting for me … to write it out for you in consecutive order.[154]

Such straightforward expressions in these books likewise bolster the authenticity of their statements.

One interesting passage from an early Christian writer, Julius Africanus (c. third century), refers to a Samaritan-born writer named Thallus, a non-believer who attempted to explain the darkness surrounding the Crucifixion[155] as an eclipse of the sun. Historians believe Thallus wrote around 54 CE; he was substantiating one of the amazing circumstances surrounding the event even as he attempted to diminish it. "Thallus, in the third book of his histories, explains away this darkness as an eclipse of the sun—unreasonably, as it seems to me."[156] Part of why it's unreasonable is that Jesus was crucified on the Passover, which always coincided with a full moon, making a solar eclipse impossible.

❖ ❖ ❖ ❖

Now, for a brief statement about archeological discoveries: At the beginning of the twentieth century, a young William Ramsay (1852–1916) traveled to ancient Asia Minor (modern Turkey) to begin his research; he was skeptical of the New Testament, believing it to have been composed by Gentile writers well into the second century. As he started his work, he intended to prove the book of Acts and the stories of Paul's journeys unhistorical and thus untrue. To his astonishment, he found Acts to be geographically and historically precise. In the end, the now famous archeologist wrote, "Luke is a historian of the first rank.... This author should be placed along with the very greatest historians."[157]

Archeology has confirmed many New Testament details and increased our confidence in its reliability. But what of its books' composition dates? Skeptics have alleged that they were written by second- or third-generation Christians, long after the actual events. What does archeology say?

Consider Paul's journeys, recorded in Acts. Luke refers to two Jews, refugees from Rome "because Claudius had commanded all the Jews to leave Rome."[158] From inscriptions, we know that this occurred in CE 51. We also know that Luke ends Acts with Paul alive and well in Rome, and we have written evidence that Paul died under Nero's persecution in CE 63–64. This means Paul's primary letters to the churches were written in the period between CE 50–64. Hence, there is no question that the gospel message—of the Resurrection, of justification by faith, and of the Holy Spirit's presence and work—was being proclaimed well within the lifetimes of the twelve apostles.

INTERNAL EVIDENCE

The third basic category for determining a document's historicity is the *internal evidence*. Internal evidence involves careful reading of the document itself, looking to see that it's free of obviously mythological material, strong contradictions in regard to dates, names, places, and facts, and other serious errors. That, it seems, is the negative side of the issue. There is also a positive side: Does the document live up to the claims that surround it, and does it reflect the reality it says it represents?

Skeptics say the presence of miracle stories in the New Testament causes it to fail the internal-evidence test. However, we must hold our judgment on validity until we look at the actual evidence. We don't reject the story of the Apollo 13 space capsule's recovery on the basis of it being associated with remarkable circumstances and narrow escapes. We know it happened because of the testimony of those who personally experienced it. So it is with the miracle stories: we must look at the testimony of those who claim to be the eyewitnesses to determine if the events are credible.[159]

Opponents of Christianity often say the Bible is "full" of contradictions. When asked to name some, they usually go in one of two directions: either they point to the miracles and imply that all miracles are impossible (and, thus, contradictory), or they point to differences in the details of the gospel accounts.

It's these latter differences Will Durant was referring to when he said, "The contradictions are of minutiae."[160] The truth is, the New Testament is a *phenomenally* coherent book: the central elements of Christ's ministry, teaching, capture, trial, interrogation, and death are completely consistent from account to account. The four Gospels show themselves to be what they claim: the recollections of four different eyewitnesses to the same events. Discrepancy of minor detail actually highlights that the books are the personal testimonies of four men who witnessed the events of Christ's life from their own individual perspective.

The Bible's detractors seek to point out the "problems" associated with it, but they fail to realize that the positive evidence for it being a revelation of God far outweighs the few questions on which they focus. While the Bible is composed of sixty-six different books written over a span of fifteen hundred years, it presents a remarkably consistent picture of the one God and His plan of redemption.

One of the most amazing Old Testament prophecies is given through Ezekiel. Almost no one disputes the authorship or dating of this book (written during the exile, soon after 600 BCE).

> Then I will sprinkle clean water on you, and will make you clean; I will cleanse you from all your filthiness and from all your idols.
>
> Moreover, I will give you a new heart and put a new spirit within you; and I will remove the heart of stone from your flesh and give you a heart of flesh.
>
> I will put My Spirit within you and cause you to walk in My statutes, and you will be careful to observe My ordinances.[161]

These verses are a concise depiction of the gospel more than *six hundred years* before it was revealed to the world in its entirety. It speaks of the cleansing promised through faith in Christ: "You shall call His name Jesus, for He will save His people from their sins."[162] It promises the transformation of a person's inner life:

"You must be born again."[163] And it tells of the Spirit's coming to indwell the believer: "This He spoke of the Spirit, whom those who believed in Him were to receive."[164]

The prophets, in particular, provide a significant connection between the Old and New Testaments. In Ezekiel and Jeremiah we have a foreshadowing of the gospel. In Isaiah we have nearly direct statements of the Incarnation, the Crucifixion, and the Resurrection. Jesus himself declared that the Old Testament was written as a testimony to His coming: "You search the Scriptures because you think that in them you have eternal life; and it is they that bear witness about me";[165] "beginning with Moses and with all the prophets, He explained to them the things concerning Himself in all the Scriptures."[166]

❖ ❖ ❖ ❖

This one book, unique from all others in history, flows fluidly, from Genesis to Revelation. The God who promised Abraham that by his seed "all the families of the earth shall be blessed"[167] also promised that by His redemptive power "a great multitude which no one could count, from every nation and all tribes and peoples and tongues, [will stand] before the throne and before the Lamb."[168] From beginning to end the Bible delivers the same promise given by the same God, whose magnificent plan of salvation is revealed throughout, from start to finish.

Another marvelous Old Testament prophecy is found in a psalm of David.

I am poured out like water,
and all my bones are out of joint;
My heart is like wax;
It is melted within me.
My strength is dried up like a potsherd,
and my tongue cleaves to my jaws;
and You lay me in the dust of death.
For dogs have surrounded me;
a band of evildoers has encompassed me;

They pierced my hands and my feet.
I can count all my bones.
They look, they stare at me;
They divide my garments among them,
and for my clothing they cast lots.[169]

More than five hundred years before crucifixion was first used as a tool of public torture and execution, we find a graphic depiction of Christ's suffering on the cross: His bones being out of joint; the piercing of His hands and feet; that His bones were not broken (the usual practice, to accelerate death by asphyxiation, was to break the convict's legs so he couldn't push up with them for breath); that the soldiers cast lots for his garments. Little wonder that the hundreds of fulfilled biblical prophecies have led so many to the Christian faith.

---

[128] Indeed, it would be only twelve years before the US Supreme Court, in response to litigation brought by the parents of ten students against the Board of Education (of Union Free School District No. 9, Hyde Park, New York), declared this prayer—and others—unconstitutional.

[129] Engel v. Vitale (1962).

[130] Abington v. Schempp (1963).

[131] John Lennon, "Imagine," from the album Imagine. Prods. Phil Spector, John Lennon, Yoko Ono, Adam McCabe. Apple, EMI: 1971.

[132] E.g., Christopher Hitchens, God Is Not Great: How Religion Poisons Everything (Toronto: Emblem Editions, 2008); and The Portable Atheist: Essential Readings for the Nonbeliever (Cambridge, MA: Da Capo Press, 2007); Richard Dawkins, The God Delusion (Boston: Mariner Books, 2008); and The Blind Watchmaker: Why the Evidence of Evolution Reveals a Universe Without Design (New York: W.W. Norton, 1996).

[133] Kenneth Mischel, "How to Make a Carnival," May 2003; paper posted @ economics.gmu.edu.

[134] See Alexis de Tocqueville, Democracy in America, trans. Henry Reeve (London: Sanders and Otley, 1835–1840).

[135] The Lemon Test, based on the 1968 Supreme Court decision in Lemon v. Kurtzman, is composed of three "prongs": (1) The government's action must have a legitimate secular purpose; (2) The government's action must not have the primary effect of either advancing or inhibiting religion; (3) The government's action must

not result in an "excessive government entanglement" with religion. If a case fails any of these tests it is considered unconstitutional.

[136] See on Brooks, William A. v. City of Elkhart at www.Findlaw.com.

[137] These are stated together in Exodus 20.

[138] Sir James George Frazier, The Golden Bough: A Study in Comparative Religion (New York/London: Macmillan and Co., 1894).

[139] Julius Wellhausen, The Composition of the Hexateuch (1876) and The History of Israel (1878), later released as Prolegomena to the History of Israel (1883).

[140] "Deutero-Isaiah" means, literally, "Second Isaiah."

[141] See Isaiah 44:28.

[142] This "between the Testaments" period spanned roughly the four hundred years before the birth of Jesus (c. 400 BCE–4 BCE).

[143] See Ezekiel 14:20.

[144] Kenneth A. Kitchen, Ancient Orient and Old Testament (Chicago: InterVarsity Press, 1966), 20.

[145] In Ernest Renan, The Life of Christ (Paris: Michael Lévy Frères, 1863).

[146] E.g., see Luke 24:13–43; John 20:19–29; Mark 16:9–14.

[147] J. P. Moreland, Scaling the Secular City (Grand Rapids: Baker Book House, 1987), 173.

[148] See Matthew 26:69–70.

[149] See Acts 2.

[150] Will Durant, Caesar and Christ, The Story of Civilization, Volume III: A History of Roman Civilization and of Christianity from Their Beginnings to A.D. 325 (New York: Simon & Schuster, 1944), 557.

[151] In Cornelius Tacitus, Annals.

[152] Flavius Josephus, The Antiquities of the Jews, xviii. 33.

[153] Eusebius of Caesarea, Ecclesiastical History, 3.39.15.

[154] See Luke 1:1, 3.

[155] See Luke 23:44–45.

[156] Julius Africanus, quoted in Josh McDowell, Evidence That Demands a Verdict (San Bernardino: Campus Crusade For Christ International, 1972), 86.

[157] Ibid., 73.

[158] See Acts 18:2.

[159] We'll do this in the next chapter.

[160] Durant, The Story of Civilization: Volume III, 557.

[161] Ezekiel 36:25–27

[162] Matthew 1:21

[163] See John 3:7.

[164] John 7:39

[165] John 5:39 ESV

[166] Luke 24:27

[167] See Genesis 12:3 ESV.

[168] See Revelation 7:9.

[169] Psalm 22:14–18

CHAPTER NINE

THE CHALLENGE OF SECULARISM (PART II)

THE CHARACTER OF CHRIST

At the center of Christianity stands the person of Jesus. It is not an exaggeration to say that the case for the faith stands or falls with the record of His life. So what do we find when we examine the record? As Will Durant noted:

> That a few simple men should in one generation have invented so powerful and appealing a personality, so lofty an ethic, and so inspiring a vision of human brotherhood, would be a miracle far more incredible than any recorded in the Gospels.[170]

Jesus Christ is set apart from every other historical figure. His character, compassion, wisdom, and love distinguish Him from anyone else who has ever lived. The philosopher Jean-Jacques Rousseau said,

> Can the person whose history the Gospels relate himself be a man? What sweetness, what

> purity in his manners! What affecting goodness in his instructions! What sublimity in his maxims! What profound wisdom in his discourses! What presence of mind, what ingenuity of justice in his replies! Yes, if the life and death of Socrates are those of a philosopher, the life and death of Jesus Christ are those of a God.[171]

We begin with His teachings, the essence of which is not "Do to others as you would have them do to you"[172] but "'*Love the Lord your God with all your heart and with all your soul and with all your strength and with all your mind'; and, 'Love your neighbor as [you love] yourself.'*"[173] Jesus first calls us, as human beings, into an intimate relationship with God; then, from the security of that relationship, into human relationships in which we have as much concern for the well-being of the other as we have for our own. There truly is no higher ethical standard. The Golden Rule is a subcategory of this greatest commandment.

Christ's example and instruction (along with the influence of the Ten Commandments and other Old Testament teaching) is firmly at the foundation of the moral and social progress we enjoy today. For instance, the English Wesleyan Revival resulted in several significant social improvements. In 1780 a layman who'd been touched by the revivals started a school for children of the poor. His goal was to lift them out of poverty by giving them the tools of education and literacy and by improving their moral and spiritual lives. He held his classes on the only day they weren't required to work in the mills. Thus the first Sunday school was established, not to provide religious education to church kids but to help poor children escape the cycle of poverty. Other believers likewise caught the vision of Robert Raikes (1736–1811), and an amazing movement was born.

In a similar fashion, John Howard (1726–1790), a friend of the Wesleys, worked tirelessly for prison reform across Europe. Also, the Clapham Sect, a group of dedicated and wealthy evangelicals in England, worked to improve and reform society, primarily focusing on the worldwide elimination of slavery.

The most famous Clapham member was William Wilberforce (1759–1833), who used his position in Parliament to help bring about the abolition of slavery in the British empire.

In the United States, evangelical Christianity was having a similar effect.

> By stressing the moral imperative to end sinful practices and each person's responsibility to uphold God's will in society, preachers like Lyman Beecher, Nathaniel Taylor, and Charles G. Finney in what came to be called the Second Great Awakening led massive religious revivals in the 1820s that gave a major impetus to the later emergence of abolitionism as well as other reforming crusades as temperance, pacifism, and women's rights.[174]

Charles Finney (1792–1875), a wonderful case in point, was a prominent figure in the Second Great Awakening; many regard him among the greatest evangelists in American history. As his concern over slavery grew, however, his emphasis changed and he spent his later years fighting for abolition. One significant accomplishment was his founding of Oberlin College, the first racially integrated college in the US.

As we've repeatedly noted, so many of our values—universal education, equality of races and genders, social justice, the rule of law, and on and on and on—flow out of our Christian heritage. Even simple elements like common courtesy, aversion to corruption, the pursuit of excellence, and public decency can be traced back to the Bible's influence upon Western values.

❖ ❖ ❖ ❖

One important underlying principle behind Christ's teaching and its influence on our society is the fear of God. Jesus never presented a strictly humanistic ethical system; He taught that our primary and ultimate allegiance must be to our heavenly Father. As a result, Western society has emphasized personal integrity and individual conscience. In this way we became an ethics-based (rather than an honor/shame-based) culture.

In an honor/shame-based culture, getting caught in the wrong and, thus, bringing shame on oneself and one's family is the worst transgression. In an ethics-based culture, one is to be moral even when nobody is looking, and conscience is more significant than reputation. We take this for granted, but it's at the foundation of our decorum and at our expectation of authenticity. We implicitly trust our public servants to be honest, not require bribes, and not steal our goods because of how highly we value honesty.

SAVIOR *AND* FRIEND

Jesus, the ultimate example of personal integrity, taught this form of unheralded righteousness: "When you give alms, do not let your left hand know what your right hand is doing, so that your alms may be in secret; and your Father who sees in secret will reward you."[175] This isn't a bizarre ethic of secret giving (or, later, secret praying); Jesus is saying that, in the end, we live our lives before an audience of one: God. Our actions must reflect our awareness of His presence rather than our concern for our reputation or status with people.

Jesus himself, when He came upon the scene as an unacclaimed rabbi, made no attempt to gain popular support or to win the endorsement of established leaders, either those of the legal class (Pharisees) or those of the priestly class (Sadducees). He had one goal: "I have come down from heaven, not to do My own will, but the will of Him who sent Me."[176]

There is limitless courage in Christ—He feared no man, and He sought no man's approval. He spoke with absolute honesty, and His allegiance was only to God. In chastising the religious leaders for their hypocrisy,[177] He made clear that their fundamental shortcoming was lack of a real human/divine relationship: "You know neither Me nor my Father; if you knew Me, you would know My Father also."[178]

The Pharisees, Israel's legal scholars and teachers, were the rabbinical class that would take the priesthood's place in spiritual leadership (after the fall of Jerusalem, in CE 70). At the time of Jesus, the Pharisees believed they were called to prepare the nation for the coming of Messiah. They fully expected that He would affirm their role; when Jesus opposed and rebuked them, they automatically considered Him a false messiah.

As the story unfolds, the New Testament plainly shows that the Pharisees had sufficient evidence for faith. They had seen and heard "the blind receive sight, the lame walk, the lepers … cleansed, and the deaf hear, the dead … raised up, [and] the poor have the Gospel preached to them."[179] Many of Christ's miracles were performed in their presence, yet they refused to believe.

In contrast, when a humble elderly priest named Simeon came to the temple one day, before him was a line of young parents bringing their children for circumcision and dedication. He had seen thousands upon thousands of these in his lifetime of worship, but now he went straight to one couple and one child. There was no visible evidence this was a special child, but Simeon knew who He was. He knew because of his personal relationship with God; thus, he held Jesus in his arms and proclaimed the significance of his life, *before* Jesus had done anything to demonstrate that He was Messiah.[180]

What was the Pharisees' problem? Once more, they lacked a vital relationship with God. They were obviously religious, but they were not spiritually connected to the one they claimed to serve. In the Shema of the Torah and the Greatest Commandment of the Gospels, both Testaments are clear:

You shall love the LORD your God
with all your heart
and with all your soul
and with all your might.[181]

❖ ❖ ❖ ❖

Love and reverence for God is central to Judeo-Christian ethics. Denying His rightful place in our lives is the central sin of humanity and the very essence of the immoral path. Jesus left no ambiguity: The first and highest human value is an authentic, personal relationship with our Maker.

From this place of allegiance to the Father, Jesus loved people like no one has before or since. As theologian Hans Küng (b. 1928) has described it:

> He belongs neither to the right or left, nor does he simply mediate between them. He really rises above them; above all alternatives, all of which he plucks up from the roots. This is his *radicalism*: the radicalism of love which, in its blunt realism, is fundamentally different from the radicalism of an ideology.[182]

One day a young woman crashed a prominent Pharisee's dinner party, to which Jesus had been invited. She came for one reason: to seek out Jesus for deliverance from a life of prostitution. Weeping, she sat at His feet, anointing them with the perfume she'd brought as a gift for Him. What's remarkable? His personality *invited* such an approach. Rather than condemn her for her many wrongs, as expected,[183] Jesus rebuked the Pharisee for his lack of compassion and his lack of openness to His ministry: "Her sins, which are many, have been forgiven, for she loved much; but he who is forgiven little, loves little."[184]

This woman sensed that in coming to Jesus she would not find condemnation and rejection but forgiveness and peace. Possibly she had seen Him serve or heard the stories of His love for and compassion toward the "poor in spirit."[185] She knew this Jesus was different from any other religious leader.

What she discovered, and what we discover in reading this story, is that, in Christ, *God is on our side.* She stands in contrast to the self-focused Pharisee, whose sins were just as grievous but less visible, and who had no felt need for forgiveness. The pride of the religious leaders had left them with awful maladies: They were hypocritical, professing righteousness but acting sinfully, and they were arrogant. Their arrogance, in fact, blinded them to their hypocrisy, and thus they were left in a desperate place: standing before the Messiah they'd hoped for all their lives but unable to recognize Him.

A song from the 60s says it well:

Jesus hung with the hard-line gang, *hmm, huhum, hmm,*
Jesus knew the songs they sang, *hmm, huhum, hmm,*
Well, Jesus hung with harlots, and he ran with the hoodlum kind,
I do believe I'd a been a friend of Jesus in his time.[186]

In hanging out with sinners, Christ never endorsed their sin. The friend of sinners called them out of sin, and by His grace they found freedom from compulsions, guilt, and regret. It's no wonder they flocked to Him, for in Jesus they found much more than acceptance: they found deliverance, healing, and liberty. The gospel doesn't leave us as we are—it has the power to transform us, to make us new creatures.[187]

And this is the radical love that Küng refers to; this is the gospel's power to set people free. In Christ, people discover and receive God's overwhelming mercy and transforming love. Napoleon Bonaparte (1769–1821) said,

> I search in vain in history to find the similar to Jesus Christ, or anything which can approach the gospel. Neither history, nor humanity, nor the ages, nor nature, offer me anything with which I am able to compare it or explain it. Here everything is extraordinary.[188]

The unimpeachable internal evidence of the Gospels is the character of the man they portray and the gospel—the good news—itself. While other moralists and moral systems agree in part with the ethics of Christ, none achieves its magnificence. How could a simple woodworker with little human training or resources have given us the world's paramount ethical paradigm unless He is, as Josh McDowell's book title says, *More than a Carpenter*?[189]

A SUPERNATURAL MORALITY

There is another crucial aspect to Christ's teachings, which He likewise lived out fully by example: they transcend our natural human tendencies, beckoning us to love others through supernatural empowerment. He called people not to weakness but to the strength required for servanthood. For example, if one of Israel's oppressors, a hated Roman soldier, required a Jew to carry his luggage from one mile marker to the next, the Jew was obligated by Roman law to do so. Christ instructed His followers not just to carry the bags for the single required mile but another mile also, willingly, as an act of kindness and service.[190]

In most cultures men are instructed to love their family and friends and to hate their enemies. In the Sermon on the Mount, Jesus goes beyond this natural human ethic to teach us that we should "love [our] enemies, and pray for those who persecute [us]."[191] This is so that we may "be sons of [our] Father who is in heaven; for He causes the sun to rise on the evil and the good, and sends rain on the righteous and the unrighteous."[192] Jesus calls us to love others and win them to Him by a *supernatural* ethic, through His transcendent, supernatural love.

EVIDENCE FOR THE RESURRECTION

C. S. Lewis described his conversion to Christianity as being "dragged, kicking and screaming into the kingdom."[193] He did not submit to Christ for the sake of the personal benefit he would receive, or for the forgiveness of sins, or for the promise of eternal life. He gave himself to Christ because he was convinced that Jesus truly is the Son of the Living God, and that as God He is entitled to our complete allegiance.

So it must be with each of us: there is only one reason to become a believer, and that is because Christianity—because *Christ*—is true. At the center of this issue is the most significant event recorded in the Gospels: the Resurrection. The validity of the faith stands or falls on the historical evidence for Jesus having been raised from the dead. The apostle Paul is very clear about what's at stake: "If Christ has not been raised, your faith is worthless."[194]

Several theories developed over the centuries to explain away the Resurrection. The first was that the disciples stole the body and then, when the tomb was found to be empty, claimed Jesus had been raised. Later opponents claimed that the first group of women who came to the tomb mistook the gardener for Jesus, so the Resurrection was just a case of mistaken identity. Others said the Resurrection was a hallucination borne from the great longing of one or more disciples. Also, some have maintained that Jesus didn't actually die on the cross—He only passed out and, in the coolness of the tomb, revived.

All these alternate explanations suffer the same problem (among others): they do not explain the most important evidence provided in the text itself, *Christ's post-resurrection appearances.* The disciples were skeptical of the first announcement that He had risen. The two followers on the road to Emmaus had heard the report of the women who first visited the tomb and found it empty, but they were unconvinced until Jesus revealed himself to them. It would take numerous encounters with Jesus to convince the disciples fully that He truly had risen.

These meetings took place at various locations, indoors and outdoors, with different groups of followers present. The appearances involve detailed and specific conversations with individual disciples. They involve contact,[195] eating,[196] and verbal interaction.[197] These intricate and specific accounts rule out the ideas of mistaken identity and hallucination. They also rule out the notion that Jesus survived the Crucifixion—as severely wounded and damaged as He would have been, the disciples would have never been able to have the encounters and experiences with Him such as described. The record is clear: *The disciples claimed to have seen not a severely injured survivor but a perfectly whole resurrected Savior.*

Given the detail and extent of the appearance stories, there really are only two possible explanations for the Resurrection. From beginning to end, either they are completely fabricated tales that the disciples foisted on the world, or they are true. Either the disciples made the whole thing up and its nothing but a big lie, or it happened and it's a fact.

THE DOCUMENTARY EVIDENCE

The documentary evidence is integral in this regard. Even the most skeptical of theologians believes the Gospels[198] were written and in circulation within thirty years of the Crucifixion, and that the gospel story of Christ's death and resurrection was presented orally nearly from the day the events occurred.[199] This means the biblical appearance stories could not have originated with anyone other than Christ's original followers. The accounts came from the mouths of the apostles themselves; thus, we must ask, were they honest men or were they liars?

To answer this, consider: why do people lie? People usually lie to gain an advantage, to cheat others, or to present a false impression that delivers fame, fortune, or both. What's remarkable about the disciples is that not one of them sought or achieved either fame or fortune in his short lifetime. None pursued personal empires or huge followings; none made himself the focus of people's attentions; all sought to point people toward Christ.

Church historian Stephen Neill (1900–1984) wrote, regarding the first-century spread of Christianity, "Nothing is more notable than the anonymity of these early missionaries."[200] We know that Christianity spread from India to Spain within the apostles' lifetimes, yet none of them appears at the story's center stage—in fact, most of what they did went unrecorded. They were too busy telling the world about Jesus to worry about writing memoirs or autobiographies.

Through the writings of the church fathers, we know that after the Passion Week events these men spent their entire lives proclaiming the gospel. Only one (John, who died in exile) was not killed for his faith in Christ. How can we explain their dedication and their deaths for the gospel's sake if it all were a lie? *They would have known*. It's one thing for a group to be indoctrinated and then to sacrifice their lives for what they have come to believe; it's another for people to lay down their lives when they have firsthand knowledge of the actual events they proclaim. It's been said, rightly, many times: *Men will not give their lives for what they know is a lie.*

The apostles themselves were cognizant of their place in history: "We were eyewitnesses of his majesty," wrote Peter.[201] "What was from the beginning, what we have heard, what we have seen with our eyes, what we have looked at and touched with our hands, concerning the Word of Life … these things we write," said John.[202] When their number was reduced after the death of Judas, they sought to replace him, and the central qualification was that the new apostle must be "a witness with us of His resurrection."[203] *They* were the ones who had lived with Christ day in and day out for three years; after His death, *they* had seen Him alive as the resurrected Savior of the world. They understood that their job from that time forward was to tell everyone that "the Word became flesh, and dwelt among us, and we saw His glory, glory as of the only begotten from the Father, full of grace and truth."[204]

In addition, the apostles' character qualities make it exceedingly difficult to see them as liars. They lived exemplary lives, in everything commending ourselves as servants of God, in much endurance, in afflictions, in hardships, in distresses, in beatings, in imprisonment, in tumults, in labors, in sleeplessness, in hunger, in purity, in knowledge, in patience, in kindness, in the Holy Spirit, in genuine love.[205]

They prized integrity and lived in the reverence of God; how could they willingly propagate a known lie? Paul said that if Christ has not been raised, then

> we are even found to be false witnesses of God, because we witnessed against God that He raised Christ, whom He did not raise, if in fact the dead are not raised.... If we have hoped in Christ in this life only, we are of all men most to be pitied.[206]

The disciples Jesus commissioned to bring His life to the world obviously understood the difference between the true and the false. Their witness is unambiguous: the story of Christ's resurrection is not something they made up but rather the central truth of the gospel that they saw and heard with their own eyes and ears.

THE RESURRECTION: HUME'S TEST FOR THE MIRACULOUS

David Hume established a list of qualifications for the verification of a miracle. According to him, a miracle had to be:

(3) Attested to by a sufficient number of men;

(4) Attested to by men of such unquestioned good sense, education, and learning, as to secure us against all delusion in themselves;

(5) Attested to by men of such undoubted integrity as to place them beyond all suspicion of any design to deceive others;

(6) Attested to by men of such credit and reputation in the eyes of mankind as to have a great deal to lose in case of being detected in any falsehood; and

(7) At the same time attesting facts performed in a public manner, and in so celebrated part of the world, as to render detection unavoidable.[207]

Hume was attempting to establish a verification standard that would be, in his view, "scientific," and, therefore, beyond the ability of either the ancients or the religious to meet. But what of the Resurrection—how *does* it compare to these standards?

(1) The apostle Paul tells us that more than five hundred people saw Jesus alive after the Resurrection; in CE 50, almost twenty years later, he noted that most of them were still alive.[208] This huge number of eyewitnesses would have made it indescribably difficult for opponents of Christianity to claim that Christ had not been raised from the dead. This appearance of Jesus before the larger group must be added to the nine other times the disciples encountered Him. The New Testament's straightforward testimony is that Jesus appeared to many people in several different contexts over a period of forty days after the Resurrection.

(2) Peter tells us that the disciples were not following "cleverly devised tales"[209] in presenting the truths of the gospel. He assures us that they were men of sufficient knowledge and common sense to be able to know the true from the false. Peter realized that in his day many people made outrageous religious claims and that in some circles "religion" and "myth" were regarded as nearly synonymous. He wanted to make it perfectly clear: the claims about Christ, including that of His resurrection, were not the product of imagination. Along with the other gospel writers, he emphasized that they were eyewitnesses; their credibility rests on their being present during the remarkable events of Christ's ministry on earth.

As well, the New Testament reveals the disciples' natural skepticism. They themselves had to be convinced, and when Thomas demanded visible proof he was probably speaking for most of them.[210]

The present-day accusation of the disciples having been superstitious, ignorant barbarians is risibly patronizing. Of course they didn't have our era's scientific knowledge, but they were as capable of common sense and logical inference as we are, and they were aware of the known limits and realities of human existence. Their initial skepticism, even in light of what appeared to be Christ's physical presence in the room with them, highlights, once again, that they knew as well as we know that dead men don't come back to life.[211]

(3) In the realm of "undoubted integrity," the New Testament simply records the apostles' comings and goings. In so doing it presents a group of people so dedicated to the cause that they're willing to sacrifice personal comfort and even risk their lives to tell the world the truth about Jesus.[212] In the end, all twelve suffered and died for the sake of the gospel. Doesn't such selfless dedication represent the highest possible level of integrity?

These men *personally* took up Christ's commission: "Go into all the world and preach the gospel."[213] The church fathers tell us the apostles divided up the known world and drew lots to see where each would go; they were the first Christian missionaries.

(4) In terms of credibility and reputation, there must have been a great deal at stake for the apostles in representing or misrepresenting the truth. Paul was well aware of this issue (likely the others were also), and their appreciation of it as ancients is more significant than ours as moderns. Hume was speaking of reputation before men, and of being seen as fools and scoundrels if discovered in a lie. Paul spoke of their reputation before God; they knew the eternal consequences of lying in God's name.[214] As we've said, Paul went even further: he understood that

their risks and sacrifices were utter folly if there is no resurrection of the dead (v. 19).

(5) Finally, as regards events occurring publicly, the events surrounding Passion Week coincided with the Jewish Passover, one of three main pilgrimage feasts for the nation of Israel. This was similar to a Muslim's pilgrimage to Mecca; Jews from everywhere made their way to Jerusalem for these sacred events. It's likely that during the week Jesus was crucified tens of thousands were assembled in the holy city. The Crucifixion would have been the talk of that Passover, and it's probable that hundreds actually saw Him upon that cross.

One evidence of this is that during Pentecost, the second pilgrimage feast of the Jewish calendar year, fifty days after Passover, several thousand Jews reacted eagerly to Peter's message about the previous Passover's events, of which they all were well aware.[215] Plainly they knew that Jesus had been crucified and that His tomb was empty because they responded readily to Peter's explanation. He assumed their common knowledge of the details: "*... just as you yourselves know.*"[216]

Furthermore, Christ's appearances took place at public places such as the Sea of Galilee[217] and the Mount of Olives.[218] As a result, Paul could say of King Herod Agrippa, "I am persuaded that none of these things [the gospel events] escape his notice, for this has not been done in a corner."[219]

❖ ❖ ❖ ❖

The apologist Josh McDowell (b. 1939) tells of an encounter with a Jewish student at UCLA; in their conversation, he discovered that the young man was a Christian. When he asked the student how he had come to believe in Jesus, he replied that he was a graduate student in classical literature and had decided one day to brush up on his koine (common) Greek. He thus began reading the book of Mark in its original language.

As he translated and read, it dawned on him that there was an unmistakable difference between Mark and the other works of literature he'd read as a classics scholar. He said, "I was used to reading mythology. I knew what it sounded like and what it felt like."[220] It quickly became clear to him that in reading Mark he was not reading myth—he was reading history. When he realized that the events of Mark's record were historical and, hence, true, he became a believer.

Other famous classical scholars have reached the same conclusion. The apologist E. M. Blaiklock (1903–1983), the translator J. B. Phillips (1906–1982), and C. S. Lewis all became Christ-followers as adults; each of their professional decisions was that the New Testament is an historical document. Lewis said,

> I have been reading poems, romances, vision-literature, legends, myths all my life. I know what they are like. I know that not one of them is like this.[221]

In reading the New Testament we encounter eyewitness testimony that is its straightforward claim for itself.

> Many other signs therefore Jesus also performed in the presence of the disciples, which are not written in this book; but these have been written that you may believe that Jesus is the Christ, the Son of God; and that believing you may have life in His name.[222]

CONCLUSION

Secularism is built upon the assumptions that (1) religion is obsolete and unnecessary and (2) religion is built upon fears and prejudices that have brought untold suffering to people throughout history. Proponents of secularism feel perfectly justified in their opposition to all things religious in public life.

This is a distorted view of religion and its impact upon the world, particularly of Christianity. Judeo-Christian values have elevated and liberated society; we abandon them at our peril. If we should have learned anything from the twentieth century, it is that people are, as the historian Mircea Eliade (1907–1986) said, "incurably religious."[223] We *are* spiritual beings, and we *do* have spiritual needs that we will seek to have met—if not in the church, then somewhere else.

We also should have learned that eliminating religion does not bring world peace. In fact, the less influence Judeo-Christian values are allowed to have on a society, the more brutal it becomes. The Soviet empire was the full-scale experiment in a completely nonreligious state, and for seventy years it demonstrated and revealed the dangers and disasters of government in a moral vacuum. Among religion's fantastic gifts are standards of morality and justice that even rulers must obey.

The Enlightenment leaders, who were near to the start of the naturalism/secularization process and who appreciated the values religion provided to society, were concerned about this very possibility. Thomas Huxley, the man who more than any other popularized Darwin's theory to the world, nonetheless had believed that the Bible should be taught in public schools because he saw no other tool available for developing honesty, compassion, and fortitude in people's lives. Julian Huxley, a major force behind the *Humanist Manifesto*, shared his father's concern and sought to find a humanistic, rationalistic "replacement" for Christian values.[224]

What's most troubling in this whole sad story of our history's last two centuries is that the church did not stand up and protect what is indivisible from its ministry to the world: the literal and historical truth of the gospel. The major Protestant denominations, and the educational institutions of both Protestant and Catholic persuasions, became allies of naturalism and secularization.

---

[170] Will Durant, Caesar and Christ, The Story of Civilization, Volume III: A History of Roman Civilization and of Christianity from Their Beginnings to A.D. 325 (New York: Simon & Schuster, 1944), 557.

[171] In Èmile: Or, On Education, Book IV (1762).

[172] Luke 6:31 NIV

[173] Luke 10:27 NIV; cf. Deuteronomy 6:5; Leviticus 19:18.

[174] www.http//college.hmco.com/readerscomp/rcah/html/ah_000300_abolitionist.htm (quotation from online Houghton Mifflin "Readers Companion").

[175] Matthew 6:3–4 NRSV

[176] John 6:38

[177] E.g., see Matthew 23:27.

[178] John 8:19

[179] Luke 7:22

[180] See Luke 2:25–35.

[181] Deuteronomy 6:5; cf. Matthew 22:37; Mark 12:30; Luke 10:27.

[182] Hans Küng, On Being a Christian (New York: Doubleday & Co., 1966), 262.

[183] See Luke 7:39.

[184] Luke 7:47

[185] See Matthew 5:3.

[186] "Friend of Jesus," source unknown.

[187] See 2 Corinthians 5:17.

[188] In John S. C. Abbott, Napoleon Bonaparte, Book II (New York: Harper & Brothers, 1885), 615. Also see Josh McDowell, Evidence That Demands a Verdict (San Bernardino, CA: Here's Life Publishers, 25th printing, June 1986), 106.

[189] More Than a Carpenter (Wheaton, IL: Tyndale House, 1977).

[190] E.g., see Matthew 5:41.

[191] Matthew 5:44

[192] Matthew 5:45

[193] In C. S. Lewis, Surprised by Joy: The Shape of My Early Life (New York/London: Harcourt Brace, 1956).

[194] 1 Corinthians 15:17

[195] See Luke 24:39.

[196] See Luke 24:43; John 21:12–14.

[197] See John 21:15–18.

[198] At least the Synoptic Gospels—Matthew, Mark, and Luke.

[199] Detailed frequently, via various media; for instance, see Frontline, "From Jesus to Christ: The First Christians—Part II," episode 1612W. PBS: first aired April 7, 1998.

[200] Stephen Neill, A History of Christian Missions (New York: Penguin Books, 1964), 22.

[201] 2 Peter 1:16

[202] 1 John 1:1, 4

[203] See Acts 1:22.

[204] John 1:14

[205] 2 Corinthians 6:4–6

[206] 1 Corinthians 15:15, 19

[207] See David Hume, An Enquiry Concerning Human Understanding (Oxford: Clarendon, 1975; orig. published 1777); and J. C. A. Gaskin, Hume's Philosophy of Religion in the Library of Philosophy and Religion (New York: Palgrave Macmillan, 1988).

[208] See 1 Corinthians 15:6.

[209] 2 Peter 1:16

[210] See John 20:24–28.

[211] See Matthew 28:16–17.

[212] E.g., see 2 Corinthians 4:1–6; 6:3–10.

[213] Mark 16:15

[214] E.g., see 1 Corinthians 15:15.

[215] See Acts 2:41.

[216] Acts 2:22

[217] See John 21:1–14.

[218] See Acts 1:4–12.

[219] Acts 26:26

[220] From McDowell, Evidence That Demands a Verdict.

[221] In Fern Seeds and Elephants and Other Essays on Christianity (Fount, 1975).

[222] John 20:30–31

[223] See Mircea Eliade and Joseph M. Kitagawa, eds., The History of Religions: Essays in Methodology (Chicago: University of Chicago Press, 1959 [original]).

[224] See Ronald W. Clark, The Huxleys (New York: McGraw-Hill Pub. Co., 1968), 83.

CHAPTER TEN

THE VORTEX OF RELATIVISM AND THE MYTH OF PLURALISM

In addition to what they overtly intend and produce, all large-scale movements also bring about unintended or at least undeclared consequences. The Enlightenment, by intention and declaration, aimed to bring "liberation" to the human race—that is, liberation from the restraints and afflictions of "old superstitions." What proponents didn't foresee—what initially would be lost or obscured in the process—was what would result from their revolution's unspoken agenda.

When we sift through all the peripherals and all the secondary elements, what *is* the ultimate reasoning behind the Enlightenment—what is the essential basis of its "faith?" Will Durant, describing the movement's beginnings, said:

When young men and women, bold with money, discovered their religion was denouncing their pleasures, they found a thousand reasons in science for denouncing their religion.[225]

The underlying purpose was similar to what eventuated from the 1960s counterculture: the removal of moral barriers perceived to hinder the pursuit of personal pleasure. Much of the twentieth century is the story of the West attempting to free itself from "Victorian" or "middle-class" morality. In reality it was throwing off Judeo-Christian virtues, the very basis for its laws and values; hence, in the name of "progress," it was undermining the foundation upon which its civilization was built. For nearly two hundred years we have acted like defiant adolescents, demanding freedom without foresight and convoluting liberty with license.

Hugh Hefner has been as vocal an advocate of the Enlightenment worldview as were Julian Huxley and John Dewey. Sigmund Freud articulated the principles of the so-called sexual revolution; the releasing of repressed desires and the casting off of persistent inhibitions were a major portion of his remedy for mental and emotional ills. Most of the century's poets, playwrights, and philosophers lived out the so-named liberated lifestyle, leading society by both word and deed into the contemporary era.

Paul Johnson (b. 1928), in his insightful book *Intellectuals*, describes the egregious contradiction between their ideals and their actual personal lives. The philosopher Rousseau, the poet Percy Shelley (1792–1822), the playwright Henrik Ibsen (1828–1906), the writers Ernest Hemingway (1899–1961) and D. H. Lawrence (1885–1930) ... these men and many others lived scandalously and immorally, often using their thoughts and theories as excuses for their selfishness. In describing Shelley, Johnson says, "He put ideas before people, and his life is a testament to how heartless ideas can be."[226]

This example is not an isolated case; many of Shelley's contemporaries lied, cheated, and betrayed their loved ones. All considered themselves above the law and above moral custom, frequently because of the perceived nobility of their notions. They claimed the prerogative to change the world, and though they promised to lead the West into a new day of freedom and fulfillment, they had a final goal of *moral* liberation.

MORAL RELATIVISM

At the Enlightenment's grounding was the premise that morality was passé. Even prior to Freud, philosophers saw moral values (particularly in the realm of sexual behavior) as unnatural and inhibiting. Many wanted emancipation; this "freedom" was behind Rousseau's scandalous treatment of his concubines and children, the adulterous relationship Karl Marx (1818–1883) had with his housemaid, and Nietzsche's death from syphilis. In a moment of deepest candor, the writer Aldous Huxley (1894–1963) said, "For myself, the philosophy of meaninglessness was essentially an instrument of liberation, sexual and political."[227]

Immorality is destructive and damaging enough; once we start down the road of removing moral restraint it's very difficult, if not impossible, to stop the car as it roars toward even more dangerous destinations. Several Western intellectuals embraced nihilism—for instance, W. B. Yeats (1865–1939), George Bernard Shaw (1856–1950), and Huxley—and found it possible (and even logical) to support genocide and eugenics.[228]

Regarding genocide, prior to World War II and the actuality of the concentration camps, these men and others made statements in support of exterminating large portions of the human race, viewing people like we view bacteria.[229] Lawrence wrote to a friend, regarding the infirm and handicapped, "If I had my way, I would build a lethal chamber as big as the Crystal Palace."[230]

Returning to the "Enlighteners," it will suffice to say there are many similar stories. George Gissing (1857–1903) married a prostitute, abused her, and finally left her "alone and destitute."[231] Wyndham Lewis (1882–1957) had three children by his mistresses and abandoned them all.[232] The distressing irony is that under Nietzsche's increasing influence, these "bringers of freedom" believed they were the race's superiors, worthy of being society's leaders. In reality, their arrogance and cruelty made them vastly inferior to those they felt at liberty to exploit.

The theologian Gordon Olson (b. 1933) has defined the broader principle behind this process of eliminating morality for the sake of "liberation," saying,

> *We do not allow ourselves to have a greater concept*
> *of God*
> *than we are willing to conform to.*[233]

RELATIVISTIC ROOTS

The belief that morals are not absolute (applying to all people at all times) but rather are relative (applying only to some people, and only in certain situations) arose from the Enlightenment's elemental assumption of uncertainty about knowledge. If the best we can hope for is agnosticism in pursuing the answers to life's great questions—such as why are we here, what's the meaning of existence, and is there a God—then how can we say what is truly right and truly wrong?

It *wasn't* the philosophers, though, who first articulated what would come to be called moral relativism. It was, rather, a group of anthropologists; in particular, the students of one very influential Columbia University professor, Franz Boas (1858–1942), who in turn had been deeply impacted by Kant's agnosticism.[234] Boas and his disciples first examined various cultures and then described dramatic differences between their respective moral values. In addition, and in particular, the writings of these anthropologists emphasized the exotic nature of non-Western values. They put a large emphasis on polygamy and variant sexual mores; they focused on taboos and even on forms of euthanasia (such as existed among the nomadic Inuit in the far Northern Hemisphere.[235]

Previous generations in the West had upheld the moral superiority of Western culture; the colonial era, broadly, was an attempt to "civilize" and educate peoples of the non-Western world. The new anthropologists instead attempted to approach cross-cultural studies from a neutral perspective. The end result was that this group of social scientists proclaimed the relativistic nature of values. Each culture has developed its own unique set of standards that apply only to that culture, and it's both impossible and inappropriate to determine whether the morals of one culture are superior to those of another.

Boas and others articulated the principles of moral relativism in the late 1940s; these statutes soon spread to other fields, like philosophy, theology, and eventually popular culture. Within a short period of time, the belief that moral values differ widely from culture to culture and that no moral system should be compared to another became commonly held. The two main tenets: (1) "Western values" are not superior to "non-Western values," and (2) no values should ever be imposed on the people of another culture.

❖ ❖ ❖ ❖

The relativists failed to notice—or, minimally, affirm—two important facts.

First, while there are variants between cultures, anyone who looks closely will see that there are far more similarities than differences. And, on a grand scale, murder, theft, deceit, and adultery among people of the same community are universally wrong. As for polygamy, while a given culture may approve of a man having more than one wife, all cultures nonetheless value and protect marriage itself. The overarching congruency demonstrates, then, that *the ultimacy of values isn't "Western" but, rather, "human."*

Second, we *intuitively* compare and contrast cultural values. For instance, who would consider a society that practices cannibalism the equal of one that does not? Furthermore, actions have consequences; the practices that result from different moral standards produce markedly differing results that can be observed and weighed. The notion that all values are equal flies in the face of actual experience. People suffer terribly and even die as a result of certain "exotic" practices, like female genital mutilation in Africa or "honor killing" in Southeast Asia.

❖ ❖ ❖ ❖

Nonetheless, in practical terms, relativism provided a convenient excuse for the abandonment of traditional morality in the 1960s and beyond. If morals are relative to culture, why not make them relative to generations within a culture? Why not consider the values of the previous generation outmoded and passé? Why not adopt a "new" morality?

The *Situation Ethics*[236] of Joseph Fletcher (1905–1991) popularized the understanding of morals as relative to time, place, and circumstance. Fletcher's book was an attempt to provide a guide for ethical decisions in a relativistic world. The pervasive problem was his assumption that there are no right answers to moral questions; as such, we don't have guidance so much as we simply must make choices and compromises.

As a result of Fletcher's influence, many schools developed "values clarification" classes, ostensibly to teach young people how to make "moral" decisions. In reality, these courses were not about clarifying values but rather about convoluting them. A typical session involved placing adolescents or pre-adolescents in small groups to discuss such disturbing dilemmas as deciding which person should be thrown from a lifeboat in order to preserve the lives of the remaining survivors. The exercises in general only reinforced the idea that there are no universally true answers to moral questions, and consequently relativism became more and more entrenched in the minds of American youth. It really is little wonder that a significant majority of college students and young adults believe there are no absolute values.

❖ ❖ ❖ ❖

There is, however, one substantial obstacle in the path of this relativistic steamroller. Earlier we observed that human beings are subject to conscience—we cannot normally break the rules of custom and culture without some type of justifying excuse. Judeo-Christian revelation presents man as made in God's image and, therefore, called to reflect His character. God is holy and just, the biblical laws are expressions of His own essence, and in Jesus Christ we see His purity and integrity lived out in human form.

This revelation is a bright light from which many shrink back. Simon & Garfunkel expressed this in "Flowers Never Bend with the Rainfall":

> I'm blinded by the light
> of God and truth and right
> and I wander in the night without direction.
> So I'll continue to continue to pretend
> my life will never end
> and flowers never bend with the rainfall.[237]

People who don't want to be held to this high standard cannot merely deny the standard; they must deny the God who *is* the standard, for if they acknowledge Him, they likewise acknowledge that they have no alibi.

In the West, shrinking back from the biblical revelation of God largely began with Deism, which posits a creator who is disengaged from his creation but who has left moral principles within the structure of nature and humanity (what Deists called the "natural law"). Again, however, the Enlightenment didn't want even that much "God," partially because Deism retained significant values, such as the sanctity of marriage. The principle of the natural law—that morality was built into the structure of the universe and the nature of humankind—still left too many restrictions people weren't willing to accept. They wanted to go further: they aimed for a designer morality by which people could pick and choose the values they wanted to keep (or jettison). For the attainment of their aims, even Deism had to go.

The agnosticism and finally the all-out atheism of modernism is the end result of the West's pursuit of unlimited "freedom." In actuality our goal was not freedom; rather, *we sought license to do whatever we want.* Remember Dostoyevsky's words?

If God does not exist,

then everything is permitted.[238]

Since the intention unquestionably has been to make sure that everything *is* permitted, we cannot have a God to interfere. A determinative reason for nihilism's stronghold over the culture is this fervor to eliminate moral restraint and thereby, hopefully, to free the conscience from inhibition.

RELATIVISM'S IMPACT ON OUR VIEW OF MAN

Closely related to the tragedy of reducing God to the level of our willingness to live rightly is this principle: *We will not allow ourselves to have a higher concept of man than we're willing to live up to.*[239] If man wants to live like an animal, then he first must believe himself to be one. But what if that's not even enough for him—what if he craves the unnatural and the perverse? Then he must find a way to posit himself as a meaningless accident in an impersonal cosmos, where choices have zero significance. This is the desperate place we've come to; this is the netherworld of nihilism. We cannot live in this no-man's-land as people; we must become beasts or worse.

Consider our contemporary view of "free speech." The First Amendment to the Constitution was intended to protect the rights of citizens to publicly state their disagreement with their leaders or their government. Over the years this right has been expanded to protect obscenity, lewd or outrageous words and actions, and even, in some cases, pornography. We seem to be attempting to use the amendment itself as a tool for achieving "everything is permitted."

This is a frightening and cynical abuse of freedom. This is saying that "liberty" is lack of restraint, no matter what else must be sacrificed. In the end, this is Western civilization saying that God does not exist, that anything goes. And yet, there *are* still places we will not go and acts we will not allow. For instance, we will not allow the abuse of children or the endangerment of public health. We *are* still capable of moral indignation.

All the same, as we persist in regression, we are gradually reducing the number of things that we're completely opposed to. In just a few decades, we have gone through public acceptance of the homosexual lifestyle to the ongoing expansion of both church- and state-sanctioned gay marriage. We're even opening the door to euthanasia in some states (though many European nations are far "ahead" of us in this regard).

These decisions and their corresponding realities raise some unavoidable questions, particularly in light of the degeneration of values that has occurred in the last several years. What will be the next stage in the progression? Will we approve of ending the life of a person suffering from an emotional disorder, like severe depression? After that, will we endorse the involuntary ending of the lives of the severely disabled or mentally ill? (There are already advocates of this position who are willing to call, publicly, for such mass euthanasia.)

In other words, moral relativism has placed us on a steep descent toward an unthinkable future. There are already segments of our society that clearly reveal the consequences of throwing away moral boundaries. Many of our inner cities suffer from rampant drug abuse, violent crime, and gang activity. The core causes for many of these maladies have a moral component, whether single-parent households due to the sky-high percentage of out-of-wedlock births, the prevalence of illicit activity as a substantial attraction to young men, or other factors.

❖ ❖ ❖ ❖

We've repeatedly seen that the Enlightenment hope—freedom through the removal of inhibitions believed to interfere with human happiness—was based on a false premise. Liberation from moral restraint is not the road to happiness. The elimination of religion leads to elimination of a high view of humankind; a low view of humankind leads to dehumanization and degradation. Many horrors have resulted directly from this calamity.

A second and equally tragic lack of foresight has been the stimulation and incitement of base desires without consideration of where they would lead us. For example, how many marriages and how many families have been shredded or shattered by our "sexual liberation"? How many relationships have been ruined through the selfish pursuit of instant gratification? How many lives have been abused, degraded, even destroyed by our cravings for "harmless entertainment"? The pursuit of release from moral restraint has never been anything but an immature fancy built upon a shortsighted appetite for immediate pleasure with little thought for the future.

Moral nihilism is a powerful intoxicant, and we have become addicts. Our tremendous resistance to any move toward restraint is symptomatic of the depth of our dependency. Notice that we have made "censorship" one of the most evil words in our vocabulary, "freedom of speech" our most cherished value. As a society we are seemingly left defenseless against influences that pull us deeper into raw hedonism.

The process is already taking us to the place where individuals who have taken the nihilistic plunge for themselves are demanding that their preferences be legitimized by everyone else. What began as the pursuit of happiness has led us to the chaos of purposelessness. The Enlightenment has given us neither freedom nor happiness; it has made us slaves and junkies.

IS NIHILISM INEVITABLE?

Relativism has truly terrifying implications for our society. As our morals have degenerated, there has been a corresponding decrease in significant social metrics. High school dropout rates have dramatically increased, and even those students staying in school have reduced achievement levels. Out-of-wedlock births are now the majority of births among both the African-American and Latino communities, and they're increasing for Caucasians.[240] Given that single-parent households are the number one determinate for lack of advancement, for drug abuse, and for juvenile crime, this statistic bodes anything but well for our next generation. We have blamed and will continue to blame these ills (and many others) on lack of funding for public education, or on inadequate social welfare programs, but the fact is that they are, at their base, moral issues that will never be solved without a rediscovery and re-embracing of moral convictions and moral choices.

Furthermore, on a grand scale, these and similar cultural disasters portend a dramatic weakening of our national character. We will never maintain our standing as a leader of the free world without the strength of character that has always been the foundation of American democracy. Moral relativism is emaciating us intellectually, as we no longer are willing to pay the price necessary for learning and thinking and growing. We prefer entertainment to education; we savor pat answers and political rhetoric while slumping in boredom when encountering careful analysis and reasoned debate.

Relativism has made us self-obsessed, both individually and corporately. We have become, as one astute observer describes, the narcissistic society. Look, for example, at how we use the Internet. An amazing amount of its traffic is toward pornography (for unshared self-gratification); increasingly, not far behind are online "communities." While the latter enable what's supposed to be meaningful networking, in fact, far more often, they've become mere vehicles for Andy Warhol's fifteen minutes of fame, embarrassing testimonies to our warped self-aggrandizement.

I'm also struck by the amazing numbers of young people who willingly define themselves by—i.e., identify themselves with—their suffering from some form of emotional and/or mental disability (anxiety disorder, depression, ADHD, and so on). I don't believe the obsession with "online connection" is coincidental. Increasingly, as people retract in self-focus, existing and functioning primarily within themselves, they're becoming more interested in "connecting" with people (actual or virtual) worlds away than they are with people sitting right next to them. That's lonely.

❖ ❖ ❖ ❖

And so, for many folks, the nihilistic conclusion *does* seem to be the only one possible. They're convinced that science has closed the door to religious faith and that they have no option but to accept a meaningless reality. To revisit Bertrand Russell's framing of the dilemma:

> *That man is the product of causes which had no provision of the end they were achieving; that his origin, his growth, his hopes, his fears, his loves and his beliefs, are but the outcome of accidental collocations of atoms; that no fire, no heroism, no intensity of thought and feeling, can preserve individual life beyond the grave; that all the labors of the ages, all devotions, all inspiration, all the noon-day brightness of human genius, are destined to extinction in the vast death of the solar system, and that the whole temple of Man's achievement must inevitably be buried beneath the debris of a universe in ruins—all these things, if not beyond dispute, are, yet so nearly certain, that no philosophy which rejects them can hope to stand. Only within the scaffolding of these truths, only on the firm foundation of unyielding despair can the soul's habitation henceforth be safely built.*[241]

This really can seem to be the one reasonable and even courageous alternative in light of naturalistic science's proclamations. How, after all, do you argue with geniuses who *guarantee* that our world is the product of purely natural processes? Earlier we noted that Francis Schaeffer called this conclusion, this consensus view of Western intellectualism, "the line of despair."[242] He also said, that, in that vein, "Rationality, including modern science, will lead only to pessimism. Man is only a machine; man is only a zero, and nothing has any final meaning."[243]

That is what we now face: we have pursued utter unrestraint at the price of the worldview upon which our civilization was built. But *is* nihilism necessary? *Has* science truly shown that there is no God and that life is just an accident of cosmic and natural forces? *Has* anthropology really proven, as said Thomas Carlyle (1795–1881), that man is just a "tool-using animal"?[244] *Must* our morals be relative, utilitarian, and shaped by cultural consensus?

Relativism can only exist where there are serious doubts about truth, and the relativism of our age is directly related to our agnosticism. Because as a society we believe that it's impossible to know what is true or false and, more practically, what is right or wrong, we have embraced a subjective and populist ("everybody's doing it") approach. The inquiry must move, then, from the question of moral values to the questions of (1) the nature of reality, and (2) our ability to know that reality.

THE MYTH OF PLURALISM

We live in an era often defined and understood as "pluralistic." Pluralism alleges that certain knowledge about the fundamental nature of reality is impossible. Pluralism maintains that all the largest-scale explanations of the principles, laws, forces, powers, and being(s) that govern the universe are founded not on sure knowledge but on best guesses. In other words, all religious and non-religious explanations of reality are nothing more than human constructions, and human constructions can carry no meaningful guarantee of being true.

One of the most famous illustrations of pluralism—which is based on the old Hindu parable of three blind men trying to describe an elephant from their narrow perspective of the single part they're touching—states that all religions and worldviews suffer from precisely that flaw: too narrow a perspective. No one can say that their belief about reality is the accurate or final description because we can know only a minuscule part of that reality, and that tiny piece of "knowledge" may give us a false impression of the larger reality we're claiming to know.

In order to avoid this problem, pluralism says we must give *all* religions and worldviews the benefit of the doubt. Who knows but that one of them actually may be true? More precisely, pluralism holds that all of them are attempts to describe the same thing, that all have some aspect of truth within them, and that all, therefore, deserve equal respect.

Pluralism leaves us with the conclusion that, at *best*, any understanding of reality is only partially true. Postmodernism expresses this view by telling us there are no "meta-narratives," or all-encompassing explanations of reality. What postmodernists mean, of course, is that while lots of meta-narratives exist, none of them are fully true, and thus no *true* meta-narrative exists.

Accordingly, it is said, there is no paradigm we can completely trust. And, from the culture's embrace of pluralism has followed both (1) a rejection of overall truth claims and (2) a selective, syncretistic combining of teachings from various religions.

This eclectic approach to the metaphysical recently was brought home to me through a conversation I had with a middle-aged man in uptown Minneapolis. He stated that he'd been raised Lutheran, and that he remains Lutheran, but that he's since added elements of Zen to his spirituality. In other words, he had become a Lutheran Buddhist.

His case is not unique; this blurring of traditional categories is increasingly common. Many have decided to create their own personalized belief system, borrowing from various perspectives the elements that, for them, most individually appeal. This smorgasbord approach to faith has many hang-ups; perhaps the biggest is that it never gets to the fundamental question of *How do I know that this amalgamation I'm creating for myself is even remotely accurate?*

Pluralism fosters this type of "creativity" precisely because it's founded on the notion that the truth question can never be truly answered. Since we're only guessing, any guess is as good as almost any other guess. "Truth," therefore, becomes a mere matter of opinion, and, worse, truth itself is granted minor status, insignificant in comparison to life's larger pragmatic issues.

Not at all coincidentally, we live in a time when people take the statement "You can be whatever you want to be" far beyond the understanding of previous generations. In the past we applied this maxim to any goal we set our mind to achieve. Today it commonly refers to any lifestyle, orientation, or ideology toward which we feel inclined. Now much more than education, vocation, and aspiration are at stake; choices about "what we want to be" involve the most fundamental dynamics of identity and of life itself.

This "expanded" take on freedom is the result of pluralism. If pluralism, as many understand it, is the belief that all philosophies and lifestyles are equal, then pluralism would allege that truth is relative—up for grabs. That is, no one knows anything "for sure," so everyone is free to choose the ideas and practices toward which he or she most personally gravitates. *Everything* lies in the realm of uncertainty.

Pluralism places an indescribably heavy burden on us as individuals, because our experiences of life depend so much upon our perceptions and our choices, without any reliable outside assistance. We saw earlier that Jean-Paul Sartre (1905–1980) detailed his own existentialism as "total responsibility in total isolation."[245] Since, according to Sartre, we're alone in the universe, we "create" our own reality through our decisions, and there is no ultimate or unchanging perspective (no God) that can help us. Anyone who thinks pluralism yields the best of all worlds should know this: A *pluralistic world is lonely.*

It's one thing to decide, for instance, what career I will pursue and whom I will marry. It's entirely another to be accountable for literally determining what is right and what is wrong, and that without any dependable extrinsic guidance. In a pluralistic construct, no one *knows*.

Are we condemned to agnostic existentialism? Is pluralism true?

THE NATURE OF REALITY

The philosophical theologian John Hick (b. 1922), one of pluralism's foremost proponents, describes ultimate reality as "beyond the scope of our human conceptual repertoire."[246] Yet, while this ultimate reality cannot be known *now*, allegedly, one day it will be made known—at the end of history. Hick speaks of this as "eschatological verification," i.e., at some future moment, the truth will be revealed.

We must assume that, except for those who are still alive at the end of time, the verification occurs for each person at the moment of death. This would mean that while reality's ultimate condition cannot be known by our current human observation, reality nevertheless exists in a singular condition. So pluralism *doesn't* theorize that reality exists in many varieties; rather, pluralism suggests that while reality is what it is, for now there are a multitude of viable human theories about what reality is like.

Accordingly, even by pluralism's own definitions, reality can't be many different ways. There must be one reality, whether known or unknown; there are not a multitude of different realities, even though there are countless perspectives on the true nature and meaning of the one reality. We may not be able to know and describe this universe in the ultimate sense, fully and completely, but this does not change the fact that it's structured the way it is. The universe exists as it presently does; that existence has determined and will continue to determine much of the reality we experience.

The definition and description of pluralism as meaning that all philosophies and lifestyles are equal is, therefore, an incorrect understanding of pluralism. Even proponents say that reality is one way, and one way only. It is *very* important for us to understand this: again, even granting pluralism's own premises, we are led to conclude that there actually is a thing called "truth."

Furthermore, since there is this something that is true, we cannot afford to accept the notion—regardless of the degree to which we can or can't know truth through our present human faculties—that anything we feel is helpful or pleasing to us is true *for us.* Instead we must ask, Can we know at least something about what's ultimately true, so that we can have hope of conforming our lives to it?

❖ ❖ ❖ ❖

Imagine the universe as a gigantic square. Within that square is a much smaller circle, which we could call the "known universe," that part of the universe we can discover directly and personally. Remember, the smaller circle is within and part of the larger square; thus our known reality accurately tells us what at least part of the universe is like. Our job is to extrapolate, from what we know of the smaller circle, the state of the much bigger square. In other words, we work from the known to reach conclusions about the unknown.

Let's begin by agreeing that as finite human beings we cannot know all with an absolute knowledge. Even collectively, our knowledge is limited. For instance, we've yet to create a spacecraft that travels to the far ends of the universe so that we can experience it firsthand. Nor are we able to time-travel and personally confirm the details of history. But does our inability to know *everything* allow us to conclude that we don't know *anything*?

The Hume- and Kant-borne skepticism that has come to dominate our culture pushes the uncertainty of knowledge to the extreme. It forces us to surmise that because we cannot have unimpeachable confidence in everything our senses reveal to us, we cannot have any confidence in them at all. Kant attempted to say, and postmodernism says today, that because we can't know everything that's in the bigger square, we can't know anything that's in the smaller circle either.

However, does not experience tell us that our senses give us an accurate picture of our world? In practice, we trust them to navigate a vehicle, to walk a flight of stairs, to thread a needle, to catch a ball. Our senses warn us of danger, enable us to view a sunset or hear a symphony, and indicate to us whether we're grasping a marble or a grape. We can't deny that even if our sensory knowledge is imperfect, it corresponds very well with our reality and is sufficient for our needs.

❖ ❖ ❖ ❖

One of the West's assumptions is that of an orderly external world we discover, through science, and use for our benefit, through technology. Remember Kant's differentiation between *phenomena* (our experiences of things) and *noumena* (things in themselves), positing our inability to "know" the latter? Science argues that we actually are closer than ever to knowing and describing the very nature of matter, energy, and space.

We'll return to this subject as we further consider the nature of reality. For now, let's agree that we *do* know—on the practical level, minimally—what's in that smaller circle of the known universe (reality). At the very least, we know enough to live our lives successfully on this planet.

In addition, there is a realm where we do know, to some degree, a thing in itself. We know ourselves, and, thus, as C. S. Lewis put it, in one facet of the universe we are "in the know."

> There is one thing, and only one, in the whole universe which we know more about than we could learn from external observation. That one thing is man. We do not merely observe men, we are men. In this case we have, so to speak, inside information; we are in the know. And because of that, we know that men find themselves under a moral law, which they did not make, and cannot quite forget even when they try, and which they know they ought to obey.[247]

What we discover on the inside, within the immaterial aspects of our personality, is a sense of right and wrong, good and evil—a core of what we call values and aspirations. We *must* ask, from where might this have come? Is it possible that at the center of reality is a Power of justice and goodness?

Even in a Kantian universe, while we cannot know with absolute certainty the ultimate condition of all reality, we can still take what we do know and draw some reliable conclusions. We would be wise to take seriously the famous words that Mark Twain (1835–1910) is supposed to have said: "It is not what I don't know that bothers me, it's what I do know."[248] What *can* be known of the world, of life, and of humanity gives us important clues about dimensions that presently seem beyond our ability to know. Best of all, it gives us insight into the person and nature of God himself.

THE ESSENTIAL SIX QUESTIONS

Looking at the smaller circle of our known universe, let's have a go at determining what's in the bigger square. Any definition of reality worth its salt must answer six foundational questions:

(1) *Where did we come from?* (What is the origin of the universe and of us?)

(2) *Why are we here?* (What is the significance of life?)

(3) *Where are we going?* (What is our fate/destiny?)

(4) *Why is there evil—and good—in the universe?* (Where did wrong and right come from?)

(5) *Why are we the way we are?* (What is the essence of human personality?)

(6) *Is there a God?* (Does He exist, and, if He does, can we know it?)

We might think these are primarily religious inquiries, because they involve reality's origin and God's existence, but every philosophy that attempts to explain life deals with them in some way. *Everyone* has a religious faith in that he or she answers these questions in the development of his or her belief system.

---

[225] Will Durant, written source unknown.

[226] See Paul Johnson, Intellectuals (New York: Harper and Row, 1989).

[227] Aldous Huxley, quoted in Josh McDowell's Evidence that Demands a Verdict (San Bernardino, CA: Campus Crusade For Christ International, 1972), xi.

[228] Eugenics is the philosophy that supports "selective breeding" to improve the human race in the same way, for instance, that a farmer seeks to improve the quality of his cattle. Eugenics had two facets: (1) people of high intelligence should choose partners of equally high intelligence to produce highly intelligent children, and (2) people of low intelligence—in particular, the retarded—should not be allowed to have children (either by forced sterilization or by execution).

[229] John Carey cites this and other examples in The Intellectuals & the Masses (New York: St. Martin's Press, 1992).

[230] Ibid., 12.

[231] Ibid., 101.

[232] Ibid., 183–84.

[233] Gordon Olson, The Truth Shall Make You Free (Franklin Park, IL: Bible Research Fellowship, 1980), T-I-8.

[234] It should be mentioned that Immanuel Kant was not a moral relativist. He believed there is an innate moral sense in humankind, and he perceived this sense of conscience to be the one and only adequate evidence for the existence of God. Kant's religious views likely were Deist, and, like all Deists of his day, he held to the absolute standard of morality of the natural law.

[235] Boas' most famous pupil was Margaret Mead (1901–1978), whose writings brought the anthropology of Eastern cultures into popular American consciousness.

[236] Joseph Fletcher, Situation Ethics: The New Morality (Philadelphia: Westminster Press, 1966).

[237] Paul Simon and Art Garfunkel, "Flowers Never Bend with the Rainfall," from the album Parsley, Sage, Rosemary, and Thyme. Columbia / Sony Music Entertainment Inc., 1966.

[238] In Fyodor Dostoyevsky, The Brothers Karamazov (orig. published 1880).

[239] Olson, The Truth Shall Make You Free, T-I-8.

[240] For example, see data available at http://www.cdc.gov/nchs/FASTATS/unmarry.htm.

[241] In Bertrand Russell, Mysticism and Logic (Minneola, NY: Dover, 2004; orig. published 1957). See also A Free Man's Worship (Portland, ME: T. B. Mosher, 1923).

[242] Francis Schaeffer, The Complete Works, 8.

[243] Francis A. Schaeffer, He Is There and He Is Not Silent (Downer's Grove, IL: InterVarsity, 1972), 38.

[244] In Thomas Carlyle and Henry Duff Traill, The Works of Thomas Carlyle, Volume 1 (London: Chapman and Hall, Ltd., 1896; orig. published 1831), 32.

[245] In Jean-Paul Sartre, Being and Nothingness (New York: Citadel, 2001; orig. published 1956).

[246] John Hick, "Response to Dr. Recher" in Islam and Christian-Muslim Relations, 16 (2005): 12.

[247] C. S. Lewis, Mere Christianity (New York: Macmillan, 1952), 33.

[248] Mark Twain, written source unknown.

CHAPTER ELEVEN

OUR ORIGIN, OUR PURPOSE, AND OUR DESTINY

WHERE DID WE COME FROM?

With all the religions in the world one might expect there would be a million different explanations of the universe's origin. In fact, there are three. Of course, each worldview has its own version, but when we boil down all the stories, there are only three broad paradigms.

ORIGINS: ANIMISM AND NATURALISM

The first option is that the universe has always been here and that we were produced by it. This is not just the evolutionary and atheistic answer, it is also the answer given by most of the ancient polytheistic ("many gods") religions and by the multitude of religions we associate with the world's tribal peoples (this, technically, is called animism[249]). Herein, the universe is the preexistent reality from which emerged everything, even the gods and goddesses.

> When on high the heavens had not been named,
> and below the land had not been called by name,
> when only Apsu the primeval, who spawned them,
> and Mummu-Tiamat, who gave birth to them all,

> mingled their waters as one; when reed thickets had not consolidated, cane-brakes were not to be found, when no god at all had been made manifest, when they had not been given a name, when there had been no fixing of their destiny, then were the gods created inside them.[250]

These are the opening lines of *Enuma Elish*, the Babylonian creation myth. It's similar to many other narratives that represent all things emerging from a primeval, preexistent universe. There are, of course, variations in the descriptions of the process and in the names of the beings that emerged. One query for us to ponder, regarding the general worldview of the ancients: Did they ever wonder where the universe *itself* came from? (We'll return to this.)

Just as animism describes all things emerging from the universe, so present-day naturalism must also say that the world and all living creatures developed from the larger universe we inhabit. The modern naturalistic view resulted from a determined effort to find a completely nonreligious explanation of the universe's origin. Required, then, by definition, was the assumption of an *eternal* universe, because there is no possible natural explanation for something arising from nothing. Also required, again by definition, was the assumption that all of the universe's "parts," including living creatures and humans, were produced through a purely natural process. Accordingly, all of us are components of the vast cosmos from which we came forth.

We've already noted many of the problems facing the modern view, among which is irreducible complexity. Just about everything the universe is supposed to have produced naturally is too complex to be accidental, and there are no known mechanisms within nature[251] to explain natural but non-accidental development from the simple to the complex. One way out of this dilemma, increasingly popular in the West, is pantheism.

ORIGINS: PANTHEISM

The idea that life emerged from the universe led eventually to a second large-scale explanation: the universe itself *is* God, or, more succinctly, God is the universe. The technical term for this is "monism," which says there is only one great reality, God; hence, individuality, separation, and distinction are only illusions. This is the essence of *pantheism* (Greek: *pan*, "everything," and *theos*, "God").

The first Western scientist to adopt a pantheistic explanation of origins was the French Jesuit Pierre Teilhard de Chardin (1881–1955). He believed that nature is "alive" and possesses within it an impulse not only toward life but also toward consciousness and, finally, toward the "Omega Point" (God)—that is, reunion with its source. Most scientists were uncomfortable with Teilhard's mysticism, but many at least agreed with the core of his idea, that nature has within it some type of directive force.[252] This view, called *vitalism*, was explained by Will Durant:

> In a large sense the materialist is right: what he meant to do, by exalting matter, was to explain his faith that there is no break in the continuity of development, that philosophers have descended from apes, and apes from protozoa, and these from supposedly inorganic substances, and these from the simplest atoms. But we cannot believe this unless we also believe that within the apparently inert body of matter … there is a principle of life, a power compelling evolution. We bridge the gap between matter and mind not by reducing mind but by raising matter.[253]

I believe this perspective will become an ever-increasing emphasis for defenders of evolution as they're compelled to provide some type of larger principle to explain both human nature and the universe's intricacy and complexity. (Even

Nietzsche wrote, "The development of matter into a thinking subject is impossible."[254])

At any rate, this argument faces serious problems. It attributes "inner directedness" to a force; the British author Gordon Rattray Taylor (1911–1981) called it the "creative life force," yet he also called it "blind."[255] If it is impersonal, it cannot be creative and it cannot be directive. Forces are unthinking and unknowing; energy is just as inadequate an explanation for irreducible complexity as is matter. That something is *immaterial* does not give it powers of *creativity*. Only intelligence and personhood are capable of this.

Upholding a "creative life force" would be like strapping oneself to a metal gurney during a thunderstorm and waiting for a bolt of lightning to remove one's appendix. Pantheism's impersonal, all-pervasive "force" is inadequate because it cannot initiate action toward an intended goal. Only persons can plan and do what they desire.

Of vitalism, C. S. Lewis wrote,

> One reason why many people find "creative evolution" so attractive is that it gives one much of the emotional comfort of believing in God and none of the less pleasant consequences. When you are feeling fit and the sun is shining and you do not want to believe that the whole universe is a mere mechanical dance of atoms, it is nice to be able to think of this great mysterious Force rolling on through the centuries and carrying you on its crest. If, on the other hand, you want to do something rather shabby, the Life-Force, being only a blind force, with no morals and no mind, will never interfere with you like that troublesome God we learned about as children. The Life-Force is a sort of tame God. You can switch it on when you want, but it will not bother you. All the thrills of religion and none of the cost. Is the Life-Force the greatest achievement of wishful thinking the world has ever seen?[256]

Though the pantheistic evolutionary model for origins possesses a certain appeal in our time because of its efforts to integrate science and spirituality, it really is a last-ditch attempt to maintain an eternal, self-originated universe—an explanation for complexity that avoids the personal Creator God.

ORIGINS: THEISM

The third possibility is that we were created by an eternally existent God. This, technically, is called *theism*. There are three primary theistic religions in the world—Judaism, Christianity, and Islam—and all three have the same root: the story of creation as written in the Old Testament. All three agree that this God is the source of all that exists. They also agree that He is personal and has revealed himself to us, both generally through His creation, and specially in the words of Scripture. The differences between the three include what they believe to be the extent and content of the Scriptures.

We have mentioned that the eighteenth century brought a tangential version of this belief, one that accepted a personal Creator and His self-revelation through nature but rejected any thought that He would seek to communicate to us, His creatures, by means of prophets or books. *Deism* aimed to acknowledge the world's complexity while disregarding other foundational theistic claims. Deism is a paradigm of convenience, calling upon a god to explain the universe but then moving him aside and so leaving nature, and us, to our own devices.

In addition, Deism's disinterested god yielded more questions than answers. Why would a personal god treat the world so impersonally? Why would the one who gave us conscience, who built a set of moral principles into the natural order—why would he be immoral through utter neglect for what he created? Because of his absence, Deism's "god" could not be worshiped, and, in the end, he wasn't worthy of our worship.

The question of our existence must deal with more than the development of the organic and of life. In the natural order, human culture and human values are without equal and without precedent precisely because they reflect the *personal*. The greatest challenge facing naturalism is explaining how the personal developed and emerged from the impersonal. And the same question could be asked of pantheism: how can the impersonal be the ultimate reality, and the personal only a temporary illusion, when the personal is necessary to explain the universe's development? Theism has a powerful strength in its declaration of the Creator from whom arose complexity, design, *and* personal beings. There is no better explanation for the existence of life and of humanity. The universe *begs* for a transcendent explanation.

Now, to return to our earlier question, as to whether the ancients ever wondered where the universe itself came from: in fact, we are coming to find out that they did. Anthropologists have discovered that their earlier explanation of human religions was incorrect: The religions of the world did *not* evolve from primitive spiritism to theism; rather, evidence from the study of the stories and beliefs of animistic peoples indicates that most degenerated *from theism to a polytheistic animism.*

These peoples' accounts often include an episode of process through which their ancient ancestors believed in and worshiped the great Creator God but eventually turned away from Him; as a result, now, as a people, they have to deal with the lesser spirits that presently rule their lives. This story, or one very much like it, appears again and again across the animistic world. (For several specific examples I recommend Don Richardson's book *Eternity in Their Hearts.*[257]) Anthropologists also have found many examples of stories about the "Sky God," of belief in a transcendent personal Creator who made all that now exists.

Did the ancients ever ask where the universe came from? The answer is yes. A personal and eternal God was the best answer then, just as it is now.

WHY ARE WE HERE?

> Whether the earth or the sun revolved around the other is a matter of profound indifference. To tell the truth, it is a futile question. On the other hand, I see many people die because they judge that life is not worth living. I see others paradoxically getting killed for ideas or illusions that give them a reason for living. I therefore conclude that the meaning of life is the most urgent of questions.[258]

Regarding the question of *why* we're here—the question of life's ultimate meaning—what are the options available through the world's philosophies and religions? While again it could seem there would be as many choices as there are worldviews, just as with the previous question there are only a few. Further, the question ultimately revolves around two possibilities: is human life meaningful, or is human life meaningless?

THE SIGNIFICANCE OF LIFE : ANIMISM AND PANTHEISM

Most animistic religions place humankind low on the scale of existence. We are obviously far below God or the gods; we do not have the power or the capacities of the spirits (ghosts, demons, angels, or whatever else we would call them); in some cultures we rank below sacred creatures or places. Think of the portrayal of humanity in the myths and in the classic literature of both the ancient and modern world: We are weak, we are mortal, and we are profane. Man is both a victim and a criminal, who finds himself in the hands of forces and circumstances over which he has no control, and his outcome is far more likely than not to be tragic. The animistic worldview regards man as ultimately insignificant, a menial servant of the gods, a being whose life's purpose is keeping spirits mollified and happy.

For pantheism, likewise, man is an expendable tool of the mysterious powers behind the universe. Most religions hold that the events and situations of our lives, in one way or another, have been predetermined, and that these completely define our destiny or fate. Among the explanations for how our destiny is preordained, for example, are: by movements and alignments of the stars and planets (astrology), by our previous-lives' actions (of which we have no conscious recollection—karma), or by the inscrutable will of God (in monotheistic Islam—*inshallah*).

To the vast majority of human beings throughout history, fate has not been kind. Only a minority on this planet lives without poverty, without consistent threat of disease, and without exposure to the constant reality of death. Accordingly, for most people, believing that they're being ruled by destiny isn't pleasant; in order to gain some small advantage in the cosmic game, humankind turned to magic. In most of the world, magic has nothing to do with stage tricks but, rather, is the serious business of aiming to avoid or alter one's fate. In this sense magic has two basic elements: divination, or discovering beforehand what has been destined, and spells or curses, which are put forward as attempts to change people, things, and/or events to suit our desires.

❖ ❖ ❖ ❖

This view of life's "significance" fills people with anxiety and uncertainty; they wait at the mercy of forces that care nothing about what happens to us. Within the New Age Movement is a sense that because something is "spiritual" it will restore meaning and transcendence to our lives. This is extremely naïve. Fate is a cruel and impersonal master that, as history demonstrates, is more inclined to leave us crushed and helpless than joyful and whole. The man who entrusts himself to fate is like the one who sets out to make his fortune by gambling—he's far more likely to lose and end in poverty than to win and achieve prosperity.

At least one faction or school of thought within almost all religions, including Christianity, has presented an insignificant or, more properly, *fatalistic* view of human life. Man, in certain theologies, is seen as a pawn on the cosmic chessboard. His destiny lies completely outside his powers; even his free will is only an illusion, as God or the gods have preordained his destiny. When "que sera, sera" is the fate of every person, resignation becomes the only option.

This view, as most broadly expressed, is called *determinism*, in that all the events of history have already been determined. We will speak more about this, particularly when we deal with the existence of evil. The problem with fatalism (and determinism) is that it makes human life in general, and each of our individual lives in particular, utterly insignificant.

THE SIGNIFICANCE OF LIFE : NATURALISM

It's little wonder that one of the Enlightenment goals was to eliminate deterministic superstition and thereby give back to man his dignity. Man, through his innate powers of reason, could determine his own future; naturalism was to be his liberation from the terrible chains of fatalism. In itself, this is a prevalent and weighty conviction in the West; in the US we even say that "any child born in this country could grow up to be president." Our emphasis on education, opportunity, and "becoming anything we want" reflect this basic presupposition about our future.

Sadly, though, the price of this freedom was the attempted elimination of religion. While that endeavor liberated the collective human mind from capricious spiritual forces, it did not elevate our place in the cosmos. It was assumed that with the elimination of the gods, man would take first place; he would become master of his destiny. But men aren't gods—we are men. And the erasing of God from our worldview left us in charge of a big, empty nothingness, with far less real power than we anticipated.

Man found himself alone in an impersonal and meaningless reality. He also rediscovered what the ancients already grasped: impotence in the face of his circumstances. No amount of self-help will enable a person to eradicate cancer or defy an earthquake. It's not surprising we have returned, through spiritualism and the New Age, to the comfort of the old gods and goddesses.

Under the influence of Nietzsche and others among the modern existential philosophers, the arts have come to reflect this awful conclusion (that man is a pointless accident in a pointless universe). This seems to me the only explanation for works like *Piss Christ*, a picture of a crucifix suspended in a jar of the "artist's" urine, on display at the New York Museum of Art. My own view is that our present-day abandonment of morality and decency in the pursuit of a mindless hedonism is actually an egregious form of escapism and denial. We are seeking to anesthetize ourselves from the horrifying realization that we rule a reality with no relevance.

THE SIGNIFICANCE OF LIFE: THEISM

I want to point out that as human beings we prefer a consequential life—we want things to matter, and we want to make a difference. Corporately, we've expended much effort, made many sacrifices, and shed a considerable amount of blood seeking to pursue and safeguard a purposeful existence. Therefore, we must ask, *why* do we prefer meaningfulness to meaninglessness?

If the Judeo-Christian worldview is correct in its view of the humane and the divine, then we have our answer: *because we are made in God's image.* The meaning of "image" has been the subject of historic debate; nevertheless, when it's combined with "likeness," the other term used in Genesis,[259] we can agree that there is a connection between our nature and God's nature. We bear a resemblance to the one who made us.

Consider the quality of intelligence—no other creature in our world has our depth or degree of it. When intelligence is combined with the physical tools we possess through our bodies, we find we can create, not on the level of the Creator but in reflection of His creativity.

There is also the quality of conscience, or moral obligation. We find this at two levels: (1) a personal conscience that seeks to guide our daily behavior, and (2) a broader concern for justice, one that opposes evil and longs for the greater good. God is just and, therefore, in our deepest aspirations, so we are as well.

It's worth noting that my generation, which sought to deny conscience and its accompanying values, was still so profoundly moved by its innate sense of justice. The counterculture attempted to create a "new morality" (it was neither new nor moral) that enabled certain types of unrestrained behavior. At the same time they stood in opposition to the war in Vietnam and the misdeeds of corporate America.

The problem is, they were contradicting their own intrinsic beliefs. If there are no personal morals, then there are no corporate morals. You can't disconnect morality from justice. If I say pragmatically that my *personal* or individual action only affects me while a *collective* or federal action could affect thousands or millions, then I don't truly understand the nature of evil. My own act of immorality affects me *and* all my circles of involvement or influence. Pollution of the soul is like environmental contamination, spreading its effects from one place (or person) to the next.

This moral sense, individual and corporate, is an undeniable aspect of human nature—we can't escape it, and that's a good thing, for without it we'd be monsters. And this characteristic certainly fits the biblical revelation of God as righteous and just.

Our ethical obligation and our longing for justice, at the *very* least, indicate our origin.

We could add our powerful need to love and be loved to Scripture's declaration that "God is love."[260] Our yearning for meaning and significance likewise says something about our connection (or desire for connection) to God. If we *were* insignificant, it wouldn't bother us so much to believe our lives had no meaning; we would know our place innately. But we're "too big for our britches." We have capacities and passions that transcend the natural order from which we're alleged to have emerged.

We could say much more about this, but the Christian belief, which is reflected in our nature, is that humankind was created by God and that creation is evidenced by the unique abilities of the human personality.

CHRISTIAN FATALISM

Earlier I raised the specter of fatalism, and yes, there is a Christian version of it, which I feel the need to explain further. Some earlier generations of believers, influenced by Reformed theology, considered every event and circumstance in life to be "God's will." Many events and circumstances, however, were nightmarish and horrific. Non-Christians, looking in at this belief and its explanation, asked, what kind of God do these people worship? And how could this God, who (among other things) takes the lives of babies, be considered a God of love?

(I don't mean to insinuate that Reformed theology does not teach a God of love, or that there is no possible explanation for the death of a child that could be reconciled with God's ultimate goodness. Both of these exist within Reformed thought; however, they're largely incomprehensible outside the interpretive framework of Reformed theology.)

It's my belief that, in stark contrast to fatalism, the Bible presents a nondeterministic picture of the universe; that is, God does not control or predetermine every event that occurs.

One crucial aspect of our nature is our capacity to choose and to initiate action. We are free moral agents. This freedom is an aspect of our creation, for God is a free agent, and for us to reflect His nature we must also be free.

Further, morality itself cannot exist if our actions are not self-chosen and therefore *our* responsibility. If our motives and actions were preprogrammed or predetermined, we would bear no responsibility for them because we wouldn't have chosen them—they would have been chosen for us. "Morality" would become a ruse, an illusory or imaginary term for the predetermined collective actions of automated robots.

Accordingly, our choices have actual significance. There's a real sense in which the existentialists are correct: you and I have the power to give meaning to our existence by the decisions we make. The fact is, true significance is only possible in such a universe. If all our actions were preordained, they'd be nothing more than the motions of puppets; they'd have the significance of lines in a script.

The biblical view is that man has been given a crucial role in the functioning of the world: we have *dominion*. This is not just the strength or authority to do as we please—dominion is properly understood as *responsibility*. There's an accountability associated with our privileges: we are to use them for good, for the good of all creation. In granting us the abilities associated with being in His image and in giving us freedom, God guaranteed the significance of our lives and our choices. We can either make the world better or we can make it worse.

THE CRUX OF OUR PURPOSE

Whether or not we like it, our lives have meaning. For good or for ill, we possess the capacity to impact at least a part of our world. Our significance is such that even our inactivity has strength: in the words thought to have been said by the Irish statesman Edmund Burke (1729–1797), "All that is necessary for the triumph of evil is that good men do nothing."[261] We have no idea how the ripples of our influence affect the reality around us. Our choices either contribute to or provide resistance against the prevailing spirit of our age.)

For example, we live in an era of extreme selfishness. Are we joining in, using the cultural consensus to give ourselves permission to live in self-obsession? Or are we committed to living unselfishly, despite what everyone else seems to be doing, because loving others as we loves ourselves is good and right?

One hero of the nineteenth century was a man who opposed the prevailing "wisdom" of his time. He was a member of Great Britain's privileged class, yet he took up the attack on an evil institution that sustained the entire financial empire: slavery. For years he fought against the opposition and even retaliation of a majority of his fellow parliamentarians; after decades that must have seemed like centuries, his perseverance finally was rewarded. At long last, William Wilberforce (1759–1833) saw slavery abolished across the British empire, just before his death. His principled stand and faithful influence convinced a majority to do away with a moral and social travesty.

❖ ❖ ❖ ❖

Why, then, *are* we here? The biblical answer to the purpose of our existence is connected with our having been made *personal* beings. We were created by love in order to love. God is love, and so love is our greatest need and our highest capacity. Love is genuine concern for someone else to the same degree we're concerned for our own well being. And love takes us beyond even this to where we would willingly sacrifice our comfort for the fulfillment of the one we love: "Greater love has no one than this, that he lay down his life for his friends."[262] True love is reflected in loving, caring, giving relationships.

Our primary relationship, the one for which we ultimately were created, is with God. Human existence and even human significance cannot be understood apart from this fundamental truth. Wrote Augustine (354–430):

Thou has made us for Thyself, O Lord,
and our restless hearts will find no rest
until we find our rest in Thee.[263]

We will not know the purpose of our existence until we come to know the one who made us. If the personal Creator is necessary to explain an indescribably complex universe, then we could expect that our meaning and our destiny would be found in a *personal* relationship with the one who made us personal beings in the first place.

The world-changing promise of God as revealed in Jesus Christ is *reconciliation*. And reconciliation means the restoration of relationship; through Christ, God has been "reconciling the world to himself."[264] Because of Jesus we've been re-enabled to have a personal relationship with the God of the universe. What was lost in the Fall is restored by faith in Christ: "This is eternal life, that they may know You, the only true God, and Jesus Christ whom You have sent."[265]

To summarize: as personal beings, an important aspect of our significance is found in our personal relationships, and Jesus Christ has provided the means by which we can be restored to a personal relationship with God himself. This in and of itself makes the gospel *good news*—in fact, it's the best news that we, the people, have ever received.

WHERE ARE WE GOING?

From the dawn of recorded history humankind has expressed a predominant belief in life after death, and until recently the numbers of those who did not affirm some type of post-death existence were very small. Many moderns, though, have said that this belief is nothing but a product of wishful thinking: We fear death, so we made up a God and a heaven to calm anxious minds. As with our other categories, humanity's views can be narrowed down to a paramount few.

OUR DESTINY: ANIMISM

The first might be called the pessimistic view of the afterlife. The ancient Romans, for example, feared death not because it was the end of existence but the end of a happy, sunny, earthly existence for an entrance into the world of the "shades." The afterlife was perceived to be a *reduced* existence, devoid of what people had always regarded as pleasures and joys. The Hebrew word *sheol* probably has some of this same sadness in its meaning.

Generally, animists seem to view an afterlife as not much different from our present existence, with the need for sustenance, material goods, relationships, and so on. One connection between our world and the realm of the dead includes the responsibility of the living to look after the well being of deceased family members. Ancestor worship, widespread across our planet, is the primary means for accomplishing this. The dead are "sent" money, food, and other provisions through sacrifice and worship at the ancestral altar.

Fear is inseparable from this belief system: for one thing, it's believed that the ghost or spirit of a neglected ancestor can make trouble for his living relatives. For another, a living elderly person lacking a vital connection to family members faces death with anything from insecurity to terror. Who will take care of him or her in the next world?

We should note that the concept of a heaven and a hell is not uniquely Judeo-Christian; many peoples around the world expect a blessed realm for the righteous and a cursed realm for the wicked. The early Greeks and/or Romans, a representative illustration, held that only a small number of the very heroic are received into the former, and only a few are so despicable as to deserve the latter. Everyone else can expect a mediocre existence in a diminished realm of being.

Significantly, animists—both ancient and modern—have seen death as a change of location but not as a change of character or nature.

OUR DESTINY: PANTHEISM

Eastern mysticism brought with it another idea entirely: the transmigration of the soul. Since God is all that exists, and since we are part of God, our independent existence in this physical universe is not our real reality, it is an illusion (called *maya*). The illusion and our commitment to it is so powerful, however, that we are unable to free ourselves from physical existence. In addition, "evil" thoughts and actions deepen our attachment to this false world and lead to the "punishment" of continued imprisonment.

In the Eastern context, "evil" is attached to such strong emotions as hatred, fear, anger, uncontrolled passion, the desire for revenge, and so forth. Buddhism, for example, heavily emphasizes "detachment," particularly from these things that keep us focused on our immediate situation and, thus, tied to this world and this life.

The result of these attachments is that humankind is condemned to an ongoing cycle of being. We are born, we live, we die, and then our soul transmigrates into another physical body, and we must face another lifetime in this "vale of tears."[266] The teaching of reincarnation is that everyone has already lived countless lifetimes; the status of each person has been determined by his or her actions in previous lifetimes (karma).

The consummate goal is to break through the illusion and escape the terrible cycle of earthly bondage. What happens at this point is described as being like a drop of water returning to the ocean: we merge with God and achieve *moksha*, union with the divine. But God is a thing, similar to the *Star Wars* "Force."

As such, we too become a thing and thereby lose both personal identity and consciousness. This seems remarkably similar to the annihilation that the atheist expects at death.

OUR DESTINY: NATURALISM

Naturalism maintains that death is the end of personal existence and consciousness. Once our bodies die, our brain ceases to function and the machine is turned off, never to be restarted. The primary impact of this in a society where naturalism is the dominant philosophy is a profound collective fear of death and an inordinate emphasis on pleasure and fulfillment *now*. Hedonism, or Epicureanism, becomes the prevailing pursuit as people seek to maximize euphoria and success in the one and only life they've been lucky enough to get.

My own feeling is that the antiwar movement in the West is founded in large part on our view of death. Since death is the worst thing that can happen to a person, war, which is all about death, is the worst of all possible events. Likewise, our emphasis on perpetuating youth and preventing the advancement of age arises from our terror of the perceived end of our personal existence.

OUR DESTINY: NEW AGE

The New Age concept of life after death is starkly reflected in the film *What Dreams May Come,*[267] as Robin Williams finds himself in the afterlife without his wife, whose despair and suicide have left her in the New Age version of hell. He and his children seek her out to change her perception of herself and her fate; the happy finale is that his love breaks through her despondency, and she's freed from her predicament. In the end, together they decide to "come back" to another earthly existence.

The New Age combines the animistic view of existence on the other side with the Eastern idea that we determine the shape and reality of our destiny by our perceptions. It also presents reincarnation as an additional set of opportunities to "get life right."

But what is the goal—dissolution into the cosmic ocean that is God? And why would one want to leave an idyllic existence, free from disease and death, to return here? In addition, if this process of self-improvement has been operating for eons, then why hasn't our world gotten progressively better as each new inhabitant returns wiser and more desirous of improving upon previous accomplishments?

Many have sought to support reincarnation by tying it to experiences of déjà vu, the feeling of going through something you know you haven't encountered before. This also has been linked with "flashbacks" to what some people think were previous lives. Nonetheless, while these experiences can seem powerful, they are also entirely subjective, and, hence, there are other possible explanations and interpretations. Subjectivity isn't intrinsically problematic, but it is troublesome, minimally, when its testimony isn't supported by other evidence, historical and/or rational.

What Dreams May Come also highlights another significant element of the New Age view of life after death: it is profoundly individualistic and impersonal. The characters entered realities on "the other side" that had been connected to their lives here. "Hell" is (in this case) depression and a wounded self-image. Heaven is ... well ... Williams, accompanied by his pet dog, literally moved into his favorite painting, of a cabin by a lake; in the afterlife, the lake and the cabin became real (as did his daughter's favorite doll house, in which she came to reside). According to the New Age, reality isn't what it is—instead, we decide what it is. We *create* the world in which we live; "truth" is "true" once we affirm and embrace it.

As the movie progressed I kept wondering, what is the source and sustenance of this existence after death? The answer is somewhat like the common agnostic perspective: *it's just there*, functioning by a set of rules that are also *just there*. But where does it all come from—who or what originated the whole thing in the first place? And who or what runs it now?

We're back again into the same conundrum: The magic and mystery that allegedly reside within and behind the universe are impersonal. We're expected to believe that these systems of spirituality are also part of a larger *natural* order that developed randomly over time? Once more we're left to wonder how the personal emerged from the impersonal, particularly when the impersonal supposedly is more ultimate than the personal.

OUR DESTINY: THEISM

The Christian answer to the question of our final destination is related to its view of God and of man. God is personal; therefore we also are personal beings, bearing His image and having consciousness. Just as our existence in this world is personal and conscious, so will be our existence after death.

God is not only personal, He is relational—probably the greatest aspect of personality is that it allows relationships. Christianity teaches that God has existed for all eternity as the Trinity: Father, Son, and Spirit. While this doctrine is difficult to understand, Trinitarianism explains one consummate aspect of God's character. "God *is* love" means that God has forever lived in relationship, for love requires another person to love and by whom to be loved. "Trinity" implies that God has lived eternally in love because He forever has been a tri-unity of persons in one Godhead.

God created humankind for relationship, and our destiny is wrapped up in that very quality of our existence. Look again at what Jesus said: "This is eternal life, *that they may know You, the only true God,* and Jesus Christ whom You have sent."[268] Heaven will not be heaven because its streets are paved with gold; heaven will be heaven because Jesus is there and because we will live with and love Him forever.

By corollary, hell will not be hell because of its terrible conditions but because it will be everlasting relational separation from God. Jesus said hell was created for the devil and his angels; people will be there only because they chose to reject Him and, therefore, refused relationship with Him.[269] C. S. Lewis presented this principle in *The Great Divorce*: for the person who has chosen to live separately from God, heaven would be worse than hell, for hell has the absence rather than the presence of God.[270]

We need to be clear: receiving eternity in heaven is not strictly about religious discipline and devotion. One of the great misconceptions of faith in Jesus Christ is that it's about people hoping to earn a life in heaven after death through moral and religious effort. That is not the gospel. God himself, in His magnificent mercy, made the way for our restoration. As Fanny Crosby (1820–1915) wrote,

Oh, perfect redemption, the purchase of blood,
to every believer the promise of God;
The vilest offender who truly believes,
that moment from Jesus a pardon receives.[271]

Entering heaven does not depend upon *religion*: it depends upon *relationship*. Again, the gospel is about reconciliation, and through Christ we can be reconciled to God. There is no way into heaven without this relationship that is ours through faith in Jesus.

We need reconciliation because sin, our sin, has broken our relationship with God.[272] When philosophers speak of the isolation and alienation of human existence, they are really describing the isolation and alienation of sin.

The LORD's hand is not so short

that it cannot save;

Nor is His ear so dull

that it cannot hear.

But your iniquities have made a separation between you and your God, and your sin has hidden His face from you.[273]

In order for us to be restored to God, sin must be dealt with. This is exactly why Christ came: "He will save His people from their sins."[274] Thus, Jesus called himself the gate[275] and the way: "I am the way, and the truth, and the life; no one comes to the Father but through Me."[276] God has provided no other remedy for sin, and apart from dealing with sin there can be no relationship with God and, hence, no possibility of eternal life in His presence. *Christ is the one and only way to God—the one and only path to the destiny for which we were created.*[277]

---

[249] Animism maintains that nature and natural forces are animated by spiritual beings and forces. Animism is the general description of the beliefs of tribal peoples, from ancient times to the present. Animism includes polytheistic and spiritist cultures and is characterized by an emphasis on magic, ancestor worship, and idolatry.

[250] H. W. F. Saggs, The Babylonians (London: The Folio Society, 1988), 330–31.

[251] Remember: evolution is not a mechanism but an unsupported assumption.

[252] See Gordon Rattray Taylor, The Great Evolution Mystery (New York: Harper & Row, 1983), 13. Taylor rejected creationism but likewise saw serious flaws with contemporary presentations of evolution. He said, "It was not by chance that living things, in all their limitless variety, appeared upon this earth. Nor was it by the working out of a preconceived plan of divine origin. Life seeks new and subtler forms of expression by a blind impulsion, an inner directedness."

[253] Will Durant, The Mansions of Philosophy (New York: Garden City Pub. Co., 1941), 68.

[254] Cited in ibid., 71.

[255] Ibid., 38.

[256] C. S. Lewis, Mere Christianity (New York: Macmillan, 1952), 35.

[257] Don Richardson, Eternity in Their Hearts: Startling Evidence of Belief in the One True God in Hundreds of Cultures Throughout the World (Ventura, CA: Regal Books, 2006).

[258] Albert Camus, in The Myth of Sisyphus (New York: Vintage Books, 1955).

[259] See Genesis 1:26–27.

[260] 1 John 4:16

[261] Edmund Burke is believed to have said these words, but he didn't write them down; or, if he did, the source has not been preserved. One possibility, also, is that the cited sentence was based on Burke's idea in Thoughts on the Cause of

Present Discontents (released in 1770) that "when bad men combine, the good must associate; else they will fall, one by one, an unpitied sacrifice in a contemptible struggle."

[262] John 15:13 NIV

[263] Augustine of Hippo, in Confessions.

[264] 2 Corinthians 5:19 NIV

[265] John 17:3

[266] From the antiphon Salve Regina.

[267] What Dreams May Come. Dir. Vincent Ward. Polygram Filmed Entertainment, 1998.

[268] John 17:3, emphasis mine.

[269] See Matthew 25:41; cf. 7:23.

[270] C. S. Lewis, The Great Divorce (New York: HarperOne, 2001; orig. published 1946).

[271] "To God Be the Glory," lyrics by Fanny Crosby. Comp. William Howard Doane. 1875.

[272] See chapter twelve.

[273] Isaiah 59:1–2

[274] See Matthew 1:21.

[275] See John 10:9 NIV.

[276] John 14:6

[277] See Acts 4:8–12.

CHAPTER TWELVE

THE EXISTENCE OF EVIL

WHERE DID WRONG AND RIGHT COME FROM?

Turning now to the fourth of our six questions, we should start by observing that sin (evil) is not a uniquely Christian theme. Every philosophy and every religion must have some type of explanation for the existence of evil. We will need to define "evil," but for now, we can say that evil is the bad things that human beings experience, both corporately and personally.

FROM WHENCE EVIL: ANIMISM

In animistic belief, evil is seen as part of the universe's inherent dualism, expressed, for example, by the yin and yang of Chinese cosmology. Herein are multitudes of intrinsic oppositional dualities: hot/cold, dark/light, male/female, good/evil, sour/sweet, and so on. Dualism seems to correspond with many of our observations of the world, and the dualistic explanation does have some qualities of wisdom, encouraging what other cultures often have called "moderation" or the "golden mean."

The main shortcoming with a dualistic interpretation of all reality, though, is the blurring and/or denial of inherent distinctions. For instance, "male" and "female" are not *just* aspects of humanity; they also are significantly distinct. Furthermore, while moderation is applicable in certain matters, there are times when it's neither necessary nor correct. I would submit, actually, that many of the greatest human accomplishments have involved a single-minded (*unidirectional*) devotion to a cause or goal.

The preeminent dualistic ideal is balance—that is, we are to not allow any one aspect to predominate. This becomes acutely problematic, though, when dualism is posited in the realm of good versus evil, for, in this regard, we intrinsically prefer one to the other. We're *not* innately dualistic about right and wrong; in fact, we put considerable effort into achieving the distinction of good over evil.

But why? Why do we, who are part of this dualistic system—which, supposedly, is intrinsically woven into the very fabric of the universe—dramatically prefer the good? Where would that come from, if reality *were* inherently dualistic?

This is where the philosophy breaks down. Strict dualism says there are two forces in the universe, opposite each other and, theoretically, equal: a force for good and a force for evil. As such, if that were true, evil would have as much chance of overcoming good as good would have of overcoming evil.

However, our own lives profoundly discredit this idea. Even those who engage in evil acts do so for the personal benefit (the "good") that they believe they will attain. Humans, in other words, actually desire a *distinction,* not a *dualism,* when it comes to good and evil.

❖ ❖ ❖ ❖

The appeal of the dualistic worldview to our present culture is that it supports the modern era's relativistic approach to morality. Dualism's blurring of distinctions fits perfectly with society's present desire to blur moral boundaries. In truth, dualism only gives us philosophical and even metaphysical support for what are, fundamentally, selfish moral compromises.

This brings us to one of the most important facets of our question. It can be argued that evil does not exist as a unique ontological reality. What we call "evil" is actually a distortion or corruption of the good; that is, a loss of or lack of the good. In other words, evil only exists because good exists, in the same way that darkness is the absence of light. Just as the level of darkness is entirely dependent on the level of light, so evil is entirely defined by and dependent upon the reality of goodness.

Evil is, in many cases, the perversion of goodness. Thus a genuine desire for, say, love, can be corrupted into an obsession that leads to the twistedness of stalking and/or assault. In the criminal's mind, crime often is justified as necessary to fulfill some type of legitimate need or as recompense for—the perceived *righting* of—some wrong done. So, misdirectedly, the robber steals because he "needs" the money, or because "those people have been getting rich off of us."

Moreover, this principle yields the result that the greater the potential for good in something, the more severe will be the damage when it is corrupted toward evil. So, for example, while marriage is highly prized for its magnanimous contributions to human happiness, divorce is catastrophic for everyone involved. And while healthy parent-child relationships are among the most meaningful and beneficial endeavors in all of life, abuse of a child by a parent causes more devastation that almost anything else.

❖ ❖ ❖ ❖

Evil is tragic, painful, and deadly. We humans passionately and viscerally hate it. Evil is cancer and AIDS and identity theft; it is injustice and murder and oppression. Humankind has been seeking throughout all history to rid itself of at least the worst of evil's manifestations. If, however, evil is an essential part of reality, as dualism posits, this becomes an impossible task—eliminating evil is like trying to rid the universe of matter itself.

Animistic and polytheistic cultures not only are dualistic, they also are fatalistic. And this has dramatic implications for the problem of evil; belief in evil's inevitability is unavoidably linked with fatalism. The predominant experience of humans throughout history has been suffering. If we examined the lives of all people who have ever lived, circumstantially, we might conclude that evil is more common than goodness.

As we have seen, too, animism presents a hierarchical view of the cosmos: the gods have all the privileges and power, while the unfortunate human masses are relegated to degrees of pain and pleasure according to their status. Since there's little chance that this state of affairs could ever change, one must simply find ways to adapt to the system. If fate is the master, a few win but most lose. Without question, animism produces a pessimistic view of life.

FROM WHENCE EVIL: PANTHEISM

I submit that a large portion of Eastern philosophy (and, in particular, Buddhism) developed in response to the aforementioned animist perspective. The East maintains that evil is an intrinsic part of the universe.[278] "God" is both good and evil; again, He/It is something like the *Star Wars* Force, with its sides of light and darkness. Eastern worldviews teach that we have an inherent preference for goodness, but they do not explain where that preference comes from. For instance, does it exist inherently in us, or does God ("the impersonal All") prefer the good, and thus does it emanate from Him/It, even though both good and evil are present within Him/It? (And again, how the impersonal could *prefer* anything is another question.)

In Eastern philosophy, karma is the explanation for the observed consequences that give rise to fatalism. People suffer because their past-life choices cause them to *deserve* suffering. Karma has been closely associated with Hinduism's caste system—a person's identity and status being consequences of his or her karma. The privileged have earned their privilege, while the downtrodden are receiving the just punishment for their sins. This paradigm is still profoundly pessimistic; an individual has little control over his present condition, which is the product of previous-life actions.

Physical, material existence, then, is a jail sentence, an imprisonment in a pain-filled world, and we've *earned* it through bad karma. In Hinduism, salvation is the final achievement of deliverance from this "illusion" into final union with God. But, again, since "God" is impersonal, we also cease to be personal and conscious.

Buddhism was born out of this same perception. Siddhartha Gautama (c. 563–483 BCE), who came to be known as the Buddha, observed that the prevalent condition of human existence is suffering. As a child and a prince, he had been shielded from woes; eventually seeing human misery changed him, and as he pursued "enlightenment," he also pursued a solution to evil.

Siddhartha's answer was *detachment:* We must, by discipline of the mind and the will, disengage ourselves from the physical world, the source of our misery and anguish. We also must practice the virtues,[279] because in so doing—by following the Path[280]—we will experience (and inflict) the least amount of pain. This is the answer likewise given by philosophical Hinduism: when we come to see and acknowledge the true nature of human existence, we find liberation from its sorrows.

The Buddhist teaching is that misery and suffering come from attachment to this life. Therefore, the path to nirvana involves the renunciation of anything that connects us to it. Siddhartha renounced wealth, privilege, comfort, even family, because he believed those things had held him captive to the desire for a continuing physical existence.

❖ ❖ ❖ ❖

In the end, Buddhism, like Hinduism, acknowledges the reality of evil. Essentially, the solution both give is "stop the world and let me get off," for the only way to escape evil is to escape this life. Yet how does this explain evil's existence? Is the answer the same as what the ancient Greeks gave—that the physical world is *inherently* evil? But how then do we explain roses and sunsets and love—aren't they a part of the physical world too? Buddhism would have to say such things are the *most* evil, because they increase our attachment to this life. In fact, though, Buddhists themselves don't do any such thing; they love sunsets and gardens as much as the rest of us. Their humanity supersedes their philosophy.

Eastern thought *does* avow that physical existence is an evil (*maya*, "illusion"). In the same way, the suffering and evil we experience in this world is *illusory;* if we only knew better and believed better, it would all go away. This view became central to the Christian Science of Mary Baker Eddy (1821–1910): We suffer pain because we think the physical world is real, but it's not. To escape the torment the world sends our way, we need only believe properly: disease is not real, poverty is not real, even death is not real.

Psychologists have a term for this: it's called *denial*. Evil is real; the Eastern answer flies in the face of human experience. What the East cannot explain is why the "illusion" is so very real, or how it became an "illusion" in the first place. Why would God, or whatever power rules our universe, play such a deceitful and hurtful trick on His/Its creatures?

FROM WHENCE EVIL: SECULARISM/ NATURALISM

At least the modern world is willing to admit that evil is real. But it simultaneously faces a huge shortcoming: it's only explanation is sheer coincidence. Evil is a human *construct* to explain events that we don't like but which nature throws our way.

Speaking of "evil" in this way is like trying to hold a runaway steamroller guilty of crushing pedestrians: it's an unintelligent, non-living machine completely unaware of anything it does for good or for ill. We, not nature, are the ones who define events with the terminology of good and evil.

Naturalism can use the words "good" and "evil," but not on the basis of naturalism. Nature is completely amoral. We human beings add the categories of moral and beneficent value to explain the circumstances of our lives. Yet, for the *nth* time, if we are the product of natural processes, from where did we get our inextricable sense of right and wrong, of good and bad? Good and evil are fundamentally personal issues. This does not mean they're only a matter of personal *opinion*; it means they're defined from a foundation of personal *existence*. An impersonal thing or force has no awareness of good and evil.

If naturalism is correct, then the only basis upon which good and evil can be understood is that of human existence. This, however, is an inadequate foundation, leading only to utilitarianism, which operates by seeking what is perceived to be the greatest good for the greatest number. For example, today, an as-yet-unborn child can become denied and destroyed when he or she is argued to be "unwanted" or "a burden to society." These are utilitarian terms, used to justify unthinkable wrongs. Who are we to know what a given life might be and become? Utilitarianism allows people to assume a God-like knowledge of present and/or future conditions. It also serves to legitimize situationalism and relativism, which merely try to choose the supposed lesser of evils in a given scenario. In the end, all of this, given the human condition, degenerates into excuses for "might makes right" and uninhibited selfishness.

❖ ❖ ❖ ❖

One primary postmodern conviction is that beliefs and perspectives within a culture end up getting determined and imposed by those in power. For example, the history of Western civilization has been dominated by the strength of European males. Accordingly, its history has been shaped by ethnocentrism and chauvinism.

The increasing (even runaway) emphases on African-American Studies, Women's Studies, and GLBT Studies at many of our universities are expressions of postmodern political correctness. Many such programs entail retroactive attempts to retell world and national history from the perspective of one or another respective group. The biggest problem with this cynical approach to the past is that the facts of history get lost (or buried) in the attempt to promote a given ideological agenda. These initiatives degenerate from the study of history to the development of propaganda, as events and results are sorted and selected to present only those that support political and ideological preference. Regarding the human condition, revisionist history does not lead to an enhanced understanding or to our collective growth.

Ultimately, again, naturalism degenerates into a nihilistic will-to-power. The contemporary deconstructions and reinventions of our history and values are symptoms of this disease. Postmodernism and its stepchild, political correctness, are built upon the reaction to this view of culture. The acquisition of power—in this case, dominating positions in education, media, and politics—allows special-interest groups to redefine right and wrong, true and false. This power then turns into the prerogative to seek limited-view standards for all of society.

Regarding evil, naturalism leaves us with no satisfactory explanation. It's simply our misfortune to be fragile, contingent personal beings in the midst of an impersonal material universe that can snuff out our helpless little lives and not even know what it's done. Likewise, nature appears to have only one value—survival—and the deeper we move into naturalism, the more our values reduce to this one element.

A BIBLICAL VIEW OF THE PROBLEM OF EVIL

As we start to examine evil from a theistic perspective, let's back up to give some definitions. There are two kinds of evil in our world: (1) human-originated evil and (2) natural or accidental evil. In some ways it's easier to fathom the first kind: people lie, cheat, steal, and perpetrate all types of wrong against their fellow man. Evil is *not* just what we personally don't like or personally wouldn't want to happen to us. We humans also are troubled when terrible things are done to others, to our environment, or to other creatures, even when those things are distant from us. We most often don't oppose evil because "it might happen to us." We oppose it because it's *wrong*. Human-originated evil is what the Bible calls "sin."

The second category, natural (accidental) evil, is represented by harmful and devastating elements that arise in nature without direct human cause. Natural evil includes earthquakes, tornados, tsunamis, and other such disasters. Many people have a telling term for these events: "acts of God." If that's true, then theism has some explaining to do. How can God be all-good *and* be the source of things or forces that cause death and destruction?

❖ ❖ ❖ ❖

We begin with this: The universe was created by an eternal, personal, intelligent, and caring God. Something *must* be eternal, and, as an explanation for our world, a personal God makes far more sense than an impersonal cosmos. We say "intelligent" and "caring" because we see God's genius in His design, His pleasure in beauty, His delight in color, taste, sound, and warmth, and His love all around us.

If God is the Creator, does that mean He also is the creator of evil? The answer to this crucial question hinges upon our previous discussion of evil's "nature." Remember: evil is the perversion of the good. A fire in a fireplace gives warmth and comfort to a home, but if that same fire goes out of control and burns down the house it causes harm and loss. In one instance, the fire is beneficial, a blessing; in the other, its corruption leads to calamity. When we speak of evil, we use words and phrases that convey this distinction—for instance, we say that something or someone is "crooked" when the action or result is evil. We thus are comparing these somethings and someones to the "straight," the standard of decency or goodness being distorted by the evil of the "crooked."

That God is *not* the creator of evil means that God only created good things. As the account in Genesis 1 proceeds, a recurring phrase is, "God saw that it was good,"[281] culminating in the final expression of approval: "And it was *very* good."[282]

In that goodness, though, was the *capacity* for the distortion of the good that is evil. God created free creatures, and while freedom unquestionably is right, it must allow for the potential entrance of wrong. Only free creatures can choose to love; in fact, real love is impossible without real freedom; likewise, freedom is also the means by which creatures can choose against love and bring great harm into the world.

This is the essence of the biblical account. God created good, free creatures, and those creatures rebelled, beginning with God's greatest angel, Lucifer.[283] Lucifer became *Satan* (which means, literally, "the adversary") and has been seeking to spread his evil opposition to God and goodness ever since.

So it is not surprising to find Satan in the Garden of Eden, seeking to entice the newly formed humans to misuse their freedom in rebellion against God. In succumbing to temptation, humankind not only corrupted themselves, they also brought corruption into the entire creation. What theologians describe as "the Fall" is this defiant choice against God; because that choice (what we call *sin*) continued and spread, evil has continued and spread.

Paul tells us that sin entered the world through the first man, Adam, and that the result of sin—death—spread to all, "because all sinned."[284] He also describes the consequences of humankind's rebellion: the entire creation has been "subjected to futility" and "corruption," and now it "eagerly" awaits the redemption of humankind, which likewise will result in its redemption.[285]

The Bible declares that God is not the author of evil—He is its absolute opponent. Evil is like a hideous, parasitic malignancy that afflicts the body of the universe; the dilemma for God was how to eradicate the cancer without destroying the patient. The *gospel* is His magnificent plan of redemption and restoration. It is entirely appropriate to call Jesus, as God incarnate, "The Great Physician."[286]

Nevertheless, one of the most common arguments against theism is the seeming contradiction between the existence of God and the existence of evil. If God is God, and if God is good, how can He allow evil?

Evil's existence often is posed as a problem for Christian belief. But God not *already* having banished evil doesn't mean he won't do exactly as He has promised: in addition, that He hasn't yet done so, "within *our* timeframe," actually has been for our inexpressible benefit.[287] Conversely, in fact, the existence of goodness, joy, and love are a confounding problem for atheism.

> Since the creation of the world His invisible attributes, His eternal power and divine nature have been clearly seen, being understood through what has been made, so that they are without excuse.[288]

❖ ❖ ❖ ❖

Genesis indicates that even in its original condition God created the world to operate non-deterministically. The very "stuff" of the universe is free—that is, God does not predetermine every event within the natural order. Yes, natural forces govern the universe's function, but there has always been a fundamental freedom in its operation. I say this for two important reasons.

First, because of this visible and apparent reality: No two snowflakes (for instance) are identical, and each creature has some level of uniqueness. The Creator threaded unparalleled variety into the very structure of the universe, yet it functions in an orderly and perpetual manner, guided by built-in forces and mechanisms.

Second, because of what God told humankind in Genesis: He commanded us to "be fruitful and multiply, and fill the earth, and *subdue* it."[289] The word "subdue" is the English rendering of the Hebrew *kabash*, which literally means "to tread down."[290] This implies that even before sin entered the world, the universe was wild and free, and that man, as God's designated caretaker, must keep creation under control.

The larger theological concept here is that the universe has a separate existence from its Creator, in the same way that an artist's painting exists separately from the artist. In other words, creation has a life of its own even as it depends entirely upon God for the continuation of that life. Paul assures us that Christ not only created all that exists, but that "in Him all things hold together."[291] We literally could not exist without God, yet He gives us freedom and being.

Another verse in Genesis implies this principle as well: It describes "God walking in the garden in the cool of the day."[292] This anthropomorphism suggests He created the universe in such a way that variety and uniqueness are built-in and self-perpetuating. Hence, even though He created the first peacock and daffodil, God can "look at" and "smell" and "touch" each subsequent peacock and daffodil and continue delighting in its one-of-a-kind beauty. He can "walk through" His universe and savor the phenomenal expressions of His creative genius *precisely* because there is a part of their uniqueness He did not directly determine—it's produced by the innate freedom He bestowed.

I believe that microevolution, the marvelous capacity for selective genetic change *within* species, is the expression of this principle placed within the core of organic nature. New forms of each type of plant and animal have developed and will continue developing from the genetic potential inherent in each species. The freedom of creation continues to delight its Creator.

LEVELS OF BEING—AND OF RESPONSIBILITY

If the universe is non-deterministic and thus inherently free, how then could it be said that God "controls" the universe? How does He *prevent* complete chaos and ultimate destruction? As we begin to answer, note that there are three levels of existence in the universe: matter, living creatures, and humankind.

God regulates the *first level of being (inorganic, organic, and energetic)* by the physical laws of nature He installed. The four main forces (strong, weak, electromagnetic, and gravitational), the laws of conservation, the laws of chemistry and biology—by design, these factors normally govern the interactions of all non-living things. The planets remain in their orbits, the sun gives off its heat and light, water evaporates and then condenses in the clouds that produce rain ... all are governed by the regular, predictable forces and laws of the natural order. These are *so* regular and predictable that we literally set our watches by them; as inanimate objects, they exist and function at the most deterministic level of the cosmic order, lacking both life and choice.

Living creatures (second level of being) have an additional facet of control (freedom), as they have another facet of existence (life). On top of the physical principles, they are governed by instinct, which in many ways mimics intelligence. Bees produce and store honey in their carefully built hives, and a spider crafts its magnificent web, not via learned behavior but from having been born with a gift. Instinct enables the creature to react to and interact with its environment, even while its actions are predetermined and predictable. So predictable, in fact, that scientists are able to study and define the expected behaviors that arise from the instincts of each creature.

Accordingly, while these actions possess the marks of intelligence—such as precise construction of detailed structures, or a specific sequence of actions to achieve a special result—the behaviors are not learned or even self-determined. They are instinctive responses to stimuli from outside the creature. The intelligence we see through instinct is not the creature's but rather the Creator's. A nonhuman creature has life but lacks choice about its behavior and role in the natural order.

With *humankind (third level of being)* comes the final dimension: *governance*. We are part of the physical world and are subject, for example, to gravity, heat, and light (first level). We are living creatures and have many of the same needs, restraints, and instincts of our fellow creatures (second level). Furthermore, we are intelligent, self-conscious, personal beings, *governed by moral statutes and personal conscience*. In creating man, God added the third-level element of will (choice, volition) to existence (first level) and life (second level). We are self-governing.

❖ ❖ ❖ ❖

Many ask why God created us this way—why didn't He make us incapable of evil? We've already seen the answer: we would be robots and not people. A robot only does what it's programmed to do. It can be programmed to mimic love—it can say, "I love you"—but its words are not its own, having been implanted there by the programmer. Without freedom and will (volition) there can be no love; God *is* love, and there is no higher virtue or value. Love is the free-will choice to love; it cannot be coerced, and an automaton cannot love. Love must arise from within the lover to be manifested toward the beloved. We could not bear God's image without the capacity to love truly and voluntarily.

Because God is free, self-governed by His own will and by the absolute goodness of His own character/essence, so we, in His image, must be free and self-governing. *However,* we were never meant to live independently of Him. The temptation of the first humans was to be "like God, knowing good and evil."[293]

I see this as meaning *to take up an independent existence and the moral responsibility that goes with it.* This choice—moral responsibility without the moral resources to fulfill it—describes the ongoing tragedy of human history. We are finite creatures, limited in our perspective and understanding, yet we have insisted on bearing the burden of determining good from evil and true from false. No wonder we've failed miserably at governing the world over which God gave us dominion.

Looking at the Genesis account, we see these very elements. God governed man by appealing to our intelligence, self-interest, and volition. He gave knowledge, in a set of instructions: "From any tree of the garden you may eat freely; but from the tree of the knowledge of good and evil you shall not eat."[294] And He gave a clear warning: "… for in the day that you eat from it you will surely die."[295] His governance was by instruction (appealing to our intelligence) and by warning (appealing to our self-interest). He left the *choice* up to us.

HUMAN EVIL

As the story of evil's entrance into the created world unfolds, the next character we encounter is Satan, having taken the form of a serpent and seeking to lure Eve into disobeying God's command. Satan *likewise* treated her as a personal and volitional being; he sought to manipulate her understanding of God and His intentions so that she would be open to making up her *own* mind about the choice before her. Implying that God had lied in order to protect His place in the universe,[296] the liar himself claimed that "knowing good and evil" would make humans equal to God—it would make them little gods, having an independent moral existence.

But we are not God. We don't know all that can be known. Constrained by our limited insight and perspective, we *cannot* know everything about what ultimately will be good and what ultimately will be evil.

Satan was trying to entice Adam and Eve into coming out from their place of dependence on God. I think he knew what was at stake: if they could be convinced that God can't be trusted, then he could lead them to break the relationship between God and man. Remember, the Bible repeatedly uses the term *reconciliation* to describe God's purpose in sending Jesus Christ. I make the connection that the primary reality lost because of sin was *relationship*—a personal relationship between the divine and the human. Once more: We were never meant to live apart from God.

❖ ❖ ❖ ❖

At the end of Genesis is the powerful story of a man who refused to participate in the sin of the parents of the human race. Joseph was victimized by the envy of his brothers, who had intended to kill him but instead sold him into slavery. As a captive, he was falsely accused of attempted rape and was cast into prison. He languished in jail, forgotten and ignored, but after a period of years he not only was released, he also was given unprecedented power.

In that position of strength, there came a time when the siblings who had done him so much harm literally were in his clutches. Instead of exacting revenge, though, Joseph developed a plan that brought about the reconciliation and restoration of his family. Joseph obviously had forgiven his brothers, but he went beyond forgiveness to a beneficent concern for their well-being.

At the end of the story, after he had provided food and a new home for his family, they still wondered if he would pay them back for their terrible crime against him. In light of the damage done to him, particularly, his willingness to forgive was anything but "normal." Calming their fears, he said,

> Do not be afraid, for am I in God's place?
>
> As for you, you meant evil against me, but God meant it for good in order to bring about this present result, to preserve many people alive.[297]

Joseph rejected the temptation to be "like God." He knew his place, as a creature dependent upon his Creator. He left the defining of good and of evil to God, realizing that, from a finite perspective, what seems evil to us may in the end turn out to be for great good, just as well as what seems good in the short term may lead in the end to great evil.

One of the most remarkable aspects of this story is the relationship between Joseph and God, even in the darkest hours.

> Joseph's master took him and put him into the jail, the place where the king's prisoners were confined; and he was there in the jail.
>
> But the LORD was with Joseph and extended kindness to him, and gave him favor in the sight of the chief jailer.[298]

The phrase "the Lord was with Joseph" or "the Lord was with him" recurs. Joseph's "secret," the facet that more than any other enabled him to swim against the flow of natural temptation, was his communion with God. I submit that this was the Creator's intention for each of us all along: We were created for this type of personal relationship with our Maker.

The folly of the human race has been to think we could *live* separately from God. To be separate from God is to be separate from life. He didn't tell us to live a certain way because He decided that would be best; He tells us to live a certain way because that way is in accordance with His very essence, and, therefore, with what is real, true, and good.

Likewise, the commandments God has given us are not arbitrary—they're based on the reality of His nature, and hence if we are to remain connected to Him we must comply. He did *not* say, "In the day that you eat from it [the tree of the knowledge of good and evil], I will kill you." He said, "In the day that you eat from it you will surely die."[299] This statute is like all the others: God's dictates are connected to the very structure of the universe (or, of reality), which in turn was born out of and exists by His very character. Thus, God didn't give this warning because He decided to establish a rule and then demand obedience. He warned Adam and Eve because the essence of their life, of their existence, was at stake.

GOD *IS* GOODNESS, GOODNESS *IS* RIGHT

Many people assume or believe that the rules of our existence are arbitrary. By "arbitrary" I mean that our divinely given guidelines for living either are *random* and have no ultimate purpose or are merely God's *preference* and therefore have no larger significance than His "likes and dislikes." There are even Christians who argue just this—that God has *decided* right and wrong, true and false, and that something is right or wrong only because God says it is.

The problem with this view is that it makes "good and evil" matters of opinion rather than eternal realities. Theists who argue for this position feel they must because to do otherwise, seemingly, is to place goodness above God. If He doesn't determine what is good, then goodness exists not only apart from Him but also as something He is subject to. But goodness isn't "apart from" or "over" God any more than love is "apart from" or "over" Him. God *is* love, and God *is* good. "Good" and "evil" are not the results of arbitrary determinations.

We know "arbitrary" when we see it. Arbitrary is preferring red over blue or chocolate over vanilla. Arbitrary is determining that men must wear a tie to church because we like the way a tie looks or because we decide that doing so is reverent. Morals aren't like this; we don't object to murder because we don't like it, we object because it's wrong—through murder an irreplaceable human life is cut short by an immoral act. The same could be said of theft, slander, adultery, deceit, abuse, racism, and arson: the prohibitions against them aren't arbitrary rules enforced by capricious omnipotence. An arbitrary standard could just as well be something else; for instance, saying all men also should wear a tie clip. By contrast, consider assault or robbery: We can't even imagine a different "morality" that still would be moral.

❖ ❖ ❖ ❖

Let's return to that question of whether the existence of a fixed, unchanging reality, to which even God is subject, thereby means that this standard, this reality, this code, is greater than He is. Once again, the answer is no. The answer is *there is no difference between God and the standard.* God *is* love. God *is* truth. Goodness is the essence of His nature. In doing good and avoiding evil, He is being true to himself. *In affirming right and opposing wrong, He is being who He is.*

John begins his gospel by telling us, "In the beginning was the Word."[300] As we continue reading, we learn that this Word actually is God himself. Another way of saying this is that God is the embodiment of His commands and instructions; He *is* what He says. Think about what we mean when we talk about being people of integrity, of truthfulness … of being a man or woman of our word. Just as God's decisions and actions never deviate from who He is, so He is, *literally*, as good as His Word.

One of the remarkable characteristics of Jesus is that He is the epitome of everything He commands His disciples to do and be. He tells them to love their enemies; He prays on the cross, at the moment of His greatest agony, at the hands of those who hated him and put him there, "Father, forgive them, for they know not what they do."[301] His apostle, Paul, instructs us to be humble by pointing directly to Jesus:

> Have this attitude in yourselves which was also in Christ Jesus,
>
> who, although He existed in the form of God,
>
> did not regard equality with God a thing to be grasped,
>
> but emptied [humbled] Himself, taking the form of a bond-servant.[302]

Jesus truly is the Word made flesh.[303]

If God has always existed, then He has always been subject to His own nature: He has always loved good and hated evil (even when evil was only the *potential* for the corruption of the good). In the same way, what is good and what is understood as evil cannot change because they are rooted in God. While our understanding of truth has changed over the centuries, if we are honest we will admit that only our opinions about morality vary, not morality itself. In actuality, we don't "break" the moral rules themselves; instead we end up broken by our transgression of them.

> Whatever a man sows, this he will also reap.
>
> For the one who sows to his own flesh will from the flesh reap corruption, but the one who sows to the Spirit will from the Spirit reap eternal life.[304]

FREEDOM IS FOUND *IN* GOD

We've already noted that Satan, in the Garden, treated man as a free moral agent. We will never be able to say, rightly, "The devil made me do it." Characteristically, he tempted and deceived, but he could not force—man was free.

Eve considered the alternatives and made a choice. Adam, deciding to join her, made the same choice. As a result, they would suffer real consequences. Again, Paul explains this in Romans: "Just as through one man sin [evil] entered into the world, and death through sin, and so death spread to all men, because all sinned."[305]

The *sin* of humankind, if I correctly understand the story, is choosing what we thought would be, and still think will be, a God-like existence of independent moral authority and responsibility. People decided they didn't and don't need God. Once again, what Adam and Eve failed to realize, and what Satan neglected to tell them, is that God *is* life, and to live apart from Him is to experience death.

Evil caused directly by humans is a consequence of human choices, from the beginning and throughout all of history. Greed, lust, and selfish ambition have produced untold suffering in our world, and we have no one to blame for it but ourselves.

NATURAL EVIL

After Adam and Eve made their decision, God sought them out and pronounced the just results. We are meant to take from this that the sin of humankind—our attempt to live apart from God—carries with it tragedy that severely impacts the entire created order: "Cursed is the ground [earth, land] because of you."[306] God gave us dominion, and He never has taken it back. The world's destiny is wrapped up in ours.

> The anxious longing of the creation waits eagerly for the revealing of the sons of God.
>
> For the creation was subjected to futility, not of its own will, but because of Him who subjected it, in hope that the creation itself also will be set free from its slavery to corruption into the freedom of the glory of the children of God.
>
> For we know that the whole creation groans and suffers the pains of childbirth together until now.[307]

We've seen that our choice against God and, thus, for evil, brought evil into the creation itself. What God had called "very good"[308] became a place in which the "very bad" could occur on a regular basis. The goodness of creation was not entirely lost—it still reflects much of its original glory—but now the beauty and the blessing are mixed with the dangerous and the deadly.

We must pay attention to the "very goodness" in God's response. Even as He pronounced humanity's punishment (pain, toil, and physical death), He also promised a day of reckoning between the woman's "seed" and the serpent.[309] Theologians consider this the first direct statement of the promise of our redemption. A descendant (*seed*) of Eve will "crush" the devil's head, even as He is "bruised" in the process. This passage is seen as a metaphor of Christ's victory upon the cross over Satan, sin, and death.

At the end of this encounter, God made coverings of skin to hide Adam and Eve's nakedness, thereby foreshadowing the one who later would come to cover our sin.[310] The rest of the

Bible is the story of God's unfolding plan to rescue humanity and the world from the curse of sin and death. From this time forward, God is at work to undo the damage done by evil.

❖ ❖ ❖ ❖

This does not change, however, that human sin brought evil into nature itself. Death, disease, and disaster all became effects of the curse upon creation. Ultimately, sin was the overthrowing of God's rule over our lives to establish our own hegemony. In taking upon ourselves the capacity (and the responsibility) to know good and evil, we claimed the ability to make our own moral decisions and live without God's assistance or guidance. In essence, we told God to leave us alone, and He did; we now live in a world devoid of His protective and beneficent presence.

We each have ratified our first parents' choice, countless times. We want control, and one prevalent reason for rejecting religion is the fear of surrendering personal autonomy. We're afraid God will prevent us from enjoying all the pleasures and benefits this world has to offer. We may not entirely reject Him (this is called "hedging our bets"), but we also cautiously keep Him at arm's length. We may even pray occasionally, but we're careful about becoming or being perceived as a fanatic. We usually want God's *help*, but we don't really want *God*.

We should not be surprised, therefore, that God is nowhere to be seen. Our separation from God is not a petulant avoidance on His part, as in, "I know where I'm not welcome." Sin has definite consequences, and separation is one: our lack of connection to (intimacy with) our Maker is both a dire warning and a sincere invitation to be reconciled.

It seems to me that God had two choices in the face of human sin: immediate judgment and thus the end of His creation, or intentional separation for the sake of His holiness. *God cannot coexist with sin:*

> Your eyes are too pure to approve evil,
>
> and You cannot look on wickedness with favor.[311]

He must either judge sin, or He must withdraw from it. Jesus, for example, quotes Daniel describing God's response to Antichrist's invasion of the future temple's Holy of Holies as "the abomination of desolation."[312] In other words, desecration leads to God's withdrawal of His presence, making the place "desolate."

The existential reality of human life—that is, our experience—is the absence of God's visible presence in the universe. For many in our culture, this is proof positive that there's no God. However, we know that invisibility isn't the same as non-existence. We have acknowledged that many things in nature itself are invisible and can only be discovered when the right "instruments" are employed. As well, many things actually may never be "seen," and we only know of them now because of the effects they produce. (E.g., high-energy physics and sub-nuclear particles are dependent upon this principle.[313])

In the same way, God is Spirit,[314] and our connection with Him is through the immaterial facet of our nature. We experience God as we relate to Him spiritually. Our conscience and our intuition, for instance, are vehicles by which God speaks to all of us.

We have already put forward the universe's complexity and posited the inadequacy of any accidental or natural explanation for it. We are faced with a mystery: There must be a God, but where is He? The biblical answer is that *He is hidden from our sight because of sin.*

---

[278] Meaning that evil does have its own ontological reality—that is to say, the East maintains evil isn't a corruption or perversion of goodness but rather exists innately and independently.

[279] The Buddhist virtues are about helping others, being honest, living simply, and doing no harm or violence.

[280] Central to the teachings of Buddhism is the Eightfold Path: the eight principles for escaping the grip of suffering and sorrow.

[281] E.g., Genesis 1:10

[282] Genesis 1:31, emphasis mine

[283] Isaiah 14:12–14 and Ezekiel 28:12–17 have been interpreted as describing the fall of Satan from his original position as the highest of the angels, the angel of worship. He chose to arrogantly exalt himself to equality with God, and in so doing lost his place of honor to become the very founder of all rebellion, deceit, and crookedness. Jesus describes him as "The thief [who] comes only to steal and kill and destroy" (John 10:10).

[284] See Romans 5:12.

[285] See Romans 8:19–23.

[286] E.g., see Luke 5:30–32.

[287] We'll get further into this in the next chapter, under "God's Mercy."

[288] Romans 1:20

[289] Genesis 1:28

[290] R. Laird Harris, Gleason L. Archer, Jr., Bruce K. Waltke, eds., Theological Wordbook of the Old Testament (Chicago: Moody, 1980), 951a.

[291] See Colossians 1:16–17.

[292] Genesis 3:8

[293] Genesis 3:5

[294] Genesis 2:16–17

[295] Genesis 2:17

[296] See Genesis 3:4–5.

[297] Genesis 50:19–20; see also 45:4–15.

[298] Genesis 39:20–21

[299] Genesis 2:17

[300] John 1:1

[301] Luke 23:34 NKJV

[302] Philippians 2:5–7

[303] See John 1:14.

[304] Galatians 6:7–8

[305] Romans 5:12

[306] Genesis 3:17; cf. Genesis 5:29; Romans 8:20–22; Hebrews 6:8.

[307] Romans 8:19–22

[308] Genesis 1:31

[309] See Genesis 3:15.

[310] See Genesis 3:21; cf. Psalm 32:1; Romans 4:7.

[311] Habakkuk 1:13

[312] Or, "the abomination that maketh desolate"—Daniel 11:31 KJV; cf. Matthew 24:15.

[313] We alluded to this in chapter five; see under "Empiricism" and "A Response to Empiricism."

[314] See John 4:24.

CHAPTER THIRTEEN

THE PERSISTENCE OF GOODNESS

So our sin has separated us from God, and we cannot see Him, but that doesn't mean He isn't present and at work in our world. For one thing, His grace is often evident in times of peril and tragedy. I remember the report of a plane crash into the Potomac River, years ago. It was wintertime; many passengers survived the impact, but the plane was starting to sink, and they needed to be saved, quickly, from the frigid water.

A helicopter arrived and lowered a cable and a collar to rescue survivors. As it hovered over the wreckage, one passenger helped others put on the collar and be pulled to safety. After the last person had been retrieved, the collar was lowered for that man, but he was gone. He gave his life to save those of his fellow passengers. His heroism stands as a tribute to the presence of good in the midst of suffering; consciously or not, in that calamity, he was the hand of God's grace. Many families to this day call him blessed.[315]

However, no vague platitude about God being "present" or "at work" in the midst of evil is a truly sufficient answer. Certainly God is not content with providing a little comfort here and there. He desires a real and final solution—and He has one.

Returning to Isaiah 59 to consider again what the Bible says about the problem of evil, I note that it reads like the works of modern existentialist philosophers:

Justice is far from us,
and righteousness does not overtake us;
We hope for light, but behold, darkness,
for brightness, but we walk in gloom.
We grope along the wall like blind men,
we grope like those who have no eyes;
We stumble at midday as in the twilight,
among those who are vigorous we are like dead men.
All of us growl like bears,
and moan sadly like doves;
We hope for justice, but there is none,
for salvation, but it is far from us.[316]

The author Henry David Thoreau (1817–1862) also was correct in that most people lead lives of "quiet desperation";[317] the term *alienation* describes much of human experience. We live in alienation from nature because there's a part of us that's not at home in this world. Humans obviously are part of the natural order, but we possess capacities that dramatically transcend the rest of nature. Our moral and spiritual qualities are such that, as long as we remain here, we will not be entirely satisfied and fulfilled.

In addition, we face peril, suffering, and death, not with resignation or acceptance, but with anger and defiance. We are the only creatures in our known world who deeply question the restraints of their existence. We live in alienation from one another and even from ourselves because we are subject to impulses we cannot control.

Paul clearly describes the human condition: "The good that I want, I do not do, but I practice the very evil that I do not want."[318] We continually betray our own best interests as our mind and conscience helplessly watch us make foolish and selfish choices. How often have we confessed that we do not understand ourselves? And the ultimate alienation is that we're separated from the one who created us.

Among the worst aspects of natural evil is the absence of a visible and tangible God. The French writer Stendhal (Henri-Marie Beyle, 1783–1842) blamed *God* for evil's presence in the world, concluding that "the only excuse for God is that He does not exist."[319] The assumption is that, because God is not empirically visible, the evils in the world show, more than anything else, that the right conclusion is to deny His existence.

❖ ❖ ❖ ❖

This is patently incorrect. *God is more moved by evil than we are.*

Now the LORD saw,
and it was displeasing in His sight that there was no justice.
And He saw that there was no man,
and was astonished that there was no one to intercede;
Then His own arm brought salvation to Him,
and His righteousness upheld Him.[320]

God's response to evil in the world was to enter time-and-place history, in the person of Jesus Christ, and confront evil at its root: human sin. The Incarnation was the means by which God identified completely with humanity, faced all our temptations without defeat, and then, by His incredible sacrifice of love, made the way for us to be restored to Him and to life. Jesus became the Last Adam,[321] the new head of the human race, by His death on the cross breaking the power of the curse of sin and death. Christ is God's antidote to the curse, and He is the only hope for every one of us fallen human beings.

What God did in Christ makes it utterly untenable to accuse Him of indifference to suffering. He bore the brunt of evil, suffering incomprehensibly in order to bear our sins in His body. God truly does *so* love the world.[322]

GOD'S MERCY

A common philosophical argument against the existence of God states the following: If God is all-good (omnibenevolent), and if God is all-powerful (omnipotent), then evil should not exist. (That is, an all-loving God *should* prevent evil, and an all-powerful God *could* prevent it.) Therefore, since evil does exist, either God is not all-good or God is not all-powerful. Another common conclusion is that God, as Christianity presents Him, simply does not exist.

This overlooks and disregards an essential aspect of God's nature. *God is also merciful.*

> The Lord is not slow about His promise, as some count slowness, but is patient toward you, not wishing for any to perish but for all to come to repentance.[323]
>
> Or do you think lightly of the riches of His kindness and tolerance and patience, not knowing that the kindness of God leads you to repentance?[324]

God has given humankind time—literally—to be restored to Him. When we ask God to put an end to evil, what we're really asking for is the end of the world. God is just and righteous; when He judges evil, He will judge *all* evil. Those who want God to put an immediate end to strife in the Middle East usually don't want Him to do the same with their own indiscretions; in essence, we ask God to take away the free will of others while leaving ours intact. Many want God to leave them alone, but we can't have it both ways—if God intervenes to prevent evil, He will prevent *all* evil, including yours and mine. God, in His mercy, is withholding His judgment so that people may have the opportunity to be reconciled to Him.

In our present state, we would find a world governed entirely by justice to be a very uncomfortable place. In fact, as there would be no room for sinners, none of us would be able to dwell there. For now, God has allowed the world to remain imperfect, permitting us who share that imperfection to live our earthly lives.

We *really* don't know what we're asking when we beseech God to eliminate evil; we are not yet ready for a fully righteous reality. Thus Paul's marvelous declaration about the future resurrection: "For this [the resurrection,] corruptible must put on incorruption."[325] God won't change the world until He first changes us!

Again, the gospel promises that "if anyone is in Christ, he is a new creature; the old things have passed away, behold, new things have come."[326] Giving our lives to Jesus brings us into renewed relationship, restores our spiritual connection, and begins our transformation, by His grace, into the person we've actually always longed to be ... the person we were made to be. In the last day, the resurrection will be this transformation's final chapter:

> Beloved, now we are children of God, and it has not appeared as yet what we will be. We know that when He appears, we will be like Him, because we will see Him just as He is.[327]

The resurrection is not just about going to heaven: it's about the complete restoration of God's image in humankind and about the inside-out transformation of our natures. The Bible promises this: on the day of Christ's return, all will be restored to the glory that was lost at the Fall.

❖ ❖ ❖ ❖

One last point concerning evil: in acknowledging our sense of alienation, we are revealing that a part of us is troubled by the world as it is. We have the feeling that something is wrong with our existence here. Albert Camus, in *The Rebel*, spoke of this as humanity's "protest" against the conditions of its present reality.[328] Francis Schaeffer referred to this as the "abnormality" of the universe;[329] we sense it, we intuit it, and though we can't really put our finger on it, we feel it—something's just not right here.

In this vein, what separates Christianity from all other religions and philosophies is the belief that evil is a tragic mistake, a profoundly poisonous cosmic deformity. When people stand up to fight against the evils in our world, they're saying that these things are not supposed to be here. They're saying that evil is wrong.

Sometimes people obey their hearts even when their belief system gives them no basis or foundation to fight injustice. For instance, in the evolutionary scheme, the strong are supposed to annihilate the weak; still, the heart's ingrained sense of compassion leads us to be concerned for plight of the vulnerable and helpless. Even an ardent evolutionist pulls for the underdog and gives willingly to charity. This is humanity—*humanness*—contradicting philosophy.

Faith in Christ gives us true grounds for the battle against evil. God is opposed to evil and injustice, and He calls us, His servants, to join His opposition. For instance, when we build hospitals and orphanages, when we look for cures for diseases and seek remedies to wrongs, we are serving Him. Viggo Olsen, a doctor who served the people of Bangladesh in the name of Christ for thirty-three years, founded the first modern medical center in that country and maintained it through the chaos of devastating warfare.[330] Olsen is just one amidst a veritable multitude of medical missionaries; this is why the emergence of Christianity in the West led to and sustained the greatest outpouring of philanthropy and the most remarkable application of knowledge to the alleviation of suffering in all of history.

THE INESCAPABLE ULTIMACY OF GOOD

Volume upon volume has been written about the problem of evil, but perhaps not as much has been said about the presence of goodness, both in the human heart and in nature. In reality, our perspective on evil often is based upon the expectation that human existence *ought* to be good. Evil stands out against a background of goodness, and it's characterized as "evil" because we experience so much we must call "good." For instance, we consider the death of a young person a tragedy because we are accustomed to people living what we consider a "full" lifetime.

In many ways, we take the good for granted—we frequently just assume "it's there" and don't consider *why*. If the universe is the result of random forces and interactions, why do we have sunsets and butterflies, and what explains kindness? "Luck" is an utterly inadequate answer.

We are wired for goodness; even atheists acknowledge that we have an internal moral compass. It's frequently claimed that one doesn't need to believe in God in order to be "good," and in a very real sense this is true—one only needs to be human to have a conscience and be compassionate. The real question is, where did our "humanness" come from?

The British biographer Ronald Clark (1916–1987) quoted the biologist Thomas Huxley and then commented on his thoughts.

> [Huxley said,] "Of moral purposes I see no trace in nature, that is an article of exclusive human manufacture—and very much to our credit.... Let us understand, once and for all, that the ethical progress of society depends, not on imitating the cosmic process, still less in running away from it, but in combating it." So although man formed the apex of the evolutionary pyramid, he was now to fight against the system which had created him—an attitude which according to [Herbert] Spencer involved "the assumption that there exists something in us which is not a product of the cosmic process."[331]

This is very much the crux of the dilemma facing evolutionary theory: how to explain human conscience and compassion. If we were products of a ruthless system, how do we account for the human heart? One Enlightenment byproduct was the development of "humanism." Not classical humanism—the study of the arts and the humanities—but rather a philosophy that sought to find a replacement for religion in creating a secular society. As mentioned before, the movement's leaders, particularly those after Darwin, understood that they were "eliminating" religion, but they also realized that religion provided something crucial to civilization: the grounding of moral values.

Why this concern? First, they understood that without a set of moral values society will degenerate into chaos. Second, they were expressing their own moral concern: human beings *ought* to be honest, to care for one another, and so on. The trouble is, as Spencer pointed out, their evolutionary philosophy gave them no basis whatsoever for this concern. *Not only were they demonstrating the influence of Christianity upon Western society, they were expressing the innate moral sense within their own natures.*

The Institute for Humanist Studies gives many examples of famous atheists who established important charitable foundations. One was Andrew Carnegie, who declared that "The man who dies rich dies disgraced."[332] Carnegie gave millions upon millions of dollars (billions, in today's currency) to build and fund thousands of libraries around the world. More recently, Warren Buffet recently gave $37 billion—almost 85 percent of his estimated net worth—to five separate foundations. And Ted Turner pledged up to $1 billion to fund the United Nations Foundation. Both Buffet and Turner are outspoken atheists, yet both they, like many other humanists,[333] affirm the reality of moral imperatives and recognize the need to do good in this broken world.[334]

As we've noted repeatedly, one humanist hope has been to ground moral values in reason. Reason, however, is insufficient; reason itself can be easily manipulated, and a moral system founded on reason will soon be co-opted in the interests of political and/or social expediency. And, for illustration, consider again what relativism did to Western morality in the last half of the twentieth century.

Even among those who outright reject the existence of God, morality goes deeper than reason; morality is a felt need of human beings. Conscience, guilt, and compassion are deep-seated aspects of our personhood, and they move people to make profound sacrifices. This is why atheists join political causes and have a sense of outrage at injustice: their human sense of *oughtness* comes shining forth. Recall how the existentialist Sartre signed the Algerian declaration against nuclear weapons testing;[335] doing so contradicted his absurdist philosophy, and he was hammered with criticism for allegedly betraying his beliefs, but he signed anyway, because he was much more than a philosopher— first and foremost, he was a person.

An intrinsic moral sense is just one symptom of goodness in humankind. Note this: one principle of the Enlightenment and also of humanism was the belief that man is basically good! It's *theism* that says people, while still bearing God's image (including His goodness), nevertheless have fallen—are sinful—and thus stand in need of redemption.

The irony is, once more, humanism has defended something for which it has no explanation. How could a meaningless universe have produced a creature that values goodness? Furthermore, since like everything else we are products of purposeless interaction between natural elements and forces, where did *value*, *good*, and *meaning* themselves originate? Why are we moved by a concerto? Why do we rejoice at a wedding? Why do we weep when our children are born? Why do we feel elation when the bad guys are defeated and the good guys restore what's right? There *is* a basic goodness within the human personality. Christianity says it's because we were made in God's likeness; humanism must say it's only an accident.

WHY ARE WE THE WAY WE ARE?

We have reached the fifth question we seek to answer: *From whence the human personality?* The ancient myths say that man was created as an afterthought by the gods, who wanted servants because they needed and enjoyed food, drink, and sleep. The gods, at least those of the Near East, were more like big, powerful, immortal people than the theistic God. To meet their constant whims and desires, they first enslaved lesser gods who had been defeated in war. Eventually, the gods being served became uncomfortable with fellow gods being so demeaned; hence, they created humans to fill the role. These tales likely reflect ancient man's feeling of helplessness and impotence in the faces of fate and nature.

THE HUMAN PERSONALITY: ANIMISM

Again, animism, in its view of humankind, is not far removed from naturalism, seeing man as a product of nature, far down on the totem pole of existence. Herein, totemism is the belief (generally) that man has a strong connection to the animal kingdom and (specifically) that a species of animal has a spiritual connection to a tribe of humans. Animism at least implies that people, along with the other elements of nature, are part of a larger natural reality than that which our physical senses perceive. In contrast to naturalism, animism can take dreams, inclinations, conscience, and values seriously.

Naturalism reduces man to make him an animal. While animism leaves man as a species of animal, it elevates nature by making it spiritual and places man in the midst of this natural/spiritual order. Even so, man is of no greater significance than many of the world's animals; in fact, man is of less significance than the spirits, gods, and goddesses. Animism lends itself strongly to the communal, hierarchical context from which it arose.

With its connection to territory and tribe, animism lends itself to ethnocentricity. In Japan, for example, Shinto[336] tells the story of the Japanese people's creation, the centrality of their islands, and the supremacy of their gods and goddesses. All other humans and all other lands are inferior, being created later and by lesser gods. In other words, such belief systems do not adequately explain *all* of humankind on *all* the earth. Animistic faith is often seen as "our" religion to the exclusion of "yours," because it is the story of "our" people and "our" culture, from which "you" are excluded.

THE HUMAN PERSONALITY: PANTHEISM

In some ways, Eastern mysticism is an attempt to give the animistic worldview a universal application. The spirits of nature and locality are combined into one great spiritual reality—the *Brahman*—which infuses and empowers everything in the cosmos. We and everything else are part of this one single reality. Like animism, pantheism maintains that nature is spiritual and alive.

So where does man fit in this scheme? The East sees "ranks" of existence:

(1) Brahman

(2) Gods and goddesses

(3) People (ranked according to karma)

(4) Living creatures

(5) Inanimate objects

Fully taking into account karma and reincarnation, *everything* must be treated with care and respect, because no one knows who or what it was in its past lives.

In practical terms, though, this has led to nothing short of large-scale class discrimination. The karma-based caste system ranks people according to the class into which they're born. If you are born Brahmin, you are of the priestly class. If you are Kshatriya, you were born to be a soldier or an administrator. If you are a Vaishya, you were born to be merchant or a farmer. If you are a Shudra, you were born to be a peasant. Those who are born beneath all these ranks are considered "the untouchables," the polluted—their lot is to suffer, to beg, and to remain in poverty.

Amazingly, because of karma and *ahimsa* (non-violence, no harm to any living thing), animals like cattle and vermin are fed and cared for while "untouchable" humans are allowed to starve. This has led to several attempted overthrows of the Hindu system, primarily by creating a new sect or, in the case of Buddhism, a new religion. Recently a segment of the large Indian Dalit population (the untouchable class) has publicly abandoned Hinduism;[337] many have embraced Buddhism and some have embraced Christianity.

The Eastern view of humanity is similar to the ancient Gnostic model: man is a lower-level, relatively insignificant creature within the larger cosmic order. Primarily, we are *physical* and, thus, are subject to the limitations and impurity connected to a material existence. From the Gnostic perspective, body/matter is inherently evil, while spirit/mind is inherently good. Because man is subject to all the "negative" emotions that bind us to physicality—because of these intrinsically "evil" manifestations of his nature—he is lowly ranked. He must go through the cycle of enlightenment and reincarnation in order to elevate his nature and escape material limitations.

THE HUMAN PERSONALITY: NEW AGE

The New Age version of this process is the ultimate expression of the self-help movement. We humans are in an ongoing personal-improvement program, circulating from lifetime to lifetime while attempting to move upward on the scale of existence from man to god and, finally, to God.

The problem, though, is that we seem to start each supposed "lifetime" from scratch, with no essential recollection of past mistakes or successes. Looking at human history, it's hard to see *any* pattern of real improvement, even among those who follow Eastern teachings. Far more people than not are born with and live out their lives having the sense that this is their first and only lifetime. Again, déjà vu occurrences are extremely rare and highly subjective. Normal human experience suggests that this life isn't one of many but rather that we really do have *one* life to live.

The postmodern popularity of the New Age largely has been due to its capacity to present a transcendent and spiritual view of nature and humanity. We are part of a vast and mysterious cosmic order, the laws and principles of which lie undiscovered, either in the writings and wisdom of the ancients, within the beliefs and practices of those peoples most in-tune with nature, or along the path of the personal spiritual pursuit.

Individuals, however, remain vulnerable to all the perspectives of "reality" from which the New Age Movement emerged. We are still subject to fate, this time determined by the condition of the cosmos when we are born. The cultural historian Richard Tarnas (b. 1950) even presents a contemporary apologetic for the study of astrology as the determinate factor in the development of modern history.[338] The New Age, for all its use of positive rhetoric, still leaves humankind in the grip of cruel fatalism.

The New Age also attempts to repackage reincarnation as a type of universal self-betterment experience. Supposedly we're reincarnated in order to improve upon our past performances. But again, we do *not* see a dramatic improvement in human behavior over recorded history's thousands of years. In addition, none of us is consciously aware of any past lives; how can we upgrade behaviors of which we have no recollection or awareness?

In the end, we are left weak and vulnerable in the midst of faceless forces we must appease and accommodate. The New Age Movement is rooted in ancient animism; the similarities in their descriptions of the human condition are no surprise.

THE HUMAN PERSONALITY: NATURALISM

As we've repeatedly seen, naturalism presents an even more pessimistic view of us: We are an accident, produced by random interactions of natural forces. Accordingly, human life has no ultimate importance; what we have is existential (experiential) and pragmatic (practical) worth to ourselves and our families and to society through our general contributions. Abortion is one example of the fallout: The state has determined that if a mother does not want her unborn child, it has no legal or philosophical ground for protecting the child's life—his or her existence fails the tests of "value" in the naturalistic order.

The molecular biologist James D. Watson (b. 1928), one of the first men to isolate and describe the DNA molecule, has argued that the severely retarded and the hopelessly insane should be euthanized. He suggests that the DNA of each pregnancy could be analyzed so as to inform us as to which deformed or "defective" children should be aborted. Watson, an atheist, sees man as an evolutionary product with no intrinsic value beyond the utilitarian worth of his normally functioning faculties. An "abnormal" person is only a burden to himself and to others.[339]

Bioethicist Peter Singer (b. 1946) takes this concept even further. Supposedly, since the individual is a natural product, he or she must be seen on equal terms with earth's other species. Singer popularized a term for the belief that humans are of a higher order of being: *speciesism* (like racism, only we "favor" our species over others).[340]

Singer has called for the elimination of laboratory testing on animals, arguing that they feel pain and that, out of empathy (since we feel pain too), we shouldn't seek to protect humans at the expense of animals. However, he has also lent his support to infanticide,[341] insisting that a baby is not a person until it begins to show signs of cognitive awareness (i.e., is several months old). It's *astonishing* that Singer's philosophical area of expertise is ethics. If you're wondering how an ethicist could be persuaded to justify murder, consider that this stance, like many others, clearly and deeply reveals the moral bankruptcy of the naturalistic worldview.

THE HUMAN PERSONALITY: THEISM

The Bible declares that humankind is a remarkable creation of the transcendent personal God. We, therefore, have a unique and significant role within the created order. Human beings reflect the personal, moral, and relational nature of our Maker. We were meant to serve Him, serve one another, and serve the creation over which He gave us stewardship.

We are both physical and spiritual beings; we are connected to both earth and heaven. This fact helps explain the many mind-boggling qualities of human conscience, intellectual aspiration, artistic expression, and religious persuasion.

Human beings are of inestimable value. Jesus tells us that "the very hairs of your head are all numbered,"[342] confirming that God is aware of and concerned about the details of our lives. David takes this even further:

> You scrutinize my path and my lying down, and
> are intimately acquainted with all my ways.[343]

God examines our goals, desires, habits, and decisions. He sees where we're going, knows our likes and dislikes, and cares about our condition and direction. I believe He is at work in every human life through circumstances, conscience, thoughts, and other influences. As Paul, speaking to the ancient Greeks in Athens, observed regarding the nature and needs of humankind, scattered across the world:

> The God who made the world and everything in it is the Lord of heaven and earth and does not live in temples built by hands. And he is not served by human hands, as if he needed anything, because he himself gives all men life and breath and everything else. From one man he made every nation of men, that they should

> inhabit the whole earth; and he determined the times set for them and the exact places where they should live. God did this so that men would seek him and perhaps reach out for him and find him, though he is not far from each one of us. "For in him we live and move and have our being." As some of your own poets have said, "We are his offspring."[344]

It is no exaggeration to say that God loves you.

THE EXISTENCE OF GOD

This brings us to the last of our six essential questions: Prior to recent times, one of humankind's indubitable convictions was the existence of a God or gods. Atheism was relatively rare; evidence for a divine creation was held to be overwhelming. Today, people look at the same world and come to an entirely different conclusion, that life was not created but, rather, it evolved.

We observed that one core Enlightenment factor was its capacity to divide and conquer the prevailing worldview, shifting the emphasis from religion's areas of strength—conscience, morals, human values—to areas vulnerable when subjected to the naturalistic presuppositions of modern science. Significantly, in their attack on belief in a divine Creator, philosophers and scholars held the biblical documents to an invalid standard, one that disregarded its historical and cultural context and denied its accounts and claims.

The Genesis creation account stands out from the other ancient stories; scholars across the board recognize and acknowledge its remarkable uniqueness. Even so, it *was* put into written form during the time all the other creation stories were in use, and it came out of the same historical culture. (All the myths were about the emergence of order from chaos, light from darkness, and life from non-life.) That the Genesis narrative's form and structure follow ancient literary patterns, using the era's language and themes, should not surprise us; it was written in that setting and to an original audience, even as it has significance for all humankind in all times.

The account's particulars are not inconsistent with what we know of the universe: a beginning in time; a structured and orderly solar system; a world created to sustain life in the waters, in the air, and on land; and humans as intelligent, responsible moral agents. The story gives us religion's highest portrayals of humankind: we are made in the image of God. Once again, that term alone, which gives us incalculable worth, is the foundation upon which the Western world established its commitment to the value of human life.

Genesis was written to answer ancient-world questions—particularly those regarding the place of man in the created order and his relationship to God. The creation account presents a demythologized universe of rivers, oceans, plants, and animals that exist as natural objects and creatures instead of as gods, goddesses, and embodied spirits. Western science itself emerged from the desacralized universe of the Judeo-Christian worldview; since the objects in nature were not inherently sacred and untouchable, they could be examined, studied, and described.

In addition, the biblical view of nature has been confirmed by human experience. As we have seen, the intricacies of human nature, human spirituality, and human culture make God's existence essentially self-evident, which explains why roughly 80 percent of Western people still affirm it despite ongoing and intense secular indoctrination.[345]

❖ ❖ ❖ ❖

While all cultures have a religious viewpoint, their particular concepts of God vary immensely. Let's briefly summarize.

Animism posits that the gods and goddesses are finite beings who have come forth from the universe. The problem is that animism's gods are too small—they can't account for the universe itself but only for the localities in which they're served and worshiped. They are imminent, but they are not transcendent.[346]

Eastern mysticism maintains that "God" is too vast and mysterious for us to begin to describe or understand; He/It is completely incomprehensible and unknowable, transcendent but not imminent.[347] The vast gap between God and us is not just moral or spiritual but also epistemological; because we are not anything like (the impersonal) God, knowledge of Him/It and relationship with Him/It are impossible. Therein, the experience of "union with God" as described in Eastern and New Age philosophy is a purely subjective sense of the infinite, an experience of utter personal insignificance in the face of the universe's (impersonal) immensity.

In other words, to find God, we lose ourselves. On the face of it, this sounds like something that could resemble Christianity: for example, "If anyone would come after me, let him deny himself and take up his cross daily and follow me."[348]However, the self-denial Christ calls for differs dramatically from absorption into God. We do not lose our identity (or, eventually, our consciousness) when we surrender to Christ; we lay down our independence, our rebellion, and our isolation, and say to the Father, as Jesus did, "Not my will, but Thine, be done."[349]

In submitting to God, we find that our unique, personal identity is *enhanced* as we enter into the life He intended for us: "Whoever would his life will lose it, but whoever loses his life for my sake will save it."[350] In following Christ, we lay down our lower ways to follow God's higher ways. We no longer live just for ourselves—we live for Him and for those to whom He gives us and sends us.

God is personal; since He made us as personal beings, we are able to *know* Him.[351] This important biblical word[352] indicates that *humans have the capacity for connection with the Creator of the universe.* At this level, in contradiction to Kierkegaard, God is *not* "wholly other,"[353] and the wonderful promise of the good news is that, by His transforming grace, "we will be like Him,"[354] forever having a personal existence and a personal relationship with the one who made us.

❖ ❖ ❖ ❖

Modernism doesn't only deny that God can be known; it denies that God even exists. We as a culture don't say this directly—collectively, we give lip service to religion, or to the spiritual realm. However, in the totality of what we say and do, one message comes through loud and clear: no God was or is involved in the past or the present of our reality.

We noted that this denial is based upon the anti-supernaturalism of David Hume and the agnosticism of Immanuel Kant. We've also said much about the down-through-the-centuries societal results of their beliefs; now we will speak directly to the issue of knowledge. Specifically, as regards the questions we're posing and the answers we're seeking, how can we trust that it's possible to know—not just to believe, but to *know*?

---

[315] There are sources for this event at en.wikipedia.org/wiki/Air_Florida_Flight_90.

[316] Isaiah 59:9–11

[317] In Henry David Thoreau, Walden: Or, Life in the Woods (Boston: Ticknor and Fields, 1854).

[318] Romans 7:19

[319] Attributed. See Stendhal (Henri-Marie Beyle), The Red and the Black (orig. published 1830).

[320] Isaiah 59:15–16

[321] See 1 Corinthians 15:45–46; Romans 5:14–19.

[322] See John 3:14–21; Romans 5:5–8.

[323] 2 Peter 3:9

[324] Romans 2:4

[325] 1 Corinthians 15:53 NKJV

[326] 2 Corinthians 5:17

[327] 1 John 3:2

[328] Albert Camus, The Rebel (New York: Vintage Books, 1956).

[329] Francis Schaeffer, The Complete Works of Francis Schaeffer: A Christian Worldview, Volume 4: "A Christian View of the Church" (Crossway, 1985), 174.

[330] See Viggo Olsen, Daktar: Diplomat in Bangladesh (Grand Rapids: Kregel, 1996; orig. published 1973); and Daktar II: A Decade of Miracles in Bangladesh (Chicago: Moody, 1987). See more info on Viggo Olsen at www.inmed.us.

[331] Ronald W. Clark, The Huxleys (New York: McGraw-Hill, 1968), 118.

[332] See "The Man Who Dies Rich Dies Disgraced," Copyright 1998, Advanced Philanthropy, Winter 1997–1998, NSFRE, Alexandria, VA; also see The Gospel of Wealth (London: F. C. Hagen & Co., 1889).

[333] E.g., see www.humaniststudies.org.

[334] See www.humaniststudies.org on "Humanist Philanthropy."

[335] Officially, the Declaration on the Right to Insubordination in the War in Algeria: The Manifesto of the 121 (1960).

[336] Shinto means "Path of the Gods," or "Way of the Spirits."

[337] A similar process took place in the early 1950s when an influential Dalit (lit: "suppressed" or "oppressed") leader, Dr. B. R. Ambedkar, converted to Buddhism along with at least a million of his people. For more information, see the Dalit Freedom Network at www.dalitnetwork.org.

[338] Richard Tarnas, Cosmos and Psyche: Intimations of a New World View (New York: Viking, 2006).

[339] See Tom Abate, "Nobel Winner's Theories Raise Uproar in Berkeley," San Francisco Chronicle, 11/13/00; Shaoni Bhattacharya, "Stupidity Should Be Cured, Says DNA Discoverer," New Scientist News Service, 2/28/03; Victoria Macdonald, "Abort Babies With Gay Genes, Says Novel Winner," The Telegraph, 2/16/07; Richard Dawkins, "Letter: Women to Decide on Gay Abortion," The Independent, 2/19/07 (sample of related reading).

[340] "Speciesism," which seems to have been coined as a term by animal psychologist Richard Ryder, became widely known through Singer's writings.

[341] Singer's appointment to the faculty at Princeton drew wide protest because of his support of euthanasia for severely retarded children. See, for example, "The Singer Solution to World Poverty" at www.nytimes.com/library/magazine/home/19990905mag-poverty-singer.html.

[342] Matthew 10:30

[343] Psalm 139:3

[344] Acts 17:24–28 NIV

[345] Again, for instance, see www.gallup.com/poll/27877/Americans-More-Likely-Believe-God-Than-Devil-Heaven-More-Than-Hell.aspx.

[346] "Imminent" implies that they are local and accessible, and that some means of communion with them is available to us.

[347] "Transcendent" signifies that He/It exists far beyond and above us, and that there is a universal, eternal reality connected to Him/It.

[348] Jesus, in Luke 9:23 ESV

[349] Luke 22:42 KJV

[350] Jesus, in Luke 9:24 ESV

[351] E.g., see John 17:3; cf. John 8:32; 1 Corinthians 2:12; 2 Corinthians 4:5–6; Ephesians 1:15–17; Philippians 1:9–11; Colossians 2:1–3; 1 Timothy 2:3–4; 2 Peter 1:2–3; 1 John 2:3, 21; 4:7, 13,16; 5:2, 13, 20.

[352] Some form of the word "to know" is used over 350 times in the New Testament.

[353] See Søren Kierkegaard, Either/Or (orig. published 1843).

[354] 1 John 3:2

CHAPTER FOURTEEN

THE QUESTION OF KNOWLEDGE

A major motivation for this book was concern over the impact upon Western culture of Immanuel Kant, one of history's most influential philosophers. Kant's *Critique of Pure Reason*, which questioned the ability of unaided human reason to answer life's ultimate questions, eventually nudged entire cultures toward believing we have no option but to *not* know (agnosticism).[355] Contemporary pluralism is built upon this "conviction," that anything which includes transcendence is outside the realm of our understanding.

Out of this, our system of public education has come to place perhaps its highest emphasis on tolerance and diversity training. Educators are instructed to be religiously neutral, presenting various customs and traditions equilaterally for the sake of combating prejudice and promoting openness.[356] In some aspects this certainly has given children and adolescents a broader comprehension of and insight into more peoples and places of our world.

At the same time, though, teachers are not allowed to present a set of moral principles. This is a serious and ominous problem for the future of our society, one that flows from the legacy of Kant's epistemology. This is the problem of our perceived inability to know.

WHAT IS TRUTH?

Parents across the country are increasingly concerned about the education their children are receiving in America's public schools. Multitudes are choosing private schools or have turned to homeschooling. Many for whom these aren't viable options are in favor of a revised system that will allow them to send their children to schools that will support and teach their values; in other words, schools that don't divorce education from the realm of right and wrong.

Our culture's public and practical agnosticism becomes particularly apparent when a group or person stands up for a specific position (usually Christian) and professes to believe and live by its truth. By "pluralists," such "exclusivists" often are deemed to be "arrogant," "arbitrary," "highly presumptive," and even "morally repugnant."[357] They are considered arrogant and repugnant because they claim to *know* truth and because many of them seek to persuade others that there is truth that applies to us all.

Society's strident emphasis on pluralism in regard to religion means, in theory, that none is to be given preferential treatment, that all worldviews are to be presented as being equal, and that educators of whatever stripe are to share information from the vantage of being disinterested observers. In fact, however, religion primarily gets avoided for the sake of avoiding controversy or causing "offense." Under the banners of tolerance and secularism we have become willing to forsake the democratic principle of majority belief.

For instance, many generations of high school football fans in Texas communities have stood for a pregame public prayer. This tradition has been perfectly fitting, too, in communities where the vast majority of citizens are Christians. Nevertheless, recent court rulings have decreed such prayers to be unconstitutional and thus forbidden.[358] In order to protect an actual or theoretical minority (it may not even exist in many small towns), a judicial restriction is imposed that people haven't requested and haven't had opportunity to ratify.

❖ ❖ ❖ ❖

Earlier we observed that pluralism has led us into profound moral confusion, especially as we apply tolerance to choices about sexuality: from the homosexual lifestyle to transgender behavior (changing one's dress and orientation and even anatomy from male to female or vice versa) to bisexual activity (having sex partners of both genders). As well, moral relativism assumes either that absolute moral values do not exist or, if they do exist, that they cannot be known. While it can be challenging to connect so many dots over a period of time that covers centuries, our current quagmire really is the consequence of Kant's agnostic view of truth.[359]

The reason for the quagmire? *Agnosticism, the belief that real and reliable knowledge is impossible, is a cop-out.* Agnosticism refuses to examine critically the evidence that *is* available and instead hides behind the excuse of whether we ever can have absolute certainty of knowledge. Agnosticism, so often an ideological façade that serves as a justifier for immoral choices, is a selfish and immature construct.

For example, to reintroduce an illustration, our inability to describe everything within the larger square of the universe does not eliminate our responsibility to pay close attention to (or our capacity to learn from) what we find within the smaller circle of our understanding and experience. Yes, there are things we don't yet know. But what about everything we *do* know?

It's important—crucial, actually—that we are humble, not prideful, about the knowledge we have. And, no matter how much we learn, there always will be more that we haven't yet learned. But the imperfection or incompletion of our knowledge does not and will not keep us from living our lives successfully and rightly. As Albert Einstein (1879–1955) said, "God does not play dice with the universe."[360] We are blessed with remarkable senses that allow us to enjoy our world; regarding the nature of reality, it seems blatantly cynical, and it is consummately irresponsible, to deny that what those senses relay to our consciousness is real and relevant.

Again, some say we don't even "know" what's in the small circle of our experience. However, the declaration that this too is an illusion or an unreality flies in the face of the simplest and most reasonable conclusion: that the objective world is real, and that our senses give us an accurate picture of it. Those who claim it's all illusory can only do so in theory; in reality, like everyone else, they must look both ways before they cross the street.

❖ ❖ ❖ ❖

Nevertheless, we still face "the agnostic issue," a central factor in our commitment to pluralism. Agnosticism lies at the heart of relativistic, philosophical postmodernism, and it's positioned at the core of our society's religious and moral uncertainty. So how do we determine what, if anything, is true and what is false? Are we condemned to live in the world described in the book of Judges, where "everyone did what was right in his own eyes"?[361]

We've mentioned already that just about everyone develops a personal conclusion about the big square of reality from his or her little circle of learning and experience. As the age of science and reason progressed, the circle kept getting smaller and smaller until all that remained were those things that could be empirically verified. But this overlooked or rejected all abstract truths—love, justice, goodness, and so on that are clearly a part of human experience and deserve to be included in the circle of our known reality. The Enlightenment's shrinkage of our circle wasn't credible; people knew innately that love is real, that justice is real, that goodness is real, even though they can't be produced in a laboratory.

So, in response, many began to search outside reason and science to find the answers to the ultimate questions. We've talked about the counterculture that lives on in the New Age Movement; what once saw expression through drugs and mysticism now manifests in the radical skepticism of philosophical postmodernism. This is a broad and fervent attempt to expand the circle by looking for knowledge beyond unaided empiricism.

We've noted also that for this the counterculture turned from the assumptions of Western culture to seek answers in the worldviews of the East. In the 1950s, beatniks (the first manifestation of the counterculture made popular by the hippies) began studying Zen Buddhism, the most philosophical and yet the most non-rational of all the Eastern traditions. In succeeding years Westerners were taken with yoga and with Transcendental Meditation. They also followed gurus, from Maharishi Mahesh Yogi (1917–2008) to Sathya Sai Baba (b. 1926).

Without question, the Eastern and Western worlds take different approaches to knowledge.

KNOWLEDGE IN THE WEST

The West prides itself in rationality, objectivity, and science. Nonetheless, again, as Kant showed, human reason alone cannot provide absolute certainty of knowledge. For one thing, reason is limited by its instruments and its perspective. With all our technology, we still do not have the capability therein to answer many of the ultimate questions—the ones we've been addressing in this book.

Another limitation for the Western approach is that our growing knowledge is in a state of constant flux, as one well-educated (or not) hypothesis gets replaced by the next. We in the West would argue that this is essential in the pursuit of truth: a new and more developed idea or theory is almost always built upon a previous idea or theory. The process of critical examination and reformulation, which is at the heart of scientific progress, *has* led us to countless discoveries and breakthroughs. But there's another side to the story, one that relates to our concern for ultimate or final knowledge about reality. For all its claims to objectivity and rationality, the West is not always objective or rational in its approach to truth.

In the mid-nineteenth century, Ignaz Semmelweis (1818–1865), a Hungarian obstetrician practicing in Austria, was deeply concerned that so many women were dying from childbirth complications in his Vienna hospital. In fact, the mothers and their babies were contracting infections because the hospital staff went from one room to the next without cleaning their hands. At this time human knowledge of germs and bacteria was in its infancy, but this doctor conducted a simple experiment: he asked the doctors and nurses to wash their hands before and after they delivered a baby.

The results were dramatic—the numbers of women and babies dying in childbirth decreased substantially. So Semmelweis published the results and encouraged the practice of washing hands in all delivery rooms. Due to this he was made the laughingstock of the medical profession; doctors and hospitals everywhere rejected his study and its conclusion because of the widespread rejection of germ theory at that time. He died a broken man, even as his work laid the foundation for the antiseptic practices we take for granted today.[362]

The point is, "experts" are human and are subject to the same self-interest, stubbornness, prejudice, and laziness that can afflict us all. Pure objectivity is a myth. People often use reason to support erroneous beliefs; we are rationalists as much as we are reasoners, and so reason is not an infallible tool for the discovery of truth.

Science is as susceptible to bias, peer pressure, and conformity to popular opinion as any other endeavor of collective humanity. Recall once more my earlier insistence that the prejudice against intelligent design as an explanation for life's origin and the bias that favors evolutionary theory are *not* based on science. People are capable of using "science" in unscientific ways, and a scientist (or a thousand scientists) arguing that something is true doesn't make it so.

REDUCTIONISM AND RESPONSE

The Western approach to truth faces an additional shortcoming: once again, it makes the circle too small. It must deny or ignore a significant dimension of human experience—for instance, all the prayers, miracles, visions, and spiritual experiences of countless people. One central component of the modern Western approach to knowledge, methodological naturalism, also is rightly called *reductionism,* for it reduces "reality" to the purely physical and reduces man to a biomechanical machine driven by electrochemical impulses and stimuli. But we know intuitively that there is more to life than the physical. This is the agonizing frustration with Western rationalism: it cuts people in half.

There is an expanding insurgency against this paradigm; for example, we've noted that Scott Peck (1936–2005) and Theodore Roszak (b. 1933) broke rank with Western academia's naturalistic/objective consensus. Peck's *The Road Less Traveled,* written as a departure from naturalistic assumptions about the human personality, was subtitled "A New Psychology of Love, Traditional Values, and Spiritual Growth."[363]

Peck was part of a significant transition that's taking place in the psychological profession. For most of the twentieth century, Sigmund Freud was considered the patriarch of the field; a majority of psychologists worked from the starting point of his assumptions. Freud was an atheist who presented a sterile view of humankind; his reductionism led psychology into the wasteland of behaviorism,[364] wherein man becomes either a trainable animal or a programmable robot. Today, as the deeply dissatisfied West moves away from this mess, psychology has replaced Freud with Carl Jung (1875–1961), Freud's chief rival during the formative years of psychoanalysis.

Psychoanalysis took psychology into the realm of the unconscious, using hypnosis, dream interpretation, and other forms of evaluating subconscious motivations. The goal of psychoanalysis was to discover hidden motivations for outward behaviors in order to help people recover from deep-seated neuroses. And psychoanalysis would open the door to the modern era's therapeutic approach to psychology.

Freud, the "inventor" of psychoanalysis, had a naturalistic (non-supernatural) view of human nature. Somehow he clung to this presupposition even as he formulated his theories about the complexity of the nonmaterial facet of the human personality. In contrast, Jung, first Freud's student and then his colleague, took the evaluation of the subconscious to its logical conclusion: that it points to a spiritual reality behind human behavior and experience.

In short, Jung believed that a naturalistic view of man is inadequate; his research told him that man is a spiritual being as well. Initially Jung was widely perceived to be unscientific and even superstitious; it was Freud who became the father of modern psychology. Several decades later, though, Jung reemerged, this time as a powerful force for defining and comprehending the human personality. Among other things, the rediscovery of Jung, the writings of Peck, and the increasing use of Gestalt therapy[365] all are unmistakable signs of the rebellion against frozen rationalism in the study of the human soul.

Likewise, in the field of the social sciences, Theodore Roszak has written extensively on the need to break away from reductionism and pseudo-objectivity and thereby to rediscover the mystery within the universe. Roszak, a major proponent of a broader, more spiritual view of nature and of the human personality, considers the presuppositions of naturalistic science a tragedy that has made the Western world a spiritual desert. Presently he is a significant spokesman for neo-paganism and for environmentalism;[366] his work additionally reveals the presence of a cultural segment that's rejecting the former consensus.

> When we challenge the finality of objective consciousness as a basis for culture, what is at issue is the size of man's life. We must insist that a culture which negates or subordinates or degrades visionary experience commits the sin of diminishing our existence.[367]

Again, people *know* they are more than biochemical machines; we *know* that personality cannot be reduced to the firing of synapses and the stimulus/response mechanism. We dream, we create, we love, and we have longings this material world cannot satisfy. Reductionism fails to account for the mannishness of man. There is a depth to us that defies the objective-rationalist explanation.

Regarding humankind's religious experiences, the folly of the modernistic West has been its assumption that because it has no interest in spirituality and no willingness to expose itself to the realities that might be there, it gets the last word on the subject. This denial is based not on unbiased research but on a prejudicial commitment to the elimination of the metaphysical. The contemporary paranoia that's allegedly about "separating" church and state is based heavily upon the fear that secularism's house of cards will be swept away with exposure to (and exposure by) the truth.

This is the dynamic that somehow has managed to pervert our freedom *of* religion into freedom *from* religion. But too many people know the reality of spiritual experience—too many prayers have been answered, too many miracles have occurred—to allow secularism any chance of sweeping away humankind's spiritual affinities. "The fool has said in his heart, 'There is no God'"[368] is as applicable today as when it was written some three thousand years ago.

KNOWLEDGE IN THE EAST

The Eastern worldview, grounded in mysticism, considers the Western approach shallow and incomplete. Life is too mysterious to be known by our puny brains, and reality won't yield its mysteries to our microscopes and Geiger counters. Truth is discovered *subjectively* (by intuition and revelation), not objectively (by examination and experiment).

In the East, God *is* everything; everything (and everyone) is God. To discover the truth, we must get in touch with the universe within us—through meditation, self-denial, and physical discipline—to receive transcendental knowledge. Truth is not something we discover with our rational minds; it's something we experience in flashes of revelation. It is ultimately an intuition, an inner sense, some form of mystical experience.

In contrast to the objectivity of the West, the East seeks truth in the subjective (intuitive, spiritual) sphere of experience because it maintains that everything in the objective (natural, physical) sphere is an illusion. Hence, rather than seeking to expand upon the sphere of objective knowledge, the East wants to replace it with experience. Rivalry between the two spheres, Eastern and Western, was a catalyst in the birth of the counter-culture.

While it was more than a little countercultural propaganda, the early 70s TV show *Kung Fu* illustrated this worldview competition. Kwai Chang Caine, the young hero, an orphaned Westerner trained in the ways of the East, returns to the West to demonstrate Eastern superiority. Caine has been trained by a blind mentor who exhibits a metaphysical gift of "sight," catching fish by hand and snatching arrows from midair.

During one episode, Caine visits a small frontier town in the American West and, as usual, has none of the equipment—he doesn't ride a horse or use a gun. In this case he has a longbow, and while he is tall and slender and lacks broad shoulders or large biceps, he alone possesses the strength and skill to string it. One night, out in the corral, he's shooting arrows—with a fencepost as his target, a hundred yards away.

Such a feat would be nearly impossible in full daylight and unthinkable at night, yet Caine draws back the bow and hits his mark dead center. A local cowboy he has befriended hollers in amazement, "How'd you do that?"

In the Western worldview everything is rational and explainable. Feats are accomplished through (for instance) technique, skill, and training. However, because Caine lives in the realm of mystery, he answers, "It is not done." His success isn't based on how rigid he keeps his left arm, on the perfection of his anchor points, or on the smoothness of his release. The rational Caine, the Caine of the West, isn't shooting the bow. The Caine of the East has released conscious control of the bow to make the impossible shot.

When he proceeds to string another arrow and it too strikes the distant post, the cowboy is completely befuddled. "I don't understand!" he bellows.

Caine's patient, Eastern-man reply is, "When you do not understand, then you will know."

This is the essence of Eastern philosophy: true understanding comes from intuition and insight. Caine isn't shooting a bow; he's engaged in a mystical experience. The experience doesn't need to be explained or comprehended—it simply must be undergone.[369]

SPIRITUAL STRENGTH: OVERSTATED AND UNDERESTIMATED

There are problems with this approach to knowledge. For one thing, its powers are greatly exaggerated and commonly misappropriated. Take the *Kung Fu* example: like countless similar visual-media accomplishments, it's entertaining fantasy. The actor, David Carradine, himself a devotee of Eastern philosophy, didn't actually shoot the arrows into the post; he could have meditated himself into a coma and not been able to hit that faraway target in the dark. The feat was an illusion, accomplished in a Western way—through technology. It was a trick, a result of special effects. The producers and directors could tell us exactly *how* the illusion of shooting the arrow into the fencepost was achieved.

Furthermore, Eastern philosophy and its close relative, the occult, invite deception. Spiritism, probably from its beginnings, has drawn countless ventriloquists and sleight-of-hand tricksters.[370] The New Age Movement has become a fertile field for con artists who seek to dupe the unsuspecting.

One internationally known "psychic," Uri Geller, who appeared on a national talk show to demonstrate his allegedly extrasensory powers, proceeded to bend a metal spoon. The skeptic James Randi, determined to expose the falsehood of such claims, then demonstrated how the spoon had been prepared beforehand and how the trick was accomplished. Later, Geller was invited back, and when presented with normal spoons to which he'd had no access before the program, his powers vanished. (He claimed there was too much "interference" in the room.)[371]

I am not saying, as those fully committed to the Western worldview must, that actions like these are all deceptions, even though a great many of them are. The supernatural *is* real; there is too much evidence in human experience to deny it. Yet such power is not easily gained and it *cannot* be controlled or predicted. As anyone who has spent time in an animistic culture knows, people do not control the spirits—the spirits control people.

Mark Andrew Ritchie's book *Spirit of the Rainforest*, a fascinating study of shamanism in South America, speaks of the power and reality of the spirits within these animistic societies; the story is told from the perspective of the men directly involved with the spirits. One of the universals of shamanism, documented by many sources (including Ritchie's book), is that shamans do not choose their profession. Shamans are chosen and called by the spirits.

This choosing takes place through a life-changing encounter between an individual and a spirit. The spirits go on to establish a lifelong relationship with their chosen ones, giving instructions, warnings, and even personal encounters. These servants recognize their place and role: they may earn "rewards" for services rendered, but the spirits are completely in charge, and the humans must do their bidding.

The idea of a magician who controls the forces beyond the physical world and bends them to his will is a fantasy of Western literature. We speak glibly of "white" magic and "black" magic in our toying with beings whose strength and intent we scarcely understand. The people who live daily in awareness of "magical" powers tell a different tale.

> The village in the jungle by the big grasslands was responsible for many children dying in our village. Toucan, their shaman, was a fierce warrior, who had killed many men. He continued to kill children in our village, and each time I killed a child in his.... I have never been to Shooting Village, but I know a lot about what happens there because I have visited so many times in the Spirit world when I kill their children. It is part of a shaman's work.... All shaman know that the spirits are happiest when we kill people.[372]

The actual realm of magic is an awful place, filled with terror, violence, shame, regret, and death. This is the arena of what the Bible calls "deceiving spirits."[373] beings who herd human disciples into cruel and fatal bondages. The Eastern/mystical world is *not* an abode of tranquility and fulfillment. A person naively exposing himself to the occult might just as well cut himself up and dive into a pool of piranhas.

THE IRRATIONALITY OF ILLUSION

In addition, the Eastern approach to knowledge is irrational. Devotees are often told to reject what their conscious mind is telling them and to operate on blind faith. Many exercises, like mantras, meditation, and yoga, are intended to empty the mind and thus open the spirit to mystical encounter. One has no way of knowing where the experiences are coming from, from good or from evil, from deceiving spirits or from friendly spirits ... or simply a figment of imagination. Cut off from reason, the East can neither confirm nor deny experience. It cannot even ask, how do I know these things are true? It cannot look to history or to evidence for validation.

What is more, many mystical experiences cannot be explained, so while they can be used to affirm anything, in the end they affirm nothing. With so many mystical philosophies in the world, how does experience validate any of them? If we say it validates them all, we are right back at contemporary relativistic agnosticism.

And so the East is syncretistic, denying each religion's claims to authority and claiming that all paths lead to God. Subjectivity cannot produce certainty because one experience is as good as another; without any objectivity, all experiences must be considered equally valid. In the East, religions cannot be compared by historical development, theology, or ethics—they must be held as various sources of mystical reality and nothing more.

As for syncretism, thorough examination of disparate beliefs leads to distinction and contradiction. The East denies contradiction and distinction as "illusion," just as it denies the reality of the physical world. This is a major weakness, this demand that we deny what's so central to our experience.

Carlos Castaneda (1925–1998), in writing about his relationship with a Mexican shaman, tells of several powerful experiences using the shaman's psychedelic drugs. Once, after coming down from his hallucination, he asked the shaman, "Did I really fly?"[374] With mystical encounters, aside from the strength of their impact, we must ask, what is their connection to reality? How do we know they're anything but an experience? How do we connect the effect (the experience) to a cause—most importantly, how do we connect it to what or who has revealed itself/himself to us?

❖ ❖ ❖ ❖

Nevertheless, anyone who approaches a mystical worldview with something of an open mind *will* find much that cannot be explained away. People have beliefs because they have real reasons for believing. Spirit-possession, trances, visions, and other supernatural experiences are widespread. One example is Shirley MacLaine (b. 1934), a skeptical Westerner who experienced phenomena among Peruvian spiritists that convinced her of the metaphysical reality and led her to become one of the leading New Age advocates in the United States.

We must not (as modernism has attempted) deny the worldview of the East. It truly won't go away. James Randi has offered a large cash reward to anyone who performs a "miracle" that he can't reproduce as a trick or prove is not an illusion. But much of what is most significant in mysticism does not have a physical manifestation. It isn't a conjurer using a wand to find water or Sai Baba filling a clay pot with ash produced from his hand that convinces people of Eastern mysteries; they're won over by premonitions, by dreams, or by other inner experiences that cannot be explained.

❖ ❖ ❖ ❖

Those committed to the Western worldview must deny the existence of anything supernatural. There is high arrogance related to their confidence in naturalism; they believe they have exposed the East and the New Age as frauds. For example, one oft-quoted study, done by a preteen girl, was an examination of nurses who used "healing touch" to sense a patient's aura and enhance recovery.[375] The girl simply wanted to determine if the nurses could sense any "aura" emanating from her hands. She placed them behind a screen, so they couldn't see her; they were to put their hands through the screen, and the girl would place her hand in proximity of either their left hand or their right hand. The nurses then were to tell her which of their hands her hand was next to.

The study showed the same results as a series of random guesses, demonstrating that the nurses could not, in a scientifically verifiable way, sense a patient's aura. It was published in a prestigious medical journal; even so, nurses continue to use—and nursing schools continue to teach—healing touch therapy. Like everything else in mysticism, there is anecdotal and experiential evidence to support it. It may not follow the rules of Western rationalism or observation science, but therein is a power and a hope, even a reality, that many find undeniable.

Virtually anyone who has spent extended time in the non-Western world has seen phenomena that cannot be explained by natural causes: trances, ordeals, spirit-possession… the list goes on. There is a reality that the West denies only out of ignorance. *However,* the supernatural reality of the East remains the realm of the irrational. Again, the mystic doesn't know the source of his or her experience, and "even Satan disguises himself as an angel of light."[376] This is the realm of deception, even and especially on the spiritual level. Deceiving spirits, demons pretending to be angels, lure human subjects into pernicious and deadly snares.

❖ ❖ ❖ ❖

So, where are we? If the rationality of the West has given no satisfactory answers to the primary questions of life, and if the mysticism of the East is ultimately deceptive and irrational, where do we turn? If neither the West nor the East has the truth, then who does?

THE THIRD OPTION

There is another alternative, one that is neither West nor East but rather is both. It has often been accused of being Western but isn't—in fact, it was first discovered and upheld in the East. Nonetheless, this view values reason and stands for objective truth; it's really just a matter of common sense.

The truth must be reasonable; it must be supported by objective evidence, whether historical, scientific, and/or logical. *Also,* the truth must be confirmed by human experience, even when that experience could be termed "mystical." In fact, without mystical confirmation, we have every right to question the validity of our belief. *Truth leads not just to understanding (West) but also to enlightenment (East).* Passionless knowledge has always been the bane of the West—knowing facts while seldom experiencing truth.

To return to our analogy of knowledge, rather than replacing the Western sphere with the Eastern sphere, it makes more sense to pursue both, because wisdom says that history and experience have clearly verified elements within both spheres. Science has changed the world and in the process confirmed the validity of many of its findings. The spiritual realm has been confirmed by the profound needs, aspirations, and realizations of all humankind.

Therefore, consider a view that includes elements of the two spheres into one expanded perspective. This alternative is Christianity, which stands apart from all other religions in that (1) it claims to be historical and that (2) its claim to historical accuracy is based on reasonable evidence, not just on the authority of its founder or of its book. The written record of Jesus Christ's life and ministry professes to be the testimony of eyewitnesses. Their documents name names and describe places; they date events using methods typical of their era.

The result is that their writings can be examined using the standard tests for any historical document. Christianity does not call people to blind or irrational faith but rather to examine the evidence and come to a reasoned faith. Of course, on top of the historical record, there are many other objective reasons for believing in Christ.

One of these is apologetics, the study of reasonable evidence for belief. An important part of Christian education and theology, apologetics is testimony to the rationality of the gospel. And writers such as C. S. Lewis (e.g., *Mere Christianity*), Francis Schaeffer (e.g., *The God Who is There*), and Josh McDowell (e.g., *Evidence that Demands a Verdict*) have pointed untold thousands of people to Christ.

IT'S NOT EITHER/OR—IT'S BOTH/AND

But Christianity is not just an ideology to be believed—it's not an abstract theology or a set of religious rituals. The moment a person places wholehearted faith in Christ, he or she is transformed. Jesus describes conversion as a momentous, life-changing experience and uses a special term to describe it: the one who puts his trust in Christ is "*born again.*"[377] Conversion is meant to be truly transcendental, and millions of converts—I include myself in this group—will tell you the power of this rebirth in describing when they became believers.

For those who do not have a dramatic conversion experience, there nonetheless will be, over time, changes in attitude, heart, and outlook that confirm God's grace at work in their lives. C. S. Lewis, for one, describes his very rational conversion in his autobiography. Lewis came to Christ expecting no spectacular event, but over time, he became, as the title of his book says, "surprised by joy."[378]

We've heard the apostle describe it thus: "If anyone is in Christ, he is a new creature; the old things passed away; behold, new things have come."[379] Elsewhere he goes further in describing this profound spiritual transformation in which people are, from that time forward, indwelt by God's Spirit.

> You have not received a spirit of slavery leading to fear again, but you have received a spirit of adoption as sons by which we cry out, "Abba! Father!"
>
> The Spirit himself bears witness with our spirit that we are children of God.[380]

Faith in Jesus Christ leads not just to knowledge (in the Western sense) but also to enlightenment (in the Eastern sense). We know in our hearts, not only in our heads, and this makes all the difference; our confidence is in both experience *and* evidence.

❖ ❖ ❖ ❖

Christianity claims to be a revealed faith, maintaining that the Bible's moral and spiritual principles are a gracious gift from God himself.

> No prophecy was ever produced by the will of man, but men spoke from God as they were carried along by the Holy Spirit.[381]

Revelation would be just another untestable religious claim but for the fact that it impinges upon and flows through history. Daniel declared that it would be sixty-nine "weeks" of years from the decree to restore Jerusalem (which most take to be the fifth-century BCE command of the Persian ruler Artaxerxes) until "Messiah will be cut off" (His rejection by the people).[382] As New Testament scholar Hugh Schonfield (1901–1988) said, this prophecy produced "Messianic Fever" in first-century Israel.[383]

In the same way, Isaiah foretold Christ's rejection by God's chosen people, His death by "piercing" and "scourging," and His role as the sin-bearer and redeemer.[384] By means of these and hundreds of other specific prophecies, the claims of revelation can be tested, and thus the principle of revelation stands as the connecting point between the objective and the subjective, between reason and faith.

Christians have no reason not to be clearheaded about their belief. Peter wrote, "We did not follow cleverly devised tales when we made known to you the power and coming of our Lord Jesus Christ, but we were eyewitnesses of His majesty."[385] The uniqueness and power of Christ's magnificent revelation is that it isn't mystical but, rather, *in and through history*. At the same time, it leads to an individual revelation within each person who accepts its claims and obeys its instructions to place faith in Him.

❖ ❖ ❖ ❖

Following Christ is both objective and subjective. It stands as the fulfillment of our aspiration; it is rational and it is spiritual, and thus it meets all our deepest needs. This is what we would expect of that which is true—that it is *holistically* true, that it meets the needs of the mind and of the spirit.

Christianity has always balanced between its Western influence and its Eastern roots. Each generation has seen various groups emphasize one side over the other to the detriment of the faith. When belief becomes too rational it can become empty and lifeless; when it becomes too mystical it can lose the accountability necessary to prevent excess and deception. Every generation must walk the fine line between head and heart, logic and experience. Faith and reason are never an either/or proposition—*both* are absolutely necessary for a balanced and complete life.

Jesus said it best: "They that worship him [God] must worship in spirit and in truth."[386] In an authentic life of faith, truth—that which squares with objective reality—cannot be ignored any more than can the inner workings of the Spirit. The theologian Clark Pinnock (b. 1937) says, "The heart cannot embrace what the mind is not convinced is true."[387] Mind and heart: *each* must be vitally involved in the pursuit of truth.

---

[355] Immanuel Kant, Critique of Pure Reason (Mineola, NY: Barnes & Noble, 2004; orig. published 1781).

[356] See, for example, tolerance.org, a website of the Southern Poverty Law Center.

[357] See Stanford Encyclopedia of Philosophy, "Religious Diversity (Pluralism)" (Stanford, CA: Revised July 2007).

[358] For instance, see "Supreme Court bans student-led prayers at football games" (June 19, 2000) at Freedomforum.org.

[359] Stanford Encyclopedia of Philosophy, op. cit. Here Philip Quinn describes the difference between a pre-Kantian view, in which truth can be assumed to be knowable, and the post-Kantian world where ultimate truth is inaccessible. In such a world, according to Quinn, exclusivist claims must be modified.

[360] Albert Einstein, "Letter to Max Born" (12/4/26) in The Born-Einstein Letters, Irene Born, trans. (New York: Walker and Co., 1971).

[361] Judges 21:25

[362] See Canadians for Health Research, at www.chrcrm.org/main, "Pioneers in Science & Medicine: Joseph Lister (1827–1912); Future Health, 1994.

[363] M. Scott Peck, The Road Less Traveled: 25th Anniversary Edition (Carmichael, CA: Touchstone Books, 2003).

[364] Behaviorism claims to be "the scientific study of human behavior." As a field of psychology, behaviorism seeks to ignore a person's inner mental state in favor of external factors as the explanation for behavior. The emphases are on stimulus/response, positive and negative reinforcement, and behavioral training as the means of changing or controlling human behavior. Most famous adherents: Ivan Pavlov (1849–1936) and B. F. Skinner (1904–1990). Behaviorism's biggest flaw: it assumes no distinction between humankind and the animals, alleging that the principles of animal training can and should be applied to people. (See Stanford Encyclopedia of Philosophy, "Behaviorism.")

[365] Gestalt is a holistic approach to therapy that endeavors to help the patient see his present condition and understand it, as it is in the moment, so that he can make the necessary changes to move forward. Gestalt, which looks at the whole person as well as his networks of relationships, developed under the influence of existential philosophy and Eastern religion, in particular Taoism and Zen Buddhism (see "An Overview of the Theory of Gestalt Therapy" at www.g-gej.org).

[366] Neo-paganism, an eclectic movement primarily influenced by animism, Wicca, and occultism, has influenced environmentalism with a more spiritual view of nature. The two are combined in eco-paganism, through its emphasis on the sanctity of the earth and of nature. This outlook directly contradicts the Enlightenment-scientific model that presents nature as an entirely material (non-spiritual) reality.

[367] Roszak, The Making of a Counter-Culture, 234.

[368] Psalm 14:1

[369] The apologist Winkie Pratney (b. 1944) presented the basic details of this narrative to the youth group of Bethany Missionary Church in Minneapolis, 1980.

[370] 16 Isaiah's mention of "the mediums and the spiritists who whisper and mutter" (Isaiah 8:19) seems to refer to their practice of changing their voice to convince

their listeners. This is not unlike the works of modern channelers who, through trickery and ventriloquism in their séances, assume different voices when they claim to be possessed.

[371] For example, see "Uri Geller and His Spoon-Bending Fraud" at skepdic.com.

[372] Mark Andrew Ritchie, Spirit of the Rainforest: A Yanomamo Shaman's Story (Chicago: Island Lake Press, 1966), 67, 69.

[373] E.g., see 1 Timothy 4:1 NIV.

[374] In Carlos Castaneda, The Teachings of Don Juan: A Yaqui Way of Knowledge (Berkeley: University of California Press, 2008; orig. published 1968).

[375] In 1998, Emily Rosa, then eleven years old, proposed the double-blind experiment to test healing touch; her study was later published in the Journal of the American Medical Association (see en.wikipedia.org/wiki/Therapeutic_Touch).

[376] 2 Corinthians 11:14

[377] See John 3:3–8.

[378] In C. S. Lewis, Surprised by Joy: The Shape of My Early Life (New York/London: Harcourt Brace, 1956).

[379] 2 Corinthians 5:17

[380] Romans 8:15–16

[381] 2 Peter 1:21 ESV

[382] See Daniel 9:24–27.

[383] See Hugh Schonfield, The Passover Plot: A New Interpretation of the Life and Death of Jesus (London: Hutchinson, 1965). Schonfield attempted in this book to contradict the Christian claims about Jesus, yet his work in many ways served to confirm Christ's uniqueness. It also confirmed the validity of the Resurrection as the best explanation for the changed lives of the disciples and their subsequent mission in establishing the church through the world.

[384] See Isaiah 53.

[385] 2 Peter 1:16

[386] John 4:24 KJV

[387] In Clark H. Pinnock, Set Forth Your Case: An Examination of Christianity's Credentials (Nutley, NJ: The Craig Press, 1967).

CHAPTER FIFTEEN

DOES CHRISTIANITY REALLY WORK?

The Bible says, "I am not ashamed of the gospel, for it is the power of God for salvation to everyone who believes."[388] Here Paul conveys that faith in Christ will bring supernatural change in our lives. The New Testament reveals the promises of remarkable peace,[389] complete removal of guilt,[390] and a renewed mind,[391] to name just a few. The question is, are these mere religious claims, or are they real experiences in the lives of real people? As Francis Schaeffer put it, is Christianity "true" truth, or is it only a pipe dream?[392]

One of the most important aspects of evangelical Christianity is that each practitioner has a personal "testimony." Evangelical faith is founded upon an individual human response to the divine promises of the gospel. Theoretically, every evangelical has been "converted" to faith in Jesus. Even children of evangelicals, at baptism, which usually occurs during the teenage years, are asked to describe the process by which they came to believe and to speak of the difference Jesus has made in their lives.

In other words, every evangelical Christian can share his or her story of conversion in terms of the miraculous changes he or she has personally experienced. In previous generations, one staple of the weekly evening church service was a time for congregants to share their testimonies of conversion and of the ongoing miraculous work of God in their lives. Without question, conversion is the common thread that sustains and perpetuates the faith. Remember that Christianity is not only historical and rational, it is also experiential and subjective. Conversion is an experiential dimension of Christian knowledge.

PROMISES AND OUTCOMES

It's illuminating to compare the list of New Testament promises with the common themes from testimonies of individual believers. For example, Christ-followers are promised a peace that "surpasses all comprehension."[393] Peace is a remarkably common, perhaps almost universal element of conversion. Typically a person will say something like, "After I prayed to receive Jesus, I felt an amazing peace flood through me."

Also, new believers frequently say, "When I gave my life to Jesus, I felt as if a great burden of guilt had been lifted from me." Another common conversion-experience phenomenon is the feeling of having been forgiven. John Wesley (1703–1791), for example, wrote of his conversion: "I felt my heart strangely warmed, I felt I did trust in Christ, Christ alone, for salvation; and an assurance was given me that he had taken away my sins, even mine, and saved me from the law of sin and death."[394]

Conversion has been documented—with startlingly consistency—in all times and in all parts of the world over the many centuries since the birth of the church. The writings of the church fathers show their experiences to be similar to those in the Middle Ages and up to the present time. Augustine's fourth-century description is similar to Raymond Lull's in the thirteenth century and to Nicky Cruz's in the twentieth. This gives strong credence to conversion as truly a transaction between God and people.

The gospel promises that believers have "the love of God … poured out within our hearts."[395] Thus, an experience related to conversion is that of being filled with love, first with God's love for us and then with a love that enables us to love others. Countless Christians can speak to this amazing reality. They feel loved and are able to give love to a level and degree they'd never known before.

A close look at the lives of believers reveals many details that seem unassailably supernatural. I am convinced that the validating experiences related to conversion produce the profound conviction that takes root in so many evangelicals. I remember my father's concern that after I converted I also became what he termed "a religious fanatic." Jesus and the truths of the gospel had become so utterly real, to me and in me.

One of the most crucial confirmations of genuine conversion is that it isn't dependent upon mood, music, or manipulation. Sadly, too much of what passes for evangelism in many churches has elements of manipulation. Jesus himself implied that an emotional experience is not necessarily a conversion experience, warning His disciples of the seed sown in unprepared soil.

> The one on whom seed was sown in the rocky places, this is the man who hears the word and immediately receives it with joy;
>
> yet he has no firm root in himself, but is only temporary, and when affliction or persecution arises because of the word, immediately he falls away.[396]

At the least, conversion cannot be *only* an emotional experience; it also must be an act of the will, a considered commitment to live for God, followed by a real transaction with Him, a trading of our life for His.

The most powerful experiences are the ones for which there is no alternative explanation. When no preacher is speaking, when no music is playing, when we're alone with no one watching—in those times, when God breaks into our consciousness, we know without any doubt that it truly is Him.

As well, conversions are often cold-blooded transactions between the Creator and the created. C. S. Lewis said,

> In the Trinity Term of 1929 I gave in, and admitted that God was God, and knelt and prayed: perhaps, that night, the most dejected and reluctant convert in England.[397]

Lewis's initial dejection was based on his realization that in believing upon God, he was surrendering his personal autonomy: God was now calling the shots. As he would later discover, though, his surrender to divine authority would reveal to him and ignite within him what he never expected: *joy*. He would describe this delight, of which any earthly pleasure is only a weak imitation, as that which he had desired all his life.[398] He did not begin searching for joy—he simply surrendered to the truth.

❖ ❖ ❖ ❖

Regarding the human tendency to fake religious/supernatural experience, we must realize that those encounters with God that have not been connected to human manipulation or manufacturing have the weightiest impact precisely because there is no confusion about the source. The Chinese preacher Watchman Nee (1903–1972) wrote extensively about this:

> We ought to remember that there is a thing before God called reality. The difficulty with many Christians is that they try to manufacture it. They attempt to produce this reality before God. With the result that they copy or imitate. What God requires, though, is trueness—the real thing manifested in our lives.[399]

For every doctrine of faith in Jesus, there is a corresponding reality. It's critical that we don't merely understand the teachings rationally and then fail to enter into the experiential reality that they explain. The understanding is an important *first* step that leads to faith (a conviction about the unseen), which, in turn, brings about the reality of which the doctrine speaks.

This is exactly what we mean by *conversion*: the discovery of the supernatural experience of God's saving grace. In the process of leading someone to faith in Christ, one chief concern of the evangelist is to see the signs of a real transaction with God. These effects may not happen right away, but in true conversion there *will* be real changes in the person's life that can only be explained as God's work.

These changes, too, are what we mean by a "testimony." I believe they are one of the means by which we become Christ's "witnesses."[400] By our firsthand interaction with the Lord, we are able to reveal to a skeptical culture the reality of the gospel's promises. Our experience of Christ makes the good news far more than words; knowing Him, and filled with His Spirit, we can stand as beacons of hope in a world filled with darkness.

SKEPTICAL EXPLANATIONS FOR CONVERSION

During his campaign for the US presidency, Jimmy Carter (b. 1924) gave an interview to *Playboy* in which he declared that he was a born-again Christian. Evangelicals knew what he was talking about: he was describing his conversion experience using the words of Jesus, who told the Pharisee Nicodemus that to enter God's kingdom he must be "born again."[401] For many other people, though, this was the first time they heard the term, and Carter's use of it created a level of curiosity.

Many either ignored it or made it into a joke, but Carter's statement nevertheless placed the specifics of Christian conversion into the public arena. For those who denied Christ's claims and/or who maintained that all religion is a manmade fantasy, this posed a dilemma. Here was a highly respected public figure claiming to have had a life-changing experience that validates not only the existence of God but also the truthfulness of the gospel. Now, if one wishes to dispute the validity of Christianity, he must be able to explain conversion, the means by which belief in Jesus has spread across the world and is the most embraced faith on earth. As one would expect, critics *have* attempted to find non-supernatural explanations.

"ADOLESCENT CRISIS"

Within weeks of Carter's interview, the journalist Bill Moyers (b. 1934) also presented a documentary on evangelical culture in the American South and, in particular, on the born-again phenomenon. His conclusion was that conversion is an emotional reaction to the confusion and guilt of adolescence, and that in "finding" Christ, teenagers find temporary relief from the anxieties related to puberty and young adulthood. Moyers himself claimed to have received Christ as a teen but said that now, as an adult, he understood the true origin of the experience.[402]

Moyers is not the first to give this explanation; psychologist G. Stanley Hall (1844–1924), historian E. T. Clark (1886–1966), and others have presented the view. Proponents of the adolescent-crisis theory believe that teenagers are vulnerable and easily manipulated by older evangelists; allegedly, because they have high anxiety related to the myriad changes of adolescence, and because they're more emotional and more subject to mood swings than adults, they thus are "open" to the evangelical message of forgiveness, peace, and joy.

The first problem with this argument is that conversion experiences aren't just emotional—there are transcendental elements that cannot be explained away as "the up-and-down of feelings." For instance, prayers are answered, attitudes are changed, habits are broken, addictions are overcome, and new believers receive an inner awareness of communion with God as an ongoing reality. Adult believers do not "outgrow" their faith precisely because they know there is much more involved than just release from teenage guilt. In this area, Moyers is part of a minority: most adults who became Christians as teens continue to uphold their convictions for the rest of their lives.

Furthermore, while within our culture the majority of evangelicals embrace faith during adolescence, this isn't the case in other societies. In most of the rest of the world, conversion is an adult phenomenon, and the same could be said historically: for instance, the Great Awakening, the Wesleyan Revival, and other such movements have taken place among adults. "Adolescence" itself is a modern invention that did not exist prior to the twentieth century; it's the extension of childhood past the age when previous generations were considered adults (thirteen-plus).

The primary reason most *North Americans* become Christians either as children or as adolescents is that churches focus their evangelistic ministry on those ages. Most US churches put on a vacation Bible school, send youth to summer Bible camps, and focus Sunday school and youth groups on leading young people to Christ. Because at this point we do not have corresponding outreach to adults, we should not be surprised that we primarily still reach youth.

A case in point is the late-twentieth-century emergence of "seeker-friendly" churches, the most well-known of which is in Illinois. Willow Creek began with a desire to reach the unchurched adults in their community. Accordingly, they designed their Sunday morning service to speak to local needs and concerns. The results have been dramatic: Willow Creek has become one of the nation's largest churches, and its model of adult evangelism is being widely applied elsewhere. The point is, conversion is neither just an adolescent phenomenon nor just an emotional experience.

"OVERSENSITIVITY"

When the pragmatist philosopher William James (1842–1910) examined religious experiences, his conclusion was a variation on Freud's view that religion is a result of human wish-fulfillment and a reaction against the fear of death. James' studies led him to posit that there are two classes of people in the world: "healthy souls" and "sick souls." He wasn't necessarily making a value judgment by these two terms; he would not, in the end, say that a so-called healthy soul was superior to a sick soul. He was trying to describe the *self-image* of the two groups: Healthy souls are those who have little sense of felt need, believing they are self-sufficient, while sick souls are well aware of their inadequacies.[403]

In many ways, James stated the obvious: religious converts *are* those who realize the necessity for God in their lives. The greatest need he identified among the "sick souls" was their clear awareness of guilt, a primary factor in their coming to Christ. Again, this is stating the obvious, for, as Jesus said in rebuking the Pharisees (self-perceived "healthy souls" who lived contentedly in self-righteousness), "It is not those who are healthy who need a physician, but those who are sick."[404]

The Pharisees were critical of Jesus for associating with "sinners," but it is to sinners—to *everyone*—that Jesus has come. The Pharisees were just as grievously sinful as those they criticized; Jesus pointed out their hypocrisy, selfishness, greed, and injustice on numerous occasions. They were unwilling to acknowledge it—their "health" was a delusion, and they needed salvation as much as each of us does.

The message is plain: "All have sinned and fall short of the glory of God."[405] Every person stands in need of His forgiveness and grace. Ironically, those who confess their need, those who are willing to be authentic and vulnerable, acknowledging their spiritual sickness—*they* receive healing and are made whole.

❖ ❖ ❖ ❖

By necessity, Christian conversion must deal with guilt and sin, humankind's greatest existential problems. Psychologists say that the number one psychosis among people is a deep burden of guilt. Whole libraries of books have been written and billions of dollars have been spent in attempting to remove guilt from our lives.

Why? Why are we so plagued by guilt? If reality is amoral and purposeless, why does man have such a strong sense of morality? Why do we feel bad when we do things that deep down we believe are wrong? This burden can't be written off as a product of social conditioning; people with little or no moral training still experience guilt. Despite many years of relativistic drift and the widespread denial of moral standards, we've been unable to eliminate human inhibition. In fact, more people than ever are struggling with depression and a lack of self-worth.

"WISH-FULFILLMENT"

Earlier we mentioned Sigmund Freud's view of religion: that it is a prop for those feeble people who are unable or unwilling to face the reality of a purely natural universe. He felt that religious belief is driven by—and, in fact, arises from—humankind's fear of death; to soothe ourselves, we invented a heavenly father figure who would protect us from the terror of the end of personal existence. Freud maintained that people turn to religion for the emotional comfort it provides, but that it's all a delusion.

Problematically, though, the religions of the world (Freud wasn't just speaking about Christianity) are not very comforting. Many require extraordinary sacrifices for seemingly little reward. Animistic religions are founded on fear of the damage that spirits can do to those who don't pacify them; Eastern mysticism is built around fear of life more than fear of death.

Pointedly, too, one would hardly invent the theistic God to salve the fear of death. His perfect, utter holiness, for fallen man, is a *cause* of the fear of death. He's no cosmic Santa Claus; His moral governorship of the universe requires atonement for transgressions. Yes, the gospel provides wondrous comfort, but at the price of a deep and abiding commitment. It is *not* wishful thinking for a rebellious human to lay down personal autonomy and receive Christ.

"GULLIBILITY"

Many believe that conversion occurs among the gullible, those who are not sufficiently intelligent or rational to discriminate between reality and fantasy, and who, therefore, are easily manipulated. In some respects, this is a left-handed way of saying Christians aren't too bright, and this aspersion has followed the faith almost from its inception. The Roman critic Celsus (c. CE second century), for example, called the early believers "only worthless and contemptible people, idiots, slaves, poor women, and children."[406]

To many in the post-Enlightenment world, the very act of belief seems irrational. People have been reluctant to place faith in what they can't see, hear, or touch; religion seems to require a willingness to suspend doubt. Jesus said as much to His followers: "Unless you are converted and become like little children, you will not enter the kingdom of heaven."[407] On the surface it can seem counterintuitive—God is nowhere to be seen.

Is religion only for the naïve? No. A look at the church reveals that countless intelligent people have followed Jesus. In the twentieth century alone, men and women such as C. S. Lewis, G. K. Chesterton (1874–1936), Malcolm Muggeridge (1903–1990), Francis Schaeffer, Madeleine L'Engle (1918–2007), John Stott (b. 1921), and Ruth Tucker (b. 1945) have shown that people of great learning and brilliance do believe. In previous generations, many of history's most amazing intellects have been Christians. Furthermore, as a result of their work and their writings, untold millions of others have been enabled to see the credibility of and evidence for the faith.

The contemporary argument that Jesus-followers are gullible is rooted in the arrogance of Western popular culture. Our pride says that we are to be sophisticated, "scientific," and even cynical. To some extent, the church has always been a counterculture, but as society has moved increasingly toward secularism, the separation has become even more pronounced. Religious faith is entirely out of step with how people want to be perceived by others; hence, culturally, believers often are the equivalent of junior high nerds.

All the same, once again, the notion that Christianity is irrational and unscientific is not based on actual facts; it's a social prejudice based on Enlightenment presuppositions. We've already shown that there is ample scientific evidence that the world could not have emerged purely as a result of accidental forces and processes and that it must have been designed.

Millions of people *have* been willing to move beyond this bias and its accompanying stigma to examine the claims of Christ. They have found in the process that Jesus is real and that the real fools are those unwilling to consider Him.

"RELIGIOUS EXPERIENCE"

A final argument is that conversion experiences are common to all religions and can be summarized as a product of the human psyche. If it could be established that these experiences are essentially psychological, there would be a non-supernatural explanation for conversion.

In reply, all religious experience is *not* the same. Many mystical encounters cannot be explained. In order to enter into them, one must either empty the mind and open oneself to the irrational or use some type of inducement. Among mystics two inducements are severe asceticism (extensive sensory deprivation) and the use of intoxicants/hallucinogens.

Christian conversion clearly is connected to the gospel and produces an explanation—that is, a person can say how, when, where, and why he or she first experienced Christ. Conversion also is directly connected to faith and leads to experiential forgiveness, peace, and transformation. Followers can tell others how they too can know Jesus, describing in specific terms what becoming a believer is like.

Conversion is not a vague feeling or sense; it always involves a conscious decision to follow Jesus. John Wesley, whose revivals opened the door for modern evangelicalism, understood that this experience was not irrational and that conversion is always conversion to a specific set of beliefs; that is, to the saving principles of the gospel (such as justification by faith). He wrote, "To renounce reason is to renounce religion," and "All irrational religion is false religion."[408]

In Christian conversion, a period of maturation is almost always required, as the new believer counts the costs of following Jesus. Studies of Christians who became lifelong followers show that most converted after as many as six opportunities to carefully consider Christ's actions and words. Only a small number made a lifelong commitment after two or fewer opportunities to hear and evaluate the good news.

THE SCIENTIFIC METHOD APPLIED TO THE GOSPEL

The postmodern assumption is that if there is a God, He can't be known. Naturalists say He isn't there. Existentialists say He is "wholly other" and beyond any potential contact or relationship. Agnostics say there may be a God but we have no way of knowing for sure.

Christianity says God *is* there, and He is *not* inaccessible or unknowable. We've already explained that in our fallen state, humankind is separated from God by sin. God is spirit—He is of a metaphysical reality. Despite these obstacles, however, the Bible speaks of knowing God. How is this possible?

When a scientist performs an experiment, he must carefully follow a set of detailed instructions to achieve a valid result. He cannot leave out a step, substitute another step, or even carry out a step imperfectly. I remember the difficulty of college lab courses. If, for instance, the test tubes weren't perfectly clean and the chemical ratios weren't precisely as prescribed, the experiment wouldn't work. Science requires careful attention to detail.

God has said that He may be found,[409] but there are conditions by which He may be known. In His perfection—as the very source of truth and goodness—He cannot reward evil and must require cleansing from sin as a condition of fellowship. In order to give us this invitation and an opportunity to be restored to Him, He has revealed that He's established a specific door of access, which He said is through the small gate on the narrow way.[410]

In pursuing God, people must be like scientists: we must be willing to follow the specific instructions that lead to the promised result of the knowledge of Him. If He truly has given us detailed directions as to how He may be found, then we must follow them carefully; else we should not expect to find Him.

The path God has established goes through His Son. Jesus said, "I am the door, if anyone enters through Me, he will be saved."[411] Christ is the one and only means of reconciliation with God, because He is the one and only antidote for sin.[412]

Humans want God to reveal himself to them on our terms. We complain that He isn't visible to our physical senses, that He doesn't prevent evil from occurring in our world, and so on. Jesus spoke to this when He confronted the Pharisees about their unwillingness to believe in Him.

> To what shall I compare … this generation, and what are they like?
>
> They are like children who sit in the market place and call to one another, and they say, "We played the flute for you, and you did not dance; we sang a dirge, and you did not weep."[413]

Jesus was pointing out that they were refusing to believe in Him because He did not meet *their* messianic expectations. They wanted God to reveal himself to them according to *their* specifications. When He didn't do what they believed Messiah should do, they rejected Him and His words. These religious leaders, with all their knowledge of the Scriptures, lacked the humility that's at the core of biblical faith. They missed Jesus—while prostitutes and tax collectors found him—because they were unwilling to do as He said:

> If anyone chooses to do God's will, he will find out whether my teaching comes from God or whether I speak on my own.[414]

We must come to God on *His* terms, through the means He has provided for us to know Him. There is no other way because there is no other resolution for what separates us from Him (sin). Just as a scientist willingly would follow the most detailed set of guidelines to successfully complete an experiment, so we must be willing to do exactly what God tells us to do in order to find Him.

Seek the LORD while He may be found,
call upon Him while He is near.
Let the wicked forsake his way
and the unrighteous man his thoughts;
and let him return to the LORD,
and He will have compassion on him,
and to our God,
for He will abundantly pardon.[415]

The pathway to God is the pathway of repentance. This is what makes coming to Him so difficult: We must relinquish our pride and admit our need. Repentance requires the willingness to acknowledge and confess our guilt. Repentance also brings us to the place of calling out to God for His mercy and asking Him to help us change our attitudes and actions. This way down is the one and only way up. When we humble ourselves before Him, we find that He raises us up to peace and joy.[416]

To know God, we must be willing to pay the price. The experience of conversion is available to *anyone* willing to take the steps of obedience revealed by Christ and laid out in the

New Testament. The reality of the gospel is affirmed every time someone places faith in Jesus and experiences His life-changing grace. It is this power that has made Christianity the most embraced faith on earth, and it's the source of the faith's continued dynamism among the peoples of nearly every nation in this world.

---

[388] Romans 1:16

[389] E.g., see John 14:27.

[390] E.g., see Hebrews 10:22.

[391] E.g., see 2 Corinthians 3:14–16.

[392] In Francis Schaeffer, The God Who Is There (Downers Grove, IL: InterVarsity, 1968).

[393] Philippians 4:7

[394] See the Wesley Center Online, "John Wesley the Methodist," at wesley.nnu.edu.

[395] Romans 5:5

[396] Matthew 13:20–21

[397] In C. S. Lewis, Surprised by Joy: The Shape of My Early Life.

[398] Ibid.

[399] Watchman Nee, Spiritual Reality or Obsession, trans. Stephen Kaung (New York: Christian Fellowship Publishers, 1970), 27.

[400] E.g., see Acts 1:8.

[401] John 3:3; see also 1 Peter 1.

[402] Bill Moyers, "A Conversation with Jimmy Carter" on U.S.A.: People and Politics. PBS: 1976.

[403] See en.wikipedia.org/wiki/The_Varieties_of_Religious_Experience.

[404] Matthew 9:12

[405] Romans 3:23

[406] Cited in Ruth A. Tucker, From Jerusalem to Irian Jaya: A Biographical History of Christian Missions, 2nd edition (Grand Rapids: Zondervan, 2004), 23. See also Bruce L. Shelley, Church History in Plain Language (Dallas: Word Publishing, 1982), 33.

[407] Matthew 18:3

[408] See the Wesley Center Online, "John Wesley the Methodist," at wesley.nnu.edu.

[409] See Isaiah 55:6.

[410] See Matthew 7:14.

[411] John 10:9

[412] See 1 Timothy 2:3–6.

[413] Luke 7:31–32

[414] John 7:17 NIV

[415] Isaiah 55:6–7

[416] See James 4:6–10; cf. Proverbs 3:34.

CHAPTER SIXTEEN

THE SUPREMACY OF FAITH

Recently a young scientist, addressing a theology class at a seminary, began by saying,

> You and I live in different worlds. I have been trained to question everything and only accept those things that can be demonstrated to be true. You, on the other hand, have been trained to believe without question.[417]

In our culture, this is a common misconception about religious belief: the assumption that "faith" is another word for "credulity." There's a popular story that once, when a Sunday school teacher asked students to describe faith, a little boy in the back stood up and said, "Faith is when you believe something even though you know it isn't true."[418] This is naturalism's attitude toward faith: that it is unsupported belief in God and the supernatural. In the mind of our scientist, all this has been proven not to exist, and for him, faith in God is the equivalent of affirming the Easter Bunny.

Our society has been led to believe that science operates on the high ground of evidence and proof. We have been led to accept that science only holds to those principles that have been carefully examined and experimentally verified. This is untrue. The scientist addressing the seminary class believes a great many things in his field "without question." He actually operates as much by faith as those students.

FAITH AND REASON

Returning to Kant for a moment, let's agree once more that reason alone cannot provide certainty because it can only take us so far in our search for answers to the ultimate questions. Again, Western science is only theorizing—guessing—when it speaks about the origin of the universe and the structure of reality. Observation science relies on empirical evidence, on firsthand, experimentally proven facts; how does someone gain firsthand knowledge about the universe's beginning? No one was there to observe it. We aren't even able to simulate it.

Science, by experiment or observation, cannot answer life's core questions—it can only surmise possibilities. Any conclusions about the nature of reality are statements of belief, not of fact, and science has as many of them as any worldview or philosophy. The aforementioned scientist, in accepting the assumptions of naturalism—that there is no God or supernatural power in the universe—has no more scientific proof for his beliefs than the seminarians do for theirs, and in the end he is making as much of a faith commitment as they are.

The biochemist Isaac Asimov (1920–1992) wrote,

> I am an atheist out and out. It took me a long time to say it. I've been an atheist for years and years, but somehow I felt it was intellectually unrespectable to say one was an atheist, because *it assumed knowledge that one didn't have.* Somehow it was better to say one was a humanist or an agnostic. I finally decided that I'm a creature of emotion as well as reason. Emotionally, I am an atheist. I don't have the evidence to prove that God doesn't exist, but I so strongly suspect that he doesn't that I don't want to waste my time.[419]

Faith is the commitment—emotionally, intellectually, and volitionally—to a given worldview's values and standards for life. Because of the real limits on human knowledge, *everyone* must make a commitment *by faith* to a chosen worldview and its associated lifestyle. In short, each person, religious or irreligious, a theologian or a scientist, lives by faith.

Faith, then, is a decision to follow a belief system that one is convinced makes sense of the world. Most people are taught the beliefs of their tribe, family, or culture. However, in our society, as education has improved and media exposure has increased, more of us are realizing we have options. We don't have to and shouldn't believe everything our parents taught us. Whether we should or shouldn't, we *can* break away from the traditions of our family or even our community.

So, amidst all the uncertainty, how do we find our way? How can we determine which of the choices before us is true? We've already agreed that there is no scientific experiment, no technological instrument that can tell us the exact nature of reality. Everyone must decide what he or she believes about what, as regards certain dimensions, is an unknown quantity. Is there *any* principle that, minimally, will help us decide if some possibility is better than the others? If we can't know for certain, can we at least know *in all likelihood*?

CERTAINTY OR CONVICTION?

Common sense tells us yes, we can. There is a connection between faith and reason; everyone must reason from the known to the unknown and, on the basis of that reasoning, commit to a set of beliefs and choices. Many people in the West still make this decision sometime during their teenage years. The writer Miriam Allen deFord (1888–1975) decided to become an atheist at thirteen,[420] and Bertrand Russell declared, "I believed in God until I was just eighteen."[421] Conversion isn't merely a religious phenomenon—unbelievers have conversion experiences too. Julian Huxley said, "For my own part, the sense of *spiritual relief* which comes from rejecting the idea of God as a supernatural being is enormous."[422]

Carl Sagan's bold opening in *Cosmos* is a statement of faith: "The Cosmos is all that is, all that was, and all that ever will be."[423] Dr. Sagan didn't know this with certainty; it was his personally held conviction (his faith). He believed he had many supporting reasons for making this a conviction, but his words weren't an expression of unquestionable fact.

Faith is always supported by reason. Faith is the end result of a reasoned analysis of the reality in which we live, or it is a set of given convictions sustained by clearly understood reasons. All of us know why we believe what we do. We frequently remind ourselves why our philosophy is best or, probably more often, why others are wrong. We usually join ourselves to those who share similar views, and we prefer to have those views constantly reinforced. At some point, the only way we can view the world is through the filter of our belief system.

❖ ❖ ❖ ❖

Consider that belief supported by reason is exactly how the Bible defines faith: "*Faith is the assurance of things hoped for, the conviction of things not seen.*"[424] The Greek noun translated "faith" is related to the infinitive *peithō*, which means "to persuade … to be convinced."[425] *Faith, biblically, means to be convinced that something is true*—it is not a "hope so" or "maybe" word but one of confidence and commitment, a word of "emotion as well as reason."

True Christian faith—the person's complete dedication to Christ—cannot exist without the full support of the powers of reason. Perhaps the greatest biblical faith story is that of Abraham's willingness to sacrifice his son Isaac at God's command.[426] Notice how the New Testament explains Abraham's faith: "He considered that God is able to raise men even from the dead."[427] Abraham used his reason to sustain his faith; he *considered*; he used his mind. We even get the word "logic" from this term's Greek root.[428] Abraham's amazing faith was rooted in the reasoning that supported his belief about God's person and power. So it is for all of us: we support our faith by our reason.

Faith is the interpreting of life's totality from the conviction that our beliefs are true. It is a deep persuasion about what we don't know in its entirety based upon what we do know. This commitment affects every thought, word, and deed in our lives; it is rightly called our *world*view. Everyone has convictions, and thus everyone lives by faith. The proper question is not "Do you have faith?" but rather "*In what* do you have faith?"

Modern thought has not, therefore, destroyed but rather has affirmed biblical faith. "We walk by faith, not by [physical, sensory] sight"[429] describes this necessity for a Christian. In fact, this is the one way by which God can be reached: "The righteous will live by his faith."[430] All humankind, therefore, is subject to the necessity of faith in regard to eternity.

"THE GREAT GAMBLE?"

History has shown time and again that it's possible for human beings to believe almost anything. Remember the Heaven's Gate cult? They trusted that within the tail of Comet Hale-Bopp, which appeared in 1997, was a spaceship coming to take them away. Only one catch: they all had to kill themselves in order to be translated to the ship. These were intelligent adults, many of them college educated, yet they forfeited their lives for a wild fable. Obviously, faith is a powerful thing. We must put the greatest of weights into and upon our consideration of whom or what we fully place it.

There are three questions we must ask of anything that demands our faith:

(1) Is this the best explanation of life and of reality as I know it?

(2) Is there sufficient evidence to warrant my complete conviction?

(3) Is it worth the risk that I will be taking in staking my very life upon it?

Note that last question. No matter in what or in whom it's placed, *faith is always a risk.* Remember, we are deciding for ourselves what the unknown is like, even as we use the known to do it. Therein lies the risk: is our choice correct? And fence-sitting doesn't work; there's as much risk in not deciding as in deciding wrongly. Every choice yields consequences, even the decision not to decide (agnosticism).

We tend to see this risk as regarding what happens at the *end* of life, but in truth it's just as crucial to what happens *during* our lives. Our worldview profoundly shapes the way we experience life, for best or for worst. This inherent risk explains why faith must never be separated from reason. We must wisely and sincerely consider our options, taking a hard look at reality to see that our beliefs are most likely to be true. As Socrates said, "The unexamined life is not worth living."[431]

Blaise Pascal (1623–1662), the French mathematician and philosopher, attempted to explain this principle in his famous "wager," wherein he pondered the best- and worst-case scenarios for those who (1) believe in God and (2) deny God's existence.[432]

For the atheist, the best case is that he's right; there is no God and thus no afterlife. His hope is for annihilation, for the end of existence. The worst case is that he's wrong; he will have lived his life as God's enemy and so will face God's judgment after death.

For the believer, if he's right he will live forever in God's presence (which will fulfill his hope). If he's wrong, and there is no God, he will face annihilation and cease to exist. Pascal's point is that the best-case scenario for the atheist is the worst-case for the believer. He wasn't saying an atheist should sell out his conscience for a possible reward or that a believer should believe for the sake of this hope alone; rather, an unbeliever should count the cost of his unbelief.

There's an atheist version of the wager as well; it suggests that the risk is not what's associated with the next world but what's connected to this one. Why miss the pleasures of this life for "pie in the sky, by and by"? If now is all there is, why deny ourselves? Better to maximize our happiness up front, since this may be all we'll get.

These examples reveal the focus and perspective of the two beliefs. The religious view centers on the risk/reward after death (where its primary hope lies); the non-religious view centers on the risk/reward before death (where all of its hope lies). Is there a way to judge further between the options? I say yes—we simply need to look at human experience to see which is most consistent with reality.

❖ ❖ ❖ ❖

My father, for most of his life, was not a deeply religious man, yet in his experiences he learned and heeded important lessons. He often reminded us, his sons, that marriage is among life's most significant institutions and was the source of profound satisfaction for him as a husband and father. He warned us that cheating and lying never produce fortune or success—only shame, regret, and poverty. His life maxim, which he frequently repeated (and, for the most part, lived out) was "virtue is its own reward."

Dad understood that doing the right thing often meant sacrificing immediate gratification for a later, more valuable reward. He knew that living morally is superior in this life; he chose it not for any possible reward *after* life but for its benefit *here*.

My dad was expressing one of the axioms of what former generations called *natural law.* Humankind learned over time that morality is superior to immorality. Therefore, people came to believe that inherent in nature and in the human personality are certain lifestyle "laws" that, if kept, produce wholeness, and, if transgressed, produce harm.

Turning back to the question at hand, the non-religious view argues that we should seek happiness *now*. However, that pursuit most often involves the rejection of crucial natural-law principles. Human experience has shown (and, unfortunately, will continue to show) that this path doesn't work—it doesn't lead to happiness. The irony is that the approach of morality and delayed gratification leads to happiness in this life *and* the promise of a heavenly reward.

In the court of history, the moral life has always produced greater satisfaction and contentment than the life of selfishness. This is a life unchained to regret, free of compulsion and addiction, and filled with love. No being on earth can be free of pain, but in the moral life are hope and strength to face troubles and trials. As Augustine declared, "He that is good is free, even though he is a slave, and he that is evil is a slave, even though he be a king."[433]

All forms of atheism—whether naturalism, secularism, agnosticism, hedonism, existentialism, and any other related -ism—carry substantial risk, not only at the end of life but also here and now. Look at the tremendous increase in human tragedy with the overthrow of moral values in the West: We ridicule "the age of Ozzie and Harriet" while we complain of rising crime, drug use, school violence, fatherless kids, and growing alienation of the young. Yet we fail to make the connection between the loss of a societal moral foundation and its escalating dysfunction. In our commitment to a secular culture, we're risking more than we can even imagine; it appears we have not been willing to tabulate the price of our choice as we rush madly toward dissolution.

❖ ❖ ❖ ❖

The question, then, is "*In what* will we have faith? The Bible calls us to faith in the personal God, who created us in His image and thus made our personality, our very nature, as a reflection of His. If this is true, no wonder we have these things we call "values," that we find inside us a law of goodness reflected in our conscience.

We find as well that the complexity and intricacy of the universe (ourselves included) essentially demands a supernatural explanation. Furthermore, anyone willing to examine the New Testament claim to be the eyewitness record of the unparalleled life, death and resurrection of Jesus Christ will find it passes all tests required of an historical document. All of this to say, once more, that Christianity is not blind faith; it is reasonable and historical (rooted in events and evidence). The declaration that the gospel is the truth is not just religious hyperbole—it is the best explanation for the all "knowns" of reality, and it truly is worth the risk of commitment.

FOUR FINAL QUESTIONS

God has given us clear and sufficient evidence of His existence and of our moral obligation. It's available to all people in all places—to embrace, to deny, or to ignore. In the end, it will not be possible to claim ignorance, and He has made plain to us that we all will be held responsible.

This evidence is related to four main issues: creation, human nature, Jesus Christ, and the Resurrection. We can state these in the form of four questions.

QUESTION ONE : WHAT WILL YOU DO WITH THE EVIDENCE FOR CREATION?

> Since the creation of the world His invisible attributes, His eternal power and divine nature, have been clearly seen, being understood through what has been made, so that they are without excuse.[434]

God's existence is self-evident in and through creation. True science should be—and, prior to the modern era, was—an act of worship as we discover God's phenomenal genius, His kindness toward His creatures, His love of beauty and joy. The Fall *has* marred this revelation; nature also reflects the tragedy of pain and death. But the presence of suffering and evil is further confirmation of the biblical record; it reveals that Scripture explains the world as it really is. And, despite the Fall, the created glory of the universe still shines through for all to see.

Some people deny this evidence by a process of rationalization and self-delusion: "The universe isn't designed, it only looks designed." They attribute, to accidental forces, creatures far too complex to be accidental. They deny the conclusion that the weight of the data for creation presents to them, and they slander their opponents for stating what's clear to any unbiased observer. In short, they "suppress the truth in unrighteousness."[435]

This dogmatic denial of the obvious does not change that we will be held accountable for what God has revealed to us. The universe cannot be explained apart from God, and He himself says this fact is plain to every person who has ever lived.

QUESTION TWO : WHAT WILL YOU DO WITH THE HUMAN PERSONALITY?

> When Gentiles, who do not have the law, do by nature things required by the law, they are a law for themselves, even though they do not have the law, since they show that the requirements of the law are written on their hearts, their consciences also bearing witness, and their thoughts now accusing, now even defending them.[436]

All human beings operate on the basis of conscience and on some level of compassion. We instinctively make moral judgments about our choices and the choices of others. While certain values vary from culture to culture, there is nonetheless an agreed-upon set of virtues that transcends cultures. Even where seemingly immoral practices are allowed, one finds that the practices are supported *within the culture* by moral reasoning.

As a restated example, for people to murder; they must believe that their enemies deserve death.[437] Virulent hatred of their enemies in many parts of the world is undergirded by misrepresentations of those enemies as inhuman and evil. As well, societies that permit polygamy do so for economic and social reasons. For instance, a wealthy man may take more than one wife in order to provide for women who have no hope of supporting themselves.

While morals may look different from outside a culture, in the rationale behind them we find the "universals" of compassion and justice. *All people are wired for morality.* The reality of conscience and the need to justify our behavior are common to all societies and all people.

Once again, Immanuel Kant considered human conscience the one irrefutable argument *for* God's existence. He denied the evidence for design (believing we "project" order and design upon the universe), but he could not deny the moral sense in our nature. He felt there was only one explanation: a moral God. Kant's view was closer to the deist or pantheist paradigm than to Christian theism, since he conceived of God as "disinterested mind." Yet, in light of man's undeniable convictions, he could not uphold a godless universe.

Human nature does stand as important evidence for God. Because we all possess it and are well aware of its presence in our lives, we are confronted every single day with the supernatural. As our humanity is revealed in the choices we make, we see our "conscience bearing witness"[438] to the reality of the divine creation. We *know* there is a sense of right and wrong within us, and we know that this sense points to the God who is its source.

QUESTION THREE : WHAT WILL YOU DO WITH JESUS?

> God, after He spoke long ago to the fathers in the prophets in many portions and in many ways,
>
> in these last days has spoken to us in His Son, whom He appointed heir of all things, through whom also He made the world.[439]

When Jesus called himself the "Son of Man," He wasn't saying He's just a human being; He was referring to the messianic prophecy of Daniel 7:13–14. Using this title, He declared His authority to forgive sins,[440] to be the Lord of the Sabbath,[441] and to be returning to earth with His angels to inaugurate the fullness of God's kingdom.[442] He told His disciples, "I and the Father are one," and "He who has seen Me has seen the Father."[443] In speaking to His generation, He professed to have seen the days of Abraham; when asked how He could be that old, He used the divine title of preexistence ("*I AM*") God used in revealing himself to Moses on Mount Sinai.[444]

Jesus Christ claimed to be the incarnation of God himself. This *alone* is not unique—Meher Baba and Sai Baba, for example, both made such claims about themselves in the twentieth century. Meher Baba died in 1969 and is revered by many as an avatar (incarnation of God, or of the Supreme Being). Sai Baba still lives in India and has amassed a large following.

Particularly in our current era of Eastern influence, it's not unheard of that someone presents himself to be God's Son. However, it was unusual for Jesus to give that declaration in the midst of monotheistic Israel. There was no precedent; there was no philosophical or theological ground for such a claim in anything but a miraculous intervention by God himself.

While anyone can announce himself as the Son of God, words are cheap, and delusions are common. It's another thing entirely to prove it. Christ absolutely convinced His followers that He is indeed who He says.

> The Word became flesh and dwelt among us, and we have seen His glory, glory as of the only Son from the Father, full of grace and truth.[445]
>
> We did not follow cleverly devised myths when we made known to you the power and coming of our Lord Jesus Christ, but we were eyewitnesses of his majesty.[446]

Christ's words and deeds substantiated his claim. The record of His ministry in the Gospels demonstrates it. His wisdom, compassion, power, and righteousness stand alone in history. No religious leader, no holy man, and no philosopher is His equal.

You have only two choices in regard to Jesus: you must either consider Him the figment of some ancient writers' imaginations, or you must believe He truly is God. For two centuries liberal theologians have attempted to discover the so-called "historical" Jesus, operating on the assumption that He was just a human being who made fantastic statements about His origin but in the end was revealed to be ordinary. Nevertheless, every attempt to demythologize Him has failed because there's not even a hint of over-inflated ego or self-delusion in the gospel accounts. There is no legitimate non-supernatural explanation for the New Testament events. The Bible is consistent in its portrayal of Jesus as the Son of God.

If the Gospels were in circulation within thirty years of the Crucifixion, the assumption that Christ's character, words, and deeds were invented by His followers becomes riddled with difficulty. Even more significant is that the New Testament records the public preaching of the very men who had experienced all the events they proclaimed. The belief that the early church "invented" Christianity does not fit the historical evidence.

What is more, the Jesus of the Gospels is beyond "inventing." His story has no precedent. Who would imagine *Him*? Born the son of a carpenter. Rejected by His own people. Betrayed by one of His disciples. Cruelly murdered by the Romans. All this so that He might be "the Lamb of God who takes away the sin of the world"?[447] *Who on earth* could have envisioned God making a way to rescue lost humanity that would be so accessible and so simple?

The gospel is *astounding;* it's not something we would or could dream up. In our ways of thinking, we'd expect God to require more than mere faith—perhaps we would need to perform extraordinary acts of contrition and compensation. The church itself has struggled with the simplicity of grace; the very nature of salvation (by faith alone, or by faith combined with works of satisfaction) once split it into Protestant and Catholic factions. Even so, the Word is clear:

> By grace you have been saved through faith; and that not of yourselves, it is the gift of God; not as a result of works, so that no one may boast.[448]

Salvation is a gift to be received in humble gratitude; it is not a privilege earned by performance.

As well, faith is not a thing in itself; what matters is faith *in* Christ and His finished work. God has publicly displayed His Son, for all the world to see, in order that the world would turn to Him for salvation. God has provided no other means; thus He has so clearly displayed Christ and His cross. One central issue related to the world's judgment will be how we responded to Jesus.

> God did not send the Son into the world to judge the world, but that the world should be saved through Him.
>
> He who believes in Him is not judged; he who does not believe has been judged already, because he

has not believed in the name of the only begotten Son of God.[449]

QUESTION FOUR : WHAT WILL YOU DO WITH THE RESURRECTION?

> What I received I passed on to you as of first importance: that Christ died for our sins according to the Scriptures, that he was buried, that he was raised on the third day according to the Scriptures, and that he appeared to Peter, and then to the Twelve. After that, he appeared to more than five hundred of the brothers at the same time.[450]

The unparalleled affirmation of the good news is the physical resurrection of Jesus Christ. This event was documented by His followers, who spent the rest of their lives proclaiming what they had seen with their own eyes: *Jesus is the risen Lord.*

The four Gospels literally make this event a matter of public record. Here is the opportunity for immortality, for everlasting life in God's presence; should not every one of us, *at the very least,* consider the possibility that it might be true?

A group of early followers once was confronted with a teaching from Jesus that made no sense to them: "Unless you eat the flesh of the Son of Man and drink His blood, you have no life in yourselves."[451] He was referring to the act of faith in His death for our redemption, but these people, at that moment, couldn't comprehend His seemingly bizarre statement.

As they walked away, Jesus turned to the core disciples who remained and asked, "You do not want to leave too, do you?"

Peter replied, "Lord, to whom shall we go? You have the words of eternal life."[452]

❖ ❖ ❖ ❖

So it is for us today. Jesus does have the words of—Jesus *is*—eternal life. Such an offer, of unending completion, of everlasting wholeness, surely requires of us a thorough consideration of its claims and its supporting evidence.

We all have heard the legend of the Spanish explorer Juan Ponce de León (1460–1521), who is said to have searched desperately for the mythical Fountain of Youth. And in one sense, minimally, we all can understand the desire that would have driven him to pursue the legend. *We all fear death; we all want to obtain immortality.*

There's a reason the gospel is called "the good news"! Freedom from the power of death is exactly what Christ offers each of us; He is the promise of life everlasting. In response, should we not at least read the New Testament, look at the claims of Jesus, and even ask God to show us if it's true?

YOU CAN KNOW

Our culture's current agnosticism is not the final word on truth. We've seen repeatedly that while our knowledge is imperfect, it's fully sufficient for us to make a decision. By any honest measure, God has given us far more than enough evidence to firmly support our faith in Him and in His Son. Ultimately, anyone who fails to believe does so because he or she doesn't want to believe, using uncertainty not as a reason but as an excuse—not from an actual lack of evidence but from avoidance of the evidence that's there.

We began by asking, "Does God exist?" The overwhelming weight of the evidence tells us that He does indeed. We also asked, "Can we know if God exists?" The answer is that Christian faith is no imaginary or illusory hope; the claims of Jesus Christ and His followers are undergirded by unprecedented and unparalleled historical and rational support. Furthermore, when we respond to the gospel as the Bible guides and instructs, we find that our faith additionally is confirmed by our own personal experience.

God's own Word promises both that He exists and that we can know He exists. But, amazingly, perhaps neither of these is the most amazing guarantee. This is because God also promises us that *we can know Him,* and that in the most wonderful and intimate way.[453] Through what He has done out of His love for us—for you, and for me—we *can* truly know Him.

When we place our faith in Jesus, we reenter personal relationship with God, whereby we begin to know and experience perfect reality. God, who by our sin had been hidden from us, again we experience as *real.* We live anew as He brings light into darkness, delights in worship, and speaks to conscience. He makes His own eternal Word read like it was written specifically to us, and through it He inspires, assures, instructs, and corrects. "Gospel" means "good news," and there is no better news than this: *through Jesus, we can know God.*

> I will not leave you as orphans; I will come to you.
>
> After a little while the world will no longer see Me, but you will see Me; because I live, you will live also.
>
> In that day you will know that I am in My Father, and you in Me, and I in you.[454]

---

[417] Adapted from an anecdote by the zoologist Mark Ridley. See The Problems of Evolution (Oxford University Press, 1985).

[418] Common vignette, source unknown.

[419] Isaac Asimov, in Free Inquiry. 2:2 (Spring 1982), 9, emphasis mine.

[420] Miriam Allen deFord, a signer of Humanist Manifesto II (1973), once said, "Humanism, in my view, must be atheistic, or it is not humanism as I understand it."

[421] Cited in James Roy Newman ed., The World of Mathematics, "Commentary on Bertrand Russell" (Minneola, NY: Dover, 2000), 385.

[422] Sir Julian Huxley, quoted in Aldous Huxley, Ends and Means: An Inquiry Into the Nature of Ideals and Into Methods Employed for Their Realization (New York: Harper, 1937), emphasis mine. See also Dinesh D'Souza, What's So Great About

Christianity, especially chapter 23, "Opiate of the Morally Corrupt: Why Unbelief Is So Appealing" (Washington, DC: Regenery, 2007).

[423] Carl Sagan, Cosmos (New York: Random, 1980), 6.

[424] Hebrews 11:1 ESV

[425] See Harold K. Moulton, The Analytical Greek Lexicon, Revised (London: Samuel Bagster & Sons, Ltd., 1977; Grand Rapids: Zondervan, 1978), 314.

[426] See Genesis 22.

[427] Hebrews 11:19

[428] See William D. Mounce, The Analytical Lexicon to the Greek New Testament (Grand Rapids: Zondervan, 1993), 302–03.

[429] 2 Corinthians 5:7

[430] Habakkuk 2:4

[431] Socrates, while on trial for heresy, in 399 BCE.

[432] Blaise Pascal, Pensées (Paris: Chez Guillaume Desprez, 1671), #233.

[433] Augustine of Hippo, City of God, trans. Marcus Dods (New York: Modern Library, 1983).

[434] Romans 1:20

[435] Romans 1:18

[436] Romans 2:14–15 NIV

[437] We broached this also in chapter four.

[438] Romans 2:15

[439] Hebrews 1:1–2

[440] See Mark 2:1–12.

[441] See Mark 2:23–28.

[442] See Mark 13:24–27.

[443] John 14:9

[444] See John 8:33–59; cf. Exodus 3:14.

[445] John 1:14 ESV

[446] 2 Peter 1:16 ESV

[447] John 1:29

[448] Ephesians 2:8–9

[449] John 3:17–18

[450] 1 Corinthians 15:3–6 NIV

[451] John 6:53

[452] John 6:67–68 NIV

[453] We noted earlier that "some form of the word 'to know' is used over 350 times in the New Testament."

[454] John 14:18–20